Cross-Border Mergers in Europe

The Cross-border Merger Directive of 26 October 2005 sets forth rules to permit and facilitate the merger of limited liability companies situated in different Member States of the European Union and the European Economic Area. It is completed by Council Directive 90/435/EEC of 23 July 1990, which provides for a common system of taxation applicable to mergers between parent companies and their subsidiaries located in different Member States, which has been replaced by Council Directive 2009/133/EC of 19 October 2009 which did not change the content (in this book referred to as the 'Merger Tax Directive'). With respect to procedural matters, the Cross-border Merger Directive refers to the Third Council Directive, which has been implemented in all Member States.

This book discusses the Cross-border Merger Directive and its implementing legislation in each Member State of the European Union and the European Economic Area. It provides companies and their advisors with useful insight into the legal framework applicable to, and the tax treatment of, cross-border mergers throughout the European Economic Area.

This book is divided into two parts. The first part analyses the Community rules laid down in the Cross-border Merger Directive and the Community rules on the tax treatment of cross-border mergers. The second part contains chapters on the implementing legislation in each Member State, prepared in accordance with a common format and contributed by a practitioner from each state. The annexes to this book contain the Cross-border Merger Directive (Annex I), the Merger Tax Directive (Annex II) and a list of the implementing legislation in each Member State (Annex III).

This is the second volume of this book which contains chapters on the Member States that are not included in the first volume.

DIRK VAN GERVEN is a partner in the Brussels office of NautaDutilh, a leading Benelux firm, and a member of the Brussels and New York Bars. He has extensive experience in all areas of corporate and financial law and is currently President of the Dutch-speaking chapter of the Brussels Bar. Dirk has published widely in the fields of corporate and financial law. Since 2003 he has been a member of the supervisory board of Belgium's Banking, Finance and Insurance Commission. Since 2010 he has been a member of the Board of Directors of CEPINA, the Belgian arbitration institute.

Law Practitioner Series

The *Law Practitioner Series* offers practical guidance in corporate and commercial law for the practitioner. It offers high-quality comment and analysis rather than simply restating the legislation, providing a critical framework as well as exploring the fundamental concepts which shape the law. Books in the series cover carefully chosen subjects of direct relevance and use to the practitioner.

The series will appeal to experienced specialists in each field, but is also accessible to more junior practitioners looking to develop their understanding of particular fields of practice.

The Consultant Editors and Editorial Board have outstanding expertise in the UK corporate and commercial arena, ensuring academic rigour with a practical approach.

Books in the series include

Good Governance for Pension Schemes
Paul Thornton and Donald Fleming

Settlement of Investment Disputes under the Energy Charter Treaty
Thomas Roe, Matthew Happold and James Dingemans QC

A Practical Guide to Private Equity Transactions
Geoff Yates and Mike Hinchliffe

Stamp Duty Land Tax
Michael Thomas; Consultant Editor David Goy QC

Accounting Principles for Lawyers
Peter Holgate

The European Company: Volume 1
General Editors: Dirk van Gerven and Paul Storm

The European Company: Volume 2
General Editors: Dirk van Gerven and Paul Storm

Capital Markets Law and Compliance: The Implications of MiFID
Paul Nelson

Reward Governance for Senior Executives
Edited by Carol Arrowsmith and Rupert McNeil

Prospectus for the Public Offering of Securities in Europe: Volume 1: European and National Legislation in the Member States of the European Economic Area
General Editor: Dirk van Gerven

Prospectus for the Public Offering of Securities in Europe: Volume 2: European and National Legislation in the Member States of the European Economic Area
General Editor: Dirk van Gerven

Common Legal Framework for Takeover Bids in Europe: Volume 1
General Editor: Dirk van Gerven

Common Legal Framework for Takeover Bids in Europe: Volume 2
General Editor: Dirk van Gerven

Accounting Principles for Non-Executive Directors
Peter A. Holgate and Elizabeth Buckley

The Law of Charitable Status
Robert Meakin

The Business Case for Corporate Governance
Ken Rushton

Cross-Border Mergers in Europe: Volume 1
General Editor: Dirk Van Gerven

Cross-Border Mergers in Europe: Volume 2
General Editor: Dirk Van Gerven

Cross-Border Mergers in Europe

VOLUME II

General Editor
DIRK VAN GERVEN

CAMBRIDGE
UNIVERSITY PRESS

CAMBRIDGE
UNIVERSITY PRESS

Shaftesbury Road, Cambridge CB2 8EA, United Kingdom

One Liberty Plaza, 20th Floor, New York, NY 10006, USA

477 Williamstown Road, Port Melbourne, VIC 3207, Australia

314–321, 3rd Floor, Plot 3, Splendor Forum, Jasola District Centre, New Delhi – 110025, India

103 Penang Road, #05–06/07, Visioncrest Commercial, Singapore 238467

Cambridge University Press is part of Cambridge University Press & Assessment, a department of the University of Cambridge.

We share the University's mission to contribute to society through the pursuit of education, learning and research at the highest international levels of excellence.

www.cambridge.org
Information on this title: www.cambridge.org/9780521487603

First published 2011

A catalogue record for this publication is available from the British Library

Library of Congress Cataloging-in-Publication data
Cross-border mergers in Europe / general editor, Dirk Van Gerven.
p. cm. – (Law practitioner series)
ISBN 978-0-521-48760-3 (Hardback)
1. Consolidation and merger of corporations–Law and legislation–
European Union countries. I. Gerven, Dirk van. II. Title. III. Series.
KJE6467.C76 2010
346.4′06626–dc22

ISBN 978-0-521-48760-3 Hardback

Contents

Contributors

FINLAND
Outi Raitasuo
Johanna Haltia-Tapio
Hannes Snellman

FRANCE
Jean-Marc Desaché
Gide Loyrette Nouel

GREECE
Tom Kyriakopoulos
Kelemenis & Co.

IRELAND
Margaret Stack
Jennifer McCarthy
Michael Greene
A&L Goodbody

ITALY
Francesco Gianni
Marco Zaccagnini
Gianni, Origoni, Grippo & Partners

LATVIA
Maris Brizgo
Raymond L. Slaidins
LAWIN Klavins & Slaidins
John JA Burke
Kazakhstan Institute of Management, Economics and Strategic Research

LITHUANIA
Irmantas Norkus
Eva Suduiko
Raidla Lejins & Norcous

LUXEMBOURG
Margaretha Wilkenhuysen
Louisa Silcox
NautaDutilh

MALTA
Adrian Gabarretta
Colm O'Connor
Nadia Cassar
Ganado & Associates

PORTUGAL
Margarida Barrocas
Marcelo Alves
Mariana Ferreira
Barrocas Advogados

REPUBLIC OF SLOVENIA
Jurij Dolžan
Matija Knapič
Samo Herič
Odvetnik Jurij Dolžan, Mitja Vidmar & Igor Zemljarič

ROMANIA
Gabriela Cacerea
Nestor Nestor Diculescu Kingston Petersen

SPAIN
Jaime Pereda Espeso

José Gabriel Martínez Paños
Uría Menéndez

SWEDEN
Jan Bertil Andersson
Jönköping International Business School, Linköping University

ICELAND
Ólafur Arinbjörn Sigurðsson
LOGOS

LIECHTENSTEIN
Alexander Appel
Moritz Blasy
Walch & Schurti

Preface

This is the second volume of the book on the Cross-border Merger Directive. The first volume contains a general discussion of the Cross-border Merger Directive and the Merger Tax Directive and chapters on the Member States that adapted their legislation first. The first volume was published by Cambridge University Press in 2010. The aim of this book is to provide a comprehensive analysis of the European legal framework on cross-border mergers and the implementing legislation in each Member State of the European Union and the European Economic Area (EEA). The Cross-border Merger Directive is made applicable through treaty to the three EEA Member States permitting cross-border mergers among companies of these states and the EU Member States.

The first volume included chapters on Austria, Belgium, Bulgaria, Cyprus, Czech Republic, Denmark, Estonia, Germany, Hungary, The Netherlands, Poland, Slovak Republic, the United Kingdom and Norway.

Volume II contains chapters on Finland, France, Greece, Ireland, Italy, Latvia, Lithuania, Luxembourg, Malta, Portugal, Republic of Slovenia, Romania, Spain, Sweden, Iceland and Liechtenstein.

Thus, taken together, the two volumes contain reports on the legal framework in all twenty-seven EU Member States and the three EEA countries. It is in consequence a useful tool for those who intend to organise a cross-border merger, or advise regularly on cross-border mergers in Europe.

This book was made possible thanks to contributions from distinguished law firms in the EU and EEA member countries. A list of these contributors is included at the beginning of each volume.

Finally, I wish to thank not only the contributors, but also those whose names are not mentioned herein, in particular Bianca Porcelli and others with NautaDutilh for their continuing support in composing this second volume.

Dirk Van Gerven
Brussels, 27 December 2010

PART V

Application in each Member State

National Reports for the EU Member States

19

Finland

OUTI RAITASUO, JOHANNA HALTIA-TAPIO
Hannes Snellman

I Introduction

1. The Cross-border Merger Directive was implemented in Finland on 31 December 2007 by acts amending the Companies Act, the Act on Cooperatives and the Act on Commercial Banks and Other Credit Institutions in the Form of a Limited Company.

II Scope of the new rules

2. The rules apply to private and public limited companies and cooperatives as well as credit institutions in the form of a limited company, a cooperative or a savings bank and such mutual real estate limited companies to which the Finnish Housing Companies Act is applied.

3. A Finnish limited liability company may participate only in a cross-border merger where the surviving company or the disappearing company qualifies as a limited liability company, as defined in the Cross-border Merger Directive. However, in the event of a parent-subsidiary merger, a Finnish limited liability company may merge into a foreign legal entity registered in another Member State and to which the laws of the said Member State are applied, if the foreign legal entity is comparable to a Finnish cooperative, cooperative bank, savings bank or mutual insurance company. A prerequisite is that the foreign legal entity owns all shares of its Finnish subsidiary.

III Cash payment

4. With regard to the merger consideration, the Companies Act is based on the assumption that the consideration is shares or securities giving an entitlement to shares issued by the receiving company. The Companies Act does not, however, limit the type of merger consideration, which may be cash or other assets. The provisions regarding equal treatment of shareholders shall be taken into consideration, if assets other than shares of the receiving company are given as merger consideration.

IV Legal consequences and enforceability of a cross-border merger

5. As a result of a cross-border merger all assets and liabilities of the disappearing companies will be considered transferred without the liquidation of the disappearing company to the receiving company upon the entry into force of the cross-border merger, i.e. with the following legal effects:

(i) the merging company will cease to exist;
(ii) the assets and liabilities, including all the rights and obligations, will be transferred to the surviving company;
(iii) the shareholders of the merging companies will become shareholders of the surviving company;
(iv) at the moment of registration of the implementation of the merger, the shareholders of the merging company and the holders of option rights and other special rights entitling to shares will become entitled to the merger consideration in accordance with the draft terms of merger. The new shares to be issued as merger consideration will carry shareholder rights as of the moment of registration; and
(v) the final settlement of accounts takes place in the merging company.

6. The transfer of all rights and obligations shall be applied also to contractual relationships in force, including but not limited to the employment contracts and employment relations existing on the date of the enforcement of the cross-border merger.

V Procedure

1 Draft terms of cross-border merger

7. The management or administrative organ of each participating company (in case of a Finnish limited liability company, the board of directors) must prepare the common draft terms of cross-border merger. The said document shall be sent to the registration authorities for registration within one month of its signing.

8. The draft terms should include the information described in Chapter 1, no. 19 of this book (i.e. the requirements under Article 5 of the Cross-border Merger Directive (see Volume I)). In addition, also the following information should be included:

(i) information on the corporate form of the companies participating in the merger and of the possible provider of merger consideration, as well as a proposal for the corporate form of a company to be established by a combination merger;
(ii) information on the registers where the foreign companies participating in the merger have been registered, and the contact details of the said registers;
(iii) an account of the reasons for the merger;
(iv) a proposal for the amendment of the articles of association, if necessary;
(v) a proposal, where appropriate, for the number of shares given as consideration broken down by share class, as well as whether new shares or treasury shares are to be issued;
(vi) a proposal for any other possible consideration and, if the consideration consists of options or other special rights entitling to shares, their terms;
(vii) a proposal for the allocation of the consideration, date of distribution and any other terms and conditions related to the distribution, as well as an account of their grounds;
(viii) an account of or a proposal for the rights of the merging company's option-holders, and the holders of any other special rights entitling to shares in the merging company, in the merger;
(ix) a proposal, where appropriate, for the increase of the share capital of the surviving company;
(x) an account of the merging company's assets, liabilities and equity and the matters influencing their valuation, the intended effect of the merger

on the balance sheet of the surviving company, and the accounting methods applicable to the merger;

(xi) a proposal for the right of the companies participating in the merger to decide on arrangements, other than those related to their normal business activities, which may affect the amount of their equity or the number of outstanding shares;

(xii) an account of any capital loans whose debtors can oppose the merger;

(xiii) an account of the number of shares of the surviving company and its parent company held by the merging company or its subsidiaries, and of the number of shares of the merging company held by companies participating in the merger;

(xiv) an account of the corporate mortgages pertaining to the assets of the companies participating in the merger;

(xv) an account of or a proposal for the special rights and benefits conferred to the supervisory board members, board members, managing directors and auditors of the companies participating in the merger, as well as to the auditor issuing the statement regarding the merger plan;

(xvi) a proposal regarding the planned date of registration of the implementation of the merger; and

(xvii) a proposal for any other possible terms of the merger.

In addition, the draft terms of merger of a credit institution shall contain an account of the commitments comparable to the capital note as well as other commitments whose creditors may object to the merger, as explained in detail in section VII of this chapter.

2 Management report

9. The management body of each merging company must prepare a written report regarding the implications of the cross-border merger for shareholders, creditors and employees.

10. The report shall be made available to shareholders and the employee representatives or, in the absence thereof, the employees directly no later than one month before the date of the general meeting scheduled to approve the merger.

11. In the event the employee representatives issue an opinion in accordance with national law, this opinion must be appended to the report.

3 Auditor's report

12. The boards of directors of the companies participating in the merger must appoint one or several chartered public accountants to issue a statement on the draft terms of merger. The statement contains an analysis of whether the merger plan includes correct and sufficient information regarding the grounds for

6

determining the consideration, and the distribution of the consideration. The statement to be issued to the acquiring company shall also indicate whether the merger is conducive to compromising the repayment of the company's debts.

13. If all shareholders of the companies participating in the merger agree, or if the matter is of a subsidiary merger, it is sufficient to issue a statement on whether the merger endangers the payment of the surviving company's debts.

14. The auditor's report shall be available for the shareholders at least one month before the general meeting called to approve the draft terms of the merger.

4 General meeting of shareholders

A Information for shareholders

15. The draft terms of the merger as well as the financial statements, the annual reports and auditor's reports of each participating company for the past three completed financial periods shall be kept available to the shareholders at the head office or website of each participating company for at least one month before the general meeting. If more than six months have passed from the end of the financial period of a public company to the signing of the draft terms of merger, the financial statements, the annual report and the auditor's report of the company dated no earlier than three months before the signing of the draft terms of merger shall be kept available at the general meeting.

16. Where appropriate, the decisions made by each company involved in the merger after the end of the latest financial period regarding the distribution of assets shall also be kept available for the shareholders. Further, the interim reports given by each company involved in the merger since the end of the latest financial period as well as a report by the board of directors on the events with an essential effect on the state of the company that have occurred after the financial statements or interim report and the auditor's statement on the draft terms of merger shall be kept available for the shareholders.

17. The above-mentioned documents shall be sent without delay to the shareholders upon their request as well as kept available at the general meeting.

18. The notice of the general meeting that is to decide on the merger shall not be delivered before the draft terms of merger have been registered. The notice shall be delivered not earlier than two months and, unless a longer period has been provided in the articles of association, no later than one month before the general meeting. In addition to the provisions of the articles of association on the notice of the general meeting, the notice shall be sent in writing to all shareholders in the merging company. The notice shall mention the shareholders' rights to demand redemption, as explained in no. 28 of this chapter. If the addresses of all rights holders with the right of redemption are not known to

the company, the notice of the right of redemption shall also be published in the Official Gazette within the same time limit.

B Shareholder approval

19. In the merging company, the general meeting will make the decision on a merger. However, in a subsidiary merger, the decision may be made by the board of directors of the merging company. In the surviving company, the board of directors shall make the decision on a merger. However, the decision shall be made by the general meeting, if shareholders with at least one-twentieth (1/20) of the shares in the company so request.

20. The general meeting that is to decide on the merger shall be held or the board of directors' decision on the merger made within four months of the registration of the draft terms of merger or the merger will lapse. In any event, the general meeting shall be held no later than one month before the due date for the creditors' right to object to the merger, unless all shareholders and, where appropriate, all holders of option rights or other special rights entitling to shares have waived their right to demand redemption.

21. The merger decision of the general meeting shall be made by qualified majority, which means that the proposal has to be supported by at least two-thirds (2/3) of the votes cast and the shares represented at the meeting. If the company has several share classes, it shall be an additional requirement for the validity of a decision that it is supported by a qualified majority within each of the share classes represented at the meeting (Chapter 5, Section 27 Companies Act). The merger can only be approved or dismissed in its entirety. If the merger is not approved in its entirety in all of the participating companies, the merger will lapse. The dismissal or the lapse of the merger must be reported to the Trade Register without delay.

5 Pre-merger certificate

22. If no creditor has objected to the merger or if it is affirmed by a court as explained in Section 29, the registration authority shall register the merger. Further, in a cross-border merger the foreign companies participating in the merger shall accept the right of redemption referred to in Section 27 and that the registration authority is provided with evidence of employee participation in the acquiring company in a manner corresponding to that provided in Article 16 of the Cross-border Merger Directive. If the assets of a Finnish company participating in a merger are subject to a business mortgage, as referred to in the Act on Business Mortgages, a prerequisite for the permission to implement the merger is that a registrable petition is pending for the mortgage being transferred to be the liability of a branch to be established in Finland, or that the mortgage has been cancelled.

8

23. If the above-mentioned criteria are fulfilled, the registration authority shall issue the merging company a certificate on the granting of the permission for the Finnish companies participating in the merger. The certificate is given only if the acquiring company is a foreign company. The registration authority shall verify and certify that the participating Finnish company has carried out the measures required for the merger and completed the statutory formalities. Further, it shall contain a reference whether any of the redemption proceedings referred to in no. 28 of this chapter are pending. The said information is important to the acquiring company, which is liable for the payment of the redemption price. The redemption procedure most likely reduces the assets of the merging company and may result in decreasing the equity below the restricted shareholders' equity.

24. After the verification, the registration authority will issue the said certificate without delay. The certificate is valid for six months. The participating companies shall send the certificate to the authority designated under the local laws of the surviving company.

6 Effects of the decision

25. The companies involved in the merger must notify the registration authorities of the implementation of the merger within six months of the decision regarding the approval of the merger, or the merger will lapse. The notification must include the following: confirmation of the boards of directors and the managing directors of the companies participating in the merger that the Companies Act has been complied with in the merger; a certificate of a certified public accountant attesting that the surviving company has received full consideration for the amount entered into its equity (if applicable), and a statement regarding the account in the merger plan; and confirmation by a board member or the managing director that the merging company's known creditors have been notified of the merger.

26. The registration authority must register the merger if the creditors have not opposed the merger. The legal effects of the merger will enter into force upon the registration of the implementation of the merger.

27. As from the registration of the cross-border merger, it cannot be declared void or be changed after the implementation of the merger.

VI Minority shareholders

28. A shareholder in the merging company may at the general meeting demand that his or her shares be redeemed; the shareholder shall be reserved the opportunity to make this demand before the decision on the merger is made (Chapter 15, Section 13 Companies Act). The said right is not applicable in subsidiary

mergers. The holder of option rights or other special rights entitling to shares may demand redemption of the rights at the general meeting that decides on the merger or verifiably file a written demand to this effect with the merging company before the general meeting. A shareholder who demands redemption shall vote against the merger decision. The redemption price shall be the price of the share at the time preceding the merger decision. The acquiring company shall be liable for the payment of the redemption price. The merging company shall without delay notify the acquiring company of any demands for redemption.

29. If no agreement is reached with the surviving company on the redemption of shares, option rights or other special rights entitling to shares or on the terms of redemption, the matter shall be submitted to arbitration.

VII Protection of creditors

30. Creditors of the merging companies whose receivables have existed before the registration of the draft terms of merger have the right to object to the merger. The registration authority shall, upon request by the merging company, issue a public summons to the creditors of the merging company, who have the right to oppose the merger by delivering a written notice to the registration authority not later than on the date specified in the summons. The merger will lapse if the merging company has not filed for the public summons within four months of the registration of the merger plan.

The merging company must send the written notification of the public summons to its known creditors not later than one month before the due date. The above-mentioned protection of creditors shall not be applied to a foreign company participating in the merger. Instead, the applicable laws regarding the protection of the creditors of the foreign company shall be applied.

In the event that the creditor has objected to the merger, the registration authority shall notify the company without delay after the due date. If a creditor objects, the merger shall lapse one month after the due date. However, the registration authority shall suspend the proceedings if the company shows that it has within one month of the due date brought an action in order to have the court affirm that the creditor has received payment or full security for the receivable, or if the company and the creditor together request that the proceedings be suspended.

VIII Employee participation

31. The Cross-border Merger Directive has in Finland been implemented in the Act on Personnel Representation in the Administration of Undertakings (24.8.1990/725 as amended, hereinafter the 'APRAU'). The implementation was enacted by an amendment to the APRAU, which entered into force on

15 December 2007. Based on the APRAU, certain parts of the SE Employee Involvement Act (13.8.2004/758 as amended, hereinafter the 'EIA') become applicable in the situation.

1 Employee participation in companies established in Finland resulting from a cross-border merger

32. Employee participation in Finnish companies is regulated by the APRAU. The APRAU shall be applied to limited liability companies, cooperatives and other economic societies, insurance companies, commercial banks, cooperative banks and savings banks that have a regular staff of at least 150 working in Finland.

33. The purpose of the APRAU is to advance the functioning of the undertaking, to intensify cooperation between the undertaking and its personnel and to increase the personnel's possibilities to exert influence in the undertaking. The personnel shall have the right to take part in the decision making in executive, supervisory or advisory bodies of the undertaking when they are handling matters of importance to the business operations, finances and the personnel's position in the undertaking.

34. As mentioned above, the APRAU may also become applicable in case of a cross-border merger. In addition, based on the APRAU, specified parts of the EIA becomes applicable if at least one of the participating companies has organised a personnel representation system as defined in the EIA. In such a case a special negotiation body shall be established to negotiate the organising of personnel representation with the competent organs of the companies involved in the merger. Based on the EIA, personnel representation is considered to be organised if an employee representative body or the employee representatives have a right to elect or appoint some of the members of the company's supervisory or administrative organ or such management groups or equivalent bodies which together cover the company's profit units, or if the employee representatives have a right to recommend or oppose the appointment of some or all of the members of the company's supervisory or administrative organ.

35. The participating companies may, however, without negotiating with the employees decide to apply the secondary rules for organising the personnel representation provided for in the EIA as of the registration of the merger.

36. If at least one of the merging companies provides for an employee participation system and, as a result of the above rules, the company resulting from the merger shall be governed by that system, it must take a legal form that allows the exercise of employee participation rights.

37. If no corresponding employee representation system is applied in any of the companies involved in the cross-border merger, there is no obligation under Finnish law to organise an employee representation system following the

merger. However, if an employee representation system is in place in any of the participating companies, a special negotiating body should be established as described above.

2 Special negotiating body ('SNB')

38. Unless a decision, as referred to above, to apply the secondary rules for organising the personnel representation provided for in the EIA has been made, the management or administrative organs of the participating companies shall as soon as possible after publishing the merger proposal take the necessary steps to start negotiations with the representatives of the companies' employees on arrangements for the involvement of employees. For the purpose of these negotiations, a special negotiating body shall be formed representing the employees of the participating companies and the concerned subsidiaries and establishments.

39. The special negotiation body may, subject to a majority of two-thirds of the representatives, representing as a minimum two-thirds of the personnel, decide not to initiate the negotiations or to discontinue the process.

40. No detailed provisions regarding the practical election process or a time limit for the election of members has been provided for in the Finnish law. However, in practice the election process is usually handled in accordance with the same practices as when other employee representatives are chosen within the company, i.e. a shop steward. The election process is to be handled by the employees themselves, not the employer.

41. As regards the obligations of the management to facilitate the appointment of members to the special negotiation body, the role of the management is limited only to provision of information to the personnel representatives. The management shall in no way interfere with the election or selection process of the Finnish members to the special negotiating body.

3 Protection of employee representatives

42. In Finland members of the special negotiation body are protected against termination of their employment in the same way as other employee representatives. Therefore, an employer shall be entitled to terminate the employment of a member of the special negotiation body on the basis of grounds related to the employee's person only if a majority of the employees whom the employee representative in question represents agree. In case of existence of collective grounds for termination, a termination of the employment of a member of the special negotiation body may only be carried out if the work of the employee representative in question ceases completely and the employer is unable to arrange work that corresponds to the person's professional skill or is otherwise suitable, or to train the person for some other work as provided for in law.

IX Tax treatment

43. Finland had implemented by 2008 the provisions regarding cross-border mergers in the Merger Tax Directive (2009/133/EC) of 19 October 2009.

44. Finnish tax law provisions regulating an income tax neutral merger apply to mergers between companies resident in two or more EU Member States, including a merger of a Finnish resident company with an acquiring company resident in another Member State if the assets of the merging company remain effectively connected to a permanent establishment of the acquiring company located in Finland.

45. A loss resulting from a merger (that is, the difference between the acquisition cost of shares and the value of net assets transferred) is not a deductible expense and a gain is not taxable income. The expenses of the transferring company are deducted in the recipient company as they would have been deducted in the transferring company.

46. The exchange of the shares in the transferring company for shares in the recipient company is not treated as a taxable event for shareholders of the transferring company. The deductible acquisition cost of the new shares received as a consideration by the shareholders of the transferring company is equal to the acquisition cost of the shares in the transferring company.

47. Cash may be used as a consideration, but it shall not exceed 10% of the nominal value of the new shares issued by the recipient company or, in the absence thereof, 10% of the value of the shares representing the share capital. The transaction is deemed to be a taxable event for shareholders to the extent that cash compensation has been used. If the cash consideration does exceed 10% of the nominal value of the new shares issued, the merger is not considered tax neutral and the merging entity is deemed to be liquidated for tax purposes. Under the Transfer Tax Act, a merger is not subject to transfer tax. However, if cash is used, the cash consideration is subject to transfer tax of 1.6% (even if the cash consideration does not exceed 10% of the nominal value of the new shares issued as consideration by the recipient company).

48. A tax loss may be carried forward during the subsequent ten tax years. When more than 50% of the shares of a limited liability company have changed ownership during the year the loss is recorded or thereafter, however, the right to carry forward is forfeited unless the regional tax office grants an exemption. Indirect ownership changes are taken into consideration when there has been a change in the ownership of a shareholder that owns at least 20% of the shares in the company in question. In the case of a merger, the acquiring company or its shareholders or both of these together must have held more than 50% of the shares of the merging company to retain the right to carry forward tax losses. No exemption is available for mergers.

20

France

JEAN-MARC DESACHÉ
Gide Loyrette Nouel

I Introduction

1. The requirements of the Cross-border Merger Directive were transposed into French law by the law no. 2008-649 dated 3 July 2008 (the 'Act'). The Act

amended the French Commercial Code (the 'Commercial Code') by inserting eight new articles (Arts. L.236-25 through L.236-32) in a newly created Section IV on cross-border mergers (*Dispositions particulières aux fusions transfrontalières*) under Chapter VI, Title III of Book II.

The Act also inserted a new Title VII in Book III, Part II of the French Labour Code on employee participation in companies resulting from cross-border mergers (*Participation des salariés dans les sociétés issues de fusions transfrontalières*).

The Act was subsequently supplemented by a series of three implementation decrees:

(i) decrees nos. 2008-1116 and 2008-1117, both dated 31 October 2008 and pertaining to employee participation in companies resulting from cross-border mergers; and
(ii) decree no. 2009-11 dated 5 January 2009, which introduced a new section under Chapter VI, Title III, Book II of the Commercial Code (Arts. R.236-13 through R.236-20).

II Scope of the new rules

2. Where one or more French companies are involved in a cross-border merger, general French merger regulations apply unless specific cross-border merger provisions of the Act provide the contrary (Art. L.236-25 of the Commercial Code). In case of conflict between the general French merger rules and the specific provisions governing cross-border mergers, the latter prevail.

3. The application of the Act is subject to two conditions: the first pertains to the type of merger that is entitled to benefit from its provisions and the second to the type of company involved in the merger process (on the French side).

4. Three types of mergers are entitled to benefit from the Act:

(i) the French *fusion-absorption* by which one or more companies are wound up without liquidation; and transfer all their assets and liabilities to another existing company, which in return issues new shares or securities as consideration for the transfer to the shareholders of the companies being absorbed. A portion of said consideration may also be paid in cash with more flexibility as under general French merger regulations (for more details concerning cash payments, see no. 6 of this chapter);
(ii) the French *fusion par création d'une société nouvelle* by which two or more companies are wound up without liquidation and transfer all their assets and liabilities to a newly created company, which issues in return new shares or securities as consideration for such transfer to the shareholders of the companies being wound up. A portion of said consideration may also be paid in cash (for more details concerning cash payments, see no. 6 of this chapter);

(iii) the French *fusion simplifiée* by which a wholly owned subsidiary is wound up without liquidation and transfers all its assets and liabilities to its parent company owning all the securities representing its share capital.

5. Article L.236-25 of the Commercial Code provides a list of corporate forms that are entitled to benefit from the specific provisions in the Act pertaining to cross-border mergers, i.e. corporations (*société anonyme*), partnerships limited by shares (*société en commandite par actions*), European companies (*société européenne*), simplified joint-stock companies (*société par actions simplifiée*) and limited liability companies (*société à responsabilité limitée*).

Several of the corporate forms mentioned above may also exist under French law but with only one sole shareholder (e.g., *enterprise unipersonnelle à responsabilité limitée, société par action simplifiée unipersonnelle*, EU subsidiary of another EU company). Despite the fact that they are not expressly listed, we believe these companies fall within the scope of the new legislation since they are mere variations of the above corporate forms.[1]

Partnerships (*société en nom collectif* and *société en commandite simple*), as well as unincorporated entities, cannot take part in cross-border mergers.

Neither agricultural companies nor economic interest groupings are included in the corporate forms provided for by Article L.236-25 of the Commercial Code; they cannot therefore benefit from the Act.

Under the Cross-border Merger Directive (Art. 3(2)), Member States were given the option of choosing whether or not to include cooperative entities (*sociétés coopératives*) within its scope. French law did not establish such exclusion. As a result, French cooperative entities incorporated under the Act n° 47-1775 of 10 September 1947 pertaining to cooperative status may take part in cross-border mergers governed by Articles. L.236-25 to L.236-32 of the Commercial Code, if having the corporate forms eligible under the Cross-border Merger Directive[2] to take part in such cross-border merger.

Companies in the process of being wound up can be involved in a cross-border merger, provided the allocation of their assets has not begun (Art. L.236-1 Commercial Code).

The Cross-border Merger Directive – and therefore the Act – does not apply to cross-border mergers involving a company whose corporate purpose is the collective investment of capital provided by the public, which operates

1 C. Cathiard, 'Le régime des fusions transfrontalières depuis la loi du 3 juillet 2008', *Droit des sociétés*, October 2008, p. 9; D. Lencou et M. Menjucq, *Les fusions transfrontalières de sociétés de capitaux: enfin une réalité mais des difficultés persistantes*, (Dalloz, 2009); *Lamy Sociétés Commerciales*, 2010, n° 1911. Contra: A. Lecourt, 'La transposition en France des fusions transfrontalières: entre innovations et espoirs déçus', *Bulletin Joly*, October 2008, n° 10, p. 806.

2 C. Cathiard, 'Le régime des fusions transfrontalières depuis la loi du 3 juillet 2008', *Droit des sociétés*, October 2008, p. 9.

on the principle of risk-spreading and the units of which are, at the holder's request, repurchased or redeemed, directly or indirectly, out of the assets of that company (Art. 3(3) Dir.). Thus open-ended public institutions for collective investment such as the *société d'investissement à capital variable* and the *société de placement à prépondérance immobilière à capital variable* are excluded from its scope.

III Consideration for the contribution

6. As regards domestic mergers, French law prohibits any cash payment in excess of 10 per cent of the total value of the consideration paid by the absorbing entity in exchange for the contribution (Art. L.236-1 Commercial Code).

However, Article L.23-26 of the Commercial Code provides that such limitation does not apply if at least one Member State in which a company involved in the merger process is located allows consideration to be paid partly in cash, such cash part exceeding 10 per cent of the share capital value of the shares attributed as a consideration for the contribution, regardless of whether the French company involved is the absorbing entity or the absorbed one.

IV Legal consequences and enforceability of a cross-border merger

7. A cross-border merger has the same legal effects as a domestic merger and thus results in:

(i) the winding up without liquidation of the absorbed or of the merging companies;
(ii) all assets and liabilities of the company being merged being transferred to the acquiring or to the new company;
(iii) the shareholders of the company being merged becoming shareholders of the acquiring or of the new company.

8. Article L.236-31 of the Commercial Code makes a distinction between cross-border mergers resulting in the incorporation of a new company and cross-border mergers known under French law as '*fusion-absorption*' (see no. 4 of this chapter). Specific provisions as to the timeframe of the merger process are provided for under the implementation decree no. 2009-11 of 5 January 2009.

A cross-border merger resulting in the incorporation of a new company registered under French law is enforceable against third parties as from the date of registration with the Trade and Commerce Registry (*Registre des commerces et des sociétés*).

In the case of a '*fusion-absorption*' (see no. 4 of this chapter), the cross-border merger becomes enforceable on the date set forth in the draft terms of the merger. However, such enforceability must occur between the delivery of the pre-merger certificate (see no. 22 of this chapter) and the end of the fiscal year during which the pre-merger certificate was delivered to the absorbing company (Art. L.236-31 Commercial Code).

When the absorbing company or the newly incorporated company has its registered office in France, the French legality scrutiny procedure of Article L.236-30 applies. Such procedure, which can be performed either by a French notary or by the clerk of the court within the jurisdiction of which the company resulting from the merger is registered, must be carried out within fifteen days from the delivery of documents required for such legality scrutiny (Art. R.236-20). The list of the required documents is provided for under Article R.236-19 (Art. R.236-20 Commercial Code).

9. A cross-border merger which has taken effect as provided for in the above paragraph cannot be judicially declared null and void (Art. L.236-31 Commercial Code).

V Procedure

1 Draft terms of the cross-border merger

10. The management or administrative organ of each of the merging companies must draw up the common draft terms of the cross-border merger, the minimum contents of which are listed in Article 5 of the Cross-border Merger Directive.

Under French law, such draft terms must include (Art. R.236-14 Commercial Code):

(i) the form, name and registered office of the merging companies and of the company resulting from the cross-border merger;
(ii) the ratio applicable to the exchange of securities or shares representing the company's capital and, as the case may be, the amount of any cash payment;
(iii) the terms for the allotment of securities or shares representing the capital of the company resulting from the merger, together with the date from which the holding of such securities or shares representing the company capital will entitle the holders to share in profits and any special conditions affecting that entitlement;
(iv) the date from which the transactions of the merging companies will be treated for accounting purposes as being those of the company resulting from the cross-border merger;
(v) the rights conferred by the company resulting from the cross-border merger on shareholders enjoying special rights or on holders of securities other than shares representing the company capital, or the measures proposed concerning them;

(vi) any special advantages granted to the experts who examine the draft terms of the cross-border mergers or to members of the administrative, management, supervisory or controlling organs of the merging companies;
(vii) information as to the evaluation of assets and liabilities transferred to the company resulting from the cross-border merger;
(viii) dates of the merging companies' accounts used to establish the conditions of the cross-border merger;
(ix) the articles of association of the company resulting from the cross-border merger;
(x) where appropriate, information on the procedures by which arrangements for the involvement of employees in the definition of their rights to participation in the company resulting from the cross-border merger are determined;
(xi) the likely repercussions of the cross-border merger on employment.

The time granted to creditors to oppose the merger will not begin to run so long as any of the above-mentioned information is missing (see no. 26 of this chapter).

11. Prior to the signing of the draft terms of the cross-border merger, the management or administrative organ of each of the merging companies must inform and consult with the work committees of the participating companies with respect to such draft.[3]

Once signed, the draft terms of the cross-border merger must be filed with the clerk of the commercial court of the judicial district where each French participating company has its registered office (Art. L.236-6 Commercial Code) and a notice relating to the cross-border merger must be published in an official newspaper entitled to publish legal notices in the departments where the participating companies are registered, and in the *Bulletin officiel des annonces civiles et commerciales.* The contents of such notices are provided for by Article R.236-15 of the Commercial Code. These formalities (the filing and the publication) must be complied with at least one month prior to the shareholders' meeting convened to vote upon the merger (Art. R.236-15 Commercial Code).

2 Management report

12. Under Article L.236-27 of the Commercial Code, the management body of each merging company must issue a written report to the company's shareholders. This report must thoroughly explain and justify the cross-border merger, especially its legal and economic aspects as regards the exchange ratio and valuation methods, which must be consistent for each company involved,

3 Art. L.2323-19 of the French Labour Code; H. Le Nabasque, 'Les fusions transfrontalières après la loi n°2008-649 du 3 juillet 2008', *Revue des sociétés*, 2008, p. 493.

and the consequences entailed by the merger for shareholders, creditors and employees (Art. R.236-16 Commercial Code).

This report is made available to the shareholders and to the staff delegates (or to the employees themselves if such delegates do not exist) at least one month prior to the shareholders' meeting convened to vote upon the merger (Arts. L.236-27 and R.236-16 Commercial Code), without prejudice to the right of the works council, if any, to be informed and consulted prior to the merger (Art. L.2323-19 French Labour Code).

If the works council, or the staff delegates in the absence thereof, has/have formally notified their opinion as to the merger at least one month prior to the shareholders' meeting convened to vote on the proposed merger, such opinion must be attached as an exhibit to the management report to the shareholders (Arts. L.236-27 and R.236-16 Commercial Code).

3 Auditor's report

13. One or more independent experts (*commissaires à la fusion*) (Art. L.236-10 Commercial Code) appointed by the competent commercial court must examine the draft terms of the merger and draft a written report, which must be made available to all shareholders of the merging companies.

As under general provisions of French law and pursuant to Article 8(2) of the Cross-border Merger Directive, the participating companies may jointly petition the president of the competent commercial court to appoint a single expert to review the draft terms of the merger and draw up a single report for the shareholders of all merging companies. The competent commercial court is that of the registered office of a merging company (Art. R.236-6 al.2 Commercial Code).

The independent expert is chosen from among the statutory auditors or the experts registered with the courts and tribunals (Art. R.225-7 al.1 Commercial Code). The statutory auditors of the merging companies may not be appointed as independent experts for the merger.

The independent experts must ensure that the relative values assigned to the shares of the companies participating in the transaction are relevant and that the share exchange ratio is fair. To that effect, they may request any information they deem necessary from the merging companies and can be assisted by any expert when it appears to be necessary (Art. L.236-10 Commercial Code).

14. The report relates the methods used to determine the share exchange ratio and indicates whether these methods are appropriate in the case at hand, the value resulting from each method and the relative importance of each method in determining the value eventually retained. The report should indicate the particular difficulties, if any, encountered in the valuation process.[4]

4 Art. 8.3 of the Cross-border Merger Directive; Art. 10.2 of Directive 78/855/EC; Art. L.236-10 of the Commercial Code.

The independent expert's report is made available to the shareholders at least one month prior to the shareholders' meeting convened to approve the draft terms of the cross-border merger (Art. R.236-3, 2° Commercial Code).

Such independent auditor's report is not required when the absorbing company holds 100 per cent of the absorbed company shares or securities (Art. L.236-11 Commercial Code), or when the shareholders of the merging companies unanimously decide to waive the requirement to draw it up (decision which should be made more than one month prior to the shareholders' meeting convened to approve the draft terms of the cross-border merger) (Art. L.236-10, II Commercial Code).

It should be noted that, except for the two situations mentioned above, French law requires such report. Thus the exception provided for by Article 15(2) of the Cross-border Merger Directive (which applies when the absorbing company holds 90% or more but less than 100% of the shares or securities representing the share capital of the absorbed company) does not apply if a French company is involved.

In case of contribution in kind, the independent expert must also prepare a report on this contribution and if the absorbing company is a *société anonyme*, the independent expert must also prepare a report on the individual benefit granted to shareholders if relevant (i.e. of the absorbed company), (Art. L.236-10 Commercial Code).

This report supplements the report on the draft terms of the merger and is made available under the same conditions.

15. The independent experts are liable to the company, the shareholders and third parties for any damage caused by their fault within the course of their mission.

4 Shareholders' meeting

A Information for shareholders

16. Certain documents need to be made available to the shareholders of each merging company for information purposes at their registered office, at least one month prior to the shareholders' meetings called to vote on the merger (Art. R.236-3 Commercial Code): the experts' report, the management's report, the draft terms of merger, the annual accounts as approved by the shareholders' meetings as well as the management reports for the past three years of all merging companies, an accounting statement prepared in accordance with the latest audited accounts (such accounts should not be more than three months old if these annual accounts relate to a fiscal year ended for more than six months).

When the merger occurs within the first months of the fiscal year but the annual accounts of the last fiscal year have not been approved yet or have been approved for less than a month, the shareholders must be provided with the annual accounts approved for the past two fiscal years and the corresponding management accounts, as well as the accounts not approved yet but certified by the statutory auditors or if they have not been decided upon by the management, an intermediary accounting statement dated less than three months.

The shareholders may obtain, upon request and free of charge, copies of all documents made available to them (Art. R.236-3 Commercial Code).

B Shareholders' approval

17. The decision of the shareholders' general meeting to approve the merger is required from all merging companies, except for a wholly owned subsidiary absorbed by its parent company (Art. L.236-11 Commercial Code).

The same conditions of quorum and majority apply as for an amendment of the articles of association (Art. L.236-2, al.2 Commercial Code), which vary depending upon the form of the company.

18. In a *société anonyme*, the cross-border merger must be voted by a special majority of two-thirds of the voting rights of the shareholders present or represented. For the shareholders' meeting to be validly held, attending or duly represented shareholders must hold one-quarter of the voting rights when first convened, or one-fifth upon the second convening (Art. L.225-96 Commercial Code).

19. In the case of a *société à responsabilité limitée*, those companies that were incorporated prior to 4 August 2005[5] are not under the same quorum requirements as those incorporated after that date.

Thus, the cross-border merger of a *société à responsabilité limitée* incorporated after 4 August 2005[6] must be approved by a majority of two-thirds of the shares held by the shareholders attending or duly represented, it being specified that the shareholders' meeting may validly deliberate only if the shareholders attending or duly represented hold one-quarter of the shares when first convened, or one-fifth upon the second convening (i.e. under the same conditions as a *société anonyme*). Articles of association may require quorum and majority rules higher than those mentioned above but not a unanimous vote (Art. L.223-30, al.3 of the Commercial Code).

For a *société à responsabilité limitée* incorporated prior to 4 August 2005,[7] the cross-border merger must be approved by the shareholders holding at least three-quarters of the shares (Art. L.223-30, al.2 Commercial Code) and there is no quorum requirement.[8] Any provisions of the articles of association requiring a higher majority would be considered null and void (Art. L.223-30, al.2 Commercial Code).

5 As a result of Law n° 2005-882 dated 2 August 2005.

6 As a result of Law n° 2005-882 dated 2 August 2005.

7 As a result of Law n° 2005-882 dated 2 August 2005.

8 *Mémento Pratique Francis Lefèbvre, Sociétés commerciales 2010*, n° 5802.

20. In a partnership limited by shares, unless otherwise specified in the articles of association, the unanimous vote of the general partners is mandatory (Art. L.226-11 Commercial Code).

21. The shareholders deciding upon the cross-border merger may decide that the merger shall be subject to the approval of the participation of employees in the company resulting from the merger (Art. L.236-28 Commercial Code).

5 Pre-merger certificate

22. Pursuant to Article L.236-6, the merging companies must file with the registry of the Tribunal within the jurisdiction in which their registered office is located a declaration of conformity by which they record all the acts carried out in order to proceed with this transaction and confirm that the transaction has been carried out in accordance with applicable rules and regulations.

The clerk of the Tribunal, as part of his duties, must establish the conformity of this declaration and issue a conformity certificate to that effect. This certificate must indicate whether an analysis or a modification process of the exchange ratio is being performed, or if an indemnification process of the minority shareholders is provided for (see no. 24 of this chapter) (Art. L.236-29 Commercial Code).

This conformity certificate must be issued by the clerk within eight days from the receipt of the certificate of conformity (Art. R.236-17 Commercial Code).

6 Legality scrutiny

23. As mentioned above (see no. 8 of this chapter), and pursuant to Article 11 of the Cross-border Merger Directive, when the absorbing company or the newly created company has its registered office in France, the French legality scrutiny procedure applies.

Under Article L.236-30, either a French notary or the clerk of the Tribunal within the jurisdiction of which the registered office of the company resulting from the merger will be located is in charge of the merger legality scrutiny process, and where appropriate, of the formation legality scrutiny process of the new company. In order to do so, he must ensure that the merging companies have approved the draft terms of merger under the same terms and conditions, and that, where applicable, the employee participation system has been set up in conformity with applicable labour law (Art. L.236-30 Commercial Code). Such verification process must be carried out within fifteen days from the receipt by the relevant recipient of the required documents listed under Article R.236-19 (see no. 8 of this chapter).

VI Minority shareholders

24. French law does not provide for any specific provisions with regard to minority shareholders who are bound by the shareholders' meeting's decision (see

nos. 17 et seq. of this chapter). The cross-border merger must be decided on the basis of the company's best interest and not solely in the best interest of a majority group.

VII Creditor protection

25. No specific provisions apply to cross-border mergers with respect to creditors' rights. As a result, applicable domestic legislation will remain enforceable in all Member States concerned.

26. As far as French companies are concerned, creditors of a merged company other than bondholders become creditors of the absorbing company, the debt remaining the same throughout the merger process (there is merely a substitution of debtor).

Those among such creditors whose claims existed prior to the publication of the draft terms of the merger (see no. 11 of this chapter) are entitled, within thirty days from the last publication, to oppose the merger (Arts. L.236-14 and R.236-8 Commercial Code). Such opposition claim must be brought before the president of the commercial court where the company has its registered office.

The competent jurisdiction may either reject such claim or order for the relevant debts to be reimbursed or, upon proposal by the absorbing company, and if deemed appropriate, for collaterals to be provided (Art. L.236-14 al 2 Commercial Code).

27. With regard to bondholders, the absorbed company may choose one of the following alternatives :

(i) the general meeting of the bondholders deliberates on the cross-border merger draft, or
(ii) the bondholders are not consulted and a reimbursement of their bonds is proposed.

If the general meeting of the bondholders approves the cross-border merger draft, the bondholders become, under the same conditions, the bondholders of the absorbing company, the decision taken by the bondholders' general meeting being enforceable against all the bondholders.

If the bondholders' general meeting does not approve the cross-border merger draft or does not validly deliberate (for example the required quorum not being achieved), the board of directors, the executive board or the executives of the absorbed company may override the bondholders' refusal but the bondholders (through the representative of the bondholders) may oppose the merger under the same conditions and effects as those described above for the creditors (Art. L.228-73 Commercial Code).

(ii) When the bondholders' general meeting is not convened to deliberate on the draft cross-border merger, the reimbursement of the bonds shall be offered to the bondholders (Art. L.236-13 Commercial Code).

The reimbursement offer is subject to several publications to ensure the good information of the bondholders. The bondholders have a three-month period as from the last formality of publicity to ask for the reimbursement of their bonds (Art. R.236-12 Commercial Code). Any bondholders who would not ask for the reimbursement of his bonds within the period mentioned above, would preserve his quality within the absorbing company, under the conditions set in the merger agreement (Art. L.236-13 Commercial Code).

VIII Rules applicable to employee participation

28. The rules governing the issue of employee participation in cross-border merger transactions are set forth in Part II, Book III, Title VII of the French Labour Code (*Participation des salariés dans les sociétés issues de fusions trans-frontalières*) (Arts. L.2371-1 through L.2375-1 French Labour Code) and were supplemented by two decrees of 31 October 2008.

1 Employee participation in companies resulting from a cross-border merger and registered in France

29. Under French company law, the articles of association of a *société anonyme* may provide for employee participation (Art L.225-27 and L.225-79 Commercial Code) on its board of directors or supervisory board, such provision being mandatory for listed *sociétés anonymes*.[9]

2 Special negotiating body ('SNB')

30. The employee participation within the company resulting from the merger is determined by a written agreement negotiated between the management and the employees through the SNB (Arts. L.2371-3 and L.2372-2 French Labour Code), unless the companies participating in the merger decide to implement employee participation according to the rules defined by the French Labour Code (Art. L.2371-3, al2 French Labour Code). The negotiations can last up to six months unless the parties exercise their option to extend the negotiations for a further six-month period (Art. L.2372-5, al2 French Labour Code).

The SNB is created as soon as practicable upon the publication of the draft terms of the merger (Art. L.2372-1, al2 French Labour Code). The SNB is composed pursuant to the rules applicable to the SNB of the European company (Art. L.2372-3 French Labour Code). If French companies, subsidiaries or establishments participating in the merger have trade unions, seats of the SNB are distributed amongst the union members employed by the merging

9 Pursuant to Arts. L.225-23 and 225-71 of the Commercial Code, one or more members of the board of directors or the supervisory board must then be elected by the general meeting of the shareholders, upon proposal of the employees holding more than 3 per cent of the company's share capital and among same employees.

companies and sitting on the works council (at the company or establishment level), if there is one, or amongst trade union representatives (*représentants syndicaux*).

If there is no trade union in the company resulting from the merger with its registered office located in France or in any French subsidiary or establishment, the employee representatives (*représentants du personnel*) in the SNB must be directly appointed by the employees in accordance with the same rules used to appoint employee representatives (*représentants du personnel*) in the works council. Thus, the SNB members may include both union representatives and employee representatives.

3 Protection of employee representatives

31. Pursuant to articles 4, 5 and 6 of the Act, SNB members enjoy the same degree of protection against dismissal as employee representatives under French law. Thus, their dismissal is subject to an opinion of the works council and prior approval of the competent state employment agent (*inspecteur du travail*).

IX Tax treatment

32. Directive 2005/19/EC does not cover the tax aspects of cross-border mergers (the 'Merger Tax Directive'), these having previously been set out in Directive 90/434 dated 23 July 1990 and then subsequently amended until the recent Directive 2009/133 of 19 October 2009 (not yet transposed into French law).

The transposition of the Merger Tax Directive will not have any consequences per se as regards the tax treatment applicable to cross-border mergers. However, it will enable cross-border mergers to be more easily implemented so as to benefit from the following tax regime.

1 Tax treatment at the level of the absorbing company

A Corporate income tax

33. Pursuant to the territoriality principle of taxation provided for by Article 209, I of the French Tax Code, a cross-border merger may have French tax implications in the case where the merger results in the transfer of an activity exercised in France or of certain French assets, regardless of the state in which the seats of the absorbing and absorbed companies are located. Despite the lack of a legal framework, cross-border mergers have been benefiting from a favourable tax regime since the Merger Tax Directive 90/434/EC of 23 July 1990, which ensures, under certain conditions, that such transactions are tax neutral as regards capital gains on the transferred assets and which considers the merger merely to be an interposed transaction. The said Directive was transposed into French law as Articles 210 OA and sub. of the French Tax Code under

which, subject to certain requirements, mergers can benefit from a tax deferral regime.

The regime is applicable to mergers that involve a foreign entity unless such foreign entity is located in a state or territory that has not entered into a tax treaty with France containing an administrative assistance clause against tax fraud and tax evasion. However, due to national sovereignty issues, specific requirements may apply to cross-border mergers in order to ensure that France maintains the right to tax latent capital gains realised on the French business activity. Beyond requirements that would be applicable to a domestic merger, the absorption of a French company by a foreign company may benefit from a deferral of the capital gains tax arising from the transfer of the assets, subject to the granting of a prior ruling by the French tax authorities. In this respect, the company may need to provide evidence of valid economic justification for the transaction and of the aim of the transaction being neither tax fraud nor tax evasion. Moreover, the company is required to show that by performing the transaction, the capital gains benefiting from the tax exemption will subsequently be subject to tax in France. From a practical point of view, this last condition requires that the foreign absorbing company create a permanent establishment in France that will book all the transferred assets on its balance sheet.

The transfer of the losses by the absorbed company to the absorbing company is subject to a ruling being granted by the French tax authorities. Such ruling is not specific to the cross-border context; however, the French tax losses transferred may only be offset against the results of a French permanent establishment of the foreign absorbing company.

As far as capital gains arising from the cancellation of the absorbed company's shares are concerned, it should be noted that the absorption of a foreign company (even if such foreign company does not have any activity in France) by a French company may give rise to the taxation of such capital gains in France depending on the provisions of the applicable tax treaty.

B Others

34. As is the case for domestic mergers, a cross-border merger is subject to a fixed registration duty of either €375 or €500 (depending on the amount of the absorbing company's share capital). However, if French real estate assets are transferred, a registration duty of 0.75 per cent is due on the fair market value of the transferred buildings.

35. As far as VAT is concerned, a merger taking place between VAT taxpayers does not trigger a payment of VAT. The absorbing company is treated as if it would continue the merged entity for VAT purposes.

2 Tax treatment at the level of the shareholders of the absorbed company

36. The merger is also tax neutral at the level of the shareholders of the absorbed company.

Attributing an absorbing company's shares to the shareholders of the absorbed company in exchange for shares in the latter company does not give rise to any taxation of the income, profits or latent capital gains of that shareholder.

The latent capital gains realised on the exchange of shares benefits from a tax deferral regime in France. The shareholders will only be taxed when selling the shares received in consideration for the transaction.

21

Greece

TOM KYRIAKOPOULOS
Kelemenis & Co.

I Introduction

1. The Cross-border Merger Directive has been implemented in Greece pursuant to law 3777/2009[1] (the 'Greek Law on Cross-border Mergers'). This law was enacted as a separate piece of corporate legislation regarding specifically cross-border mergers, which is supplemented by relevant provisions of existing company legislation, depending on the type of legal form.

II Scope of the new rules

2. The Greek Law on Cross-border Mergers applies to all Greek limited liability companies, as these are set out in the First Company Law Directive

1 Greek Government Gazette Issue A, no. 127 of 28 July 2009.

(68/151/EEC) (i.e. *societes anonymes* (ανώνυμες εταιρίες), private limited liability companies (εταιρίες περιορισμένης ευθύνης) and limited partnerships by shares (ετερόρρυθμες κατά μετοχές εταιρίες)[2] and to European companies (SE) whose seat is located in Greece. Moreover, the Greek Law on Cross-border Mergers also applies to companies with share capital and having legal personality, possessing separate assets, which alone serve to cover its debts, and subject, under national law governing it, to conditions concerning guarantees such as are provided for by the First Company Law (68/151/EEC) for the protection of the interests of members and other third parties.

The provisions of the Greek Law on Cross-border Mergers apply to mergers of one or more Greek companies, as per above, with one or more limited liability companies established according to the law of another Member State of the European Union and which have their registered office, central administration or principal place of business within the Community or when the company resulting from the cross-border merger of companies from different Member States has its registered address in Greece (Art. 1(2) Greek Law on Cross-border Mergers).

3. The Greek Law on Cross-border Mergers does not apply to cross-border mergers involving a company the object of which is the collective investment of capital provided by the public, which operates on the principle of risk-spreading and the units of which are, at the holders' request, repurchased or redeemed, directly or indirectly, out of the assets of that company (Art. 1(3) Greek Law on Cross-border Mergers). Under Greek law, such companies are governed by the law 3283/2004.

III Cash payment

4. By exception to the provisions of Article 68 of Greek Codified Law 2190/1920 regarding Greek *societes anonymes* restricting the amount of cash payable to shareholders upon merger, the Greek Law on Cross-border Mergers permits the payment of cash exceeding 10 per cent of the nominal value or, in the absence thereof, the accounting value of the securities or shares representing the capital of the company arising from the cross-border merger, provided the law of the Member State of one of the participating companies so allows (Art. 2(3) Greek Law on Cross-border Mergers).

IV Legal consequences and enforceability of a cross-border merger

5. In accordance with Article 12(1) and (2) of the Greek law, once the cross-border merger has been registered with the General Commercial Register maintained

2 First Council Directive 68/151/EEC of 9 March 1968 on coordination of safeguards which, for the protection of the interests of members and others, are required by Member States of companies within the meaning of the second paragraph of Article 58 of the Treaty, with a view to making such safeguards equivalent throughout the Community (OJ L65, 14.3.1968, p. 8).

with the Greek Ministry of Development (now called the Ministry of Economy, Competitiveness and Marine), the following legal consequences apply:

(i) all assets and liabilities of the companies being acquired are transferred to the acquiring company without liquidation of the acquired companies;
(ii) the partners or shareholders of the companies being acquired become partners or shareholders of the acquiring company; and
(iii) the companies being acquired cease to exist without liquidation.

Following the registration of the cross-border merger with the General Commercial Register, the merger can no longer be held as null and void (Art. 15 Greek Law on Cross-border Mergers) by anyone.

There is no exchange of shares issued by the acquiring company in consideration for shares in the company/companies being acquired in the following cases:

(i) when the shares in the company/companies being acquired are owned by the acquiring company or by third parties acting in their own name but on behalf of the acquiring company; or
(ii) when the shares in the company/companies being acquired are owned by the companies themselves or by third parties acting in their own name but on behalf of the company/companies being acquired.

6. If, in the case of a cross-border merger, Greek law requires the completion of special formalities before the transfer of certain assets, rights and obligations belonging to the merging becomes effective against third parties, these formalities are carried out by the company resulting from the cross-border merger (Art. 12(3) Greek Law on Cross-border Mergers).

The rights and obligations of the merging companies arising from contracts of employment or from employment relationships and existing at the date on which the cross-border merger takes effect are transferred to the company resulting from the cross-border merger on the date on which the cross-border merger is registered with the General Commercial Register (Art. 12(4) Greek Law on Cross-border Mergers).

V Procedure

1 The draft terms of the cross-border merger

7. The management or administrative bodies of each of the merging companies must draw up the common draft terms of the cross-border merger. In accordance with Article 3 of the Greek Law on Cross-border Mergers, the common draft terms of cross-border merger must include at least the following:

(i) the legal form, name and registered office of the merging companies and the respective data for the company resulting from the cross-border merger;

(ii) the ratio applicable to the exchange of securities or shares representing the company capital and the amount, if applicable, of any cash payment;
(iii) the terms for the allotment of securities or shares representing the capital of the company resulting from the cross-border merger;
(iv) the likely repercussions of the cross-border merger on the labour situation of the employees;
(v) the date from which the holding of securities or shares representing the company capital will entitle the holders to share in profits and any special conditions affecting that entitlement;
(vi) the date from which the transactions of the merging companies will be treated for accounting purposes as being those of the company resulting from the cross-border merger;
(vii) the rights conferred by the company resulting from the cross-border merger on members enjoying special rights or on holders of securities other than shares representing the company capital, or the measures proposed concerning them;
(viii) any special advantages granted to the experts who examine the draft terms of the cross-border merger or to members of the administrative, management, supervisory or controlling organs of the merging companies;
(ix) the statutes of the company resulting from the cross-border merger;
(x) where appropriate, information on the procedures by which arrangements for the involvement of employees in the definition of their rights to participation in the company resulting from the cross-border merger are determined pursuant to Article 14 of the Greek Law on Cross-border Mergers;
(xi) information on the evaluation of the assets and liabilities which are transferred to the company resulting from the cross-border merger;
(xii) dates of the merging companies' accounts used to establish the conditions of the cross-border merger.

In the event a parent company merges with its wholly owned subsidiary, items (ii), (iii) and (v) above can be omitted (Art. 13(a) Greek Law on Cross-border Mergers).

In accordance with Article 76(1) of the Greek Codified Law on *public limited liability companies*, members of the Board of Directors of the merging companies can be held liable to the shareholders of these companies or to third parties for any damage resulting from the preparation and conclusion of the merger.

8. According to Article 4 of the Greek Law on Cross-border Mergers, a Greek company participating in a cross-border merger, either as the acquiring or acquired company, must first submit the common draft terms of the cross-border merger for review by the Department of Public Limited Liability Companies and Credit within the General Secretariat of Commerce of the

Ministry of Development. Following the review, the common draft terms are filed with the General Commercial Register held in the General Secretariat of Commerce at least one (1) month before the shareholders' meeting is convened to decide on the cross-border merger. In addition, an extract of the common draft terms must be published in the Greek Government Gazette, which must contain the following information:

(i) the type, name and registered office of every merging company;
(ii) the register in which the documents referred to in Article 3(2) of the First Company Law Directive (68/151/EEC) are filed in respect of each merging company, and the number of the entry in that register;
(iii) an indication, for each of the merging companies, of the arrangements made for the exercise of the rights of creditors and of any minority members of the merging companies and the address at which complete information on those arrangements may be obtained free of charge.

2 Management report

9. In accordance with Article 5 of the Greek Law on Cross-border Mergers, the management or administrative organ of the Greek merging company must draw up a report intended for the shareholders' meeting explaining and justifying the legal and economic aspects of the cross-border merger and explaining the implications of the cross-border merger for members, creditors and employees.

Where the management or administrative organ of the merging Greek company receives, in a timely fashion, an opinion from the representatives of the employees, as provided for under Presidential Decree 240/2006, that opinion shall be appended to the report.

The Management report is filed with the General Commercial Register held in the General Secretariat of Commerce at least one month before the shareholders' meeting is convened.

10. The report must be made available to the members and to the representatives of the employees or, where there are no such representatives, to the employees themselves, not less than one month before the date of the shareholders' meeting.

11. In accordance with Article 76(1) of the Greek Codified Law on public limited liability companies, members of the board of directors of the merging companies can be held liable to the shareholders of these companies or to third parties for any damage resulting from the preparation and conclusion of the merger.

3 Auditor's report

12. In accordance with Article 6(1) of the Greek Law on Cross-border Mergers, an independent auditor's report intended for the partners/shareholders (depending

on the legal form of the company) is drawn up for each merging company. The auditors may be individuals or legal entities.

In accordance with Article 6(2) of the Greek Law on Cross-border Mergers, as an alternative to auditors operating on behalf of each of the merging companies, one or more independent experts, appointed for that purpose at the joint request of the companies by a judicial or administrative authority in the Member State of one of the merging companies or of the company resulting from the cross-border merger or approved by such an authority, may examine the common draft terms of the cross-border merger and draw up a single written report to all the members. In Greece, the appropriate above administrative authority for the appointment of the aforementioned independent auditors is the Department of Sociétés Anonymes and Credit within the General Secretariat of Commerce of the Ministry of Development.

If all the partners/shareholders of each of the companies involved in the cross-border merger have so agreed, neither an examination of the common draft terms of cross-border merger by independent auditors nor an audit report is required (Art. 6(4) Greek Law on Cross-border Mergers).

An auditor's report is also not required in the event of a merger by absorption of a wholly owned subsidiary (Art. 13(a) Greek Law on Cross-border Mergers).

13. According to the Greek Law on Cross-border Mergers and Corporate Law, the auditors' report must include the following:

(i) If, in the opinion of the auditors, the exchange ratio between the shares of the company or companies being absorbed and the shares issued by the company absorbing is fair and reasonable. It should be noted that the auditors do not determine the exchange ratio but simply provide their assessment on the ratio.

(ii) The total value of all the contributing assets and liabilities of the company or companies being absorbed and the change this will have on the capital of the absorbing company, resulting from the merger. According to Greek law, the report must also: include the description of each contribution; make reference to the valuation methods that have been applied; and certify whether the values deriving from the application of these valuation methods correspond to the number and nominal value of the shares that will be issued against the contributions or where the par value is not known, to the book value, taking also into consideration the difference above par which may arise from the issue of the shares.

(iii) The method or methods used for the determination of the proposed exchange ratio between the shares.

(iv) A statement on whether the method or methods followed are appropriate for the specific case or cases, the values resulting from the application of each method and an opinion of the importance given to certain methods for the determination of these values, as well as a description of any difficulties that have arisen during the valuation.

The auditors have the right to request from each merging company all information they consider necessary for the discharge of their duties (Art. 6(3) Greek Law on Cross-border Mergers).

14. The independent auditor's report must be drawn up for each merging company and made available not less than one month before the date of the general meeting.

4 General meeting of shareholders

A Information for shareholders

15. According to an application by analogy of relevant provisions of Greek company law 2190/20, at least one month before the shareholders' meeting convenes in order to decide on the common draft terms of cross-border merger, every shareholder has the right to be informed of the contents of at least the following documents, at the seat of the company:

(i) the management report and the auditor's report;
(ii) the common draft terms of cross-border merger;
(iii) the annual financial statements, including the management reports issued by the Board of Directors, for the last three fiscal years of each merging company; and
(iv) if the draft terms of cross-border merger are dated more than six months after the close of the last fiscal year to which the latest annual accounts relate, an accounting statement (temporary balance sheet) for each merging company dated no earlier than three months prior to the date of the draft terms of cross-border merger.

16. Following a written application by any interested shareholder, the company must deliver or send at no cost full copies or abstracts of the above documents.

B Shareholder approval

17. After taking note of the management and auditors' reports, the general meeting of each of the merging companies shall decide on the approval of the common draft terms of cross-border merger. However, for the absorption of a wholly owned subsidiary by its parent company, shareholder approval is not required at the level of the subsidiary (Art. 13(a) Greek Law on Cross-border Mergers).

18. As concerns Greek companies participating in cross-border mergers, a reinforced quorum and majority is required according to the legal form of the entity, as follows.

For Greek public limited liability companies, the shareholders' meeting requires a quorum and validly meets when two-thirds of the paid up share capital is present or represented at the meeting. If no such quorum is achieved during the first meeting, a quorum of one-half of the paid up share capital is required. If no such quorum is achieved during the second meeting, a quorum of one-third of the paid up share capital is required. Decisions are validly taken by a majority of two-thirds of the votes represented at the shareholders' meeting.

For Greek private limited liability companies, the shareholders' meeting of partners can take a valid decision regarding a cross-border merger if it achieves a majority of at least three-quarters of partners representing at least three-quarters of the capital. It should be noted that the change of nationality requires a unanimous decision of all partners.

For Greek limited partnerships by shares, a unanimous decision of all partners is required.

19. According to an application by analogy of relevant provisions of Greek company laws 2190/20 and 3190/55, the decision of the shareholders' meetings on the merger together with the relevant agreement must be drawn up in the form of a notarial deed, which must be filed with the Ministry of Development and published in the Greek Government Gazette.

20. If there are different classes of shares and if the merger results in a change of their respective rights, the quorum and special majority requirements must be met for each class of shares. If any company participating in the cross-border merger has creditors holding convertible corporate bonds, the decision regarding the merger has to be approved by these creditors as well.

21. The general meeting of a merging company may decide to make its decision subject to express ratification of the arrangements with respect to the participation of employees in the company resulting from the merger (Art. 7(4) Greek Law on Cross-border Mergers).

5 Pre-merger certificate

22. The Greek Administrative authority competent to review the legality of the cross-border merger as regards that part of the procedure which concerns the merging companies subject to Greek law is the Department of Public Limited Liability Companies and Credit within the General Secretariat of Commerce of the Ministry of Development (now called the Ministry of Economy, Competitiveness and Marine).

The aforementioned authority must issue, without delay, to the merging companies subject to Greek law, a certificate attesting to the proper completion of the pre-merger acts and formalities.

23. The above authority may issue the aforementioned certificate even if a compensation procedure is pending for the minority members in connection with the ratio applicable to the exchange of shares, in accordance with Article 8(1)(b)

of the Greek Law on Cross-border Mergers. The certificate must, however, indicate that the procedure is pending. The decision in the procedure shall be binding on the company resulting from the cross-border merger and all its members.

6 Effects of the decision

24. The Greek Administrative authority competent to review the legality and approve the cross-border merger as regards that part of the procedure which concerns the completion of the cross-border merger in Greece and, where appropriate, the formation of a new company resulting from the cross-border merger in Greece, is the Department of Public Limited Liability Companies and Credit within the General Secretariat of Commerce of the Ministry of Development. The above authority ensures in particular that the merging companies have approved the common draft terms of cross-border merger in the same terms and, where appropriate, that arrangements for employee participation have been determined in accordance with Article 14 of the Greek Law on Cross-border Mergers (Art. 10(1) Greek Law on Cross-border Mergers).

25. To that end each merging company that is not subject to Greek law shall submit to the Department of Public Limited Liability Companies and Credit within the General Secretariat of Commerce of the Ministry of Development the pre-merger certificate within six months of its issue together with the common draft terms of cross-border merger approved by the general meeting (Art. 10(2) Greek Law on Cross-border Mergers).

In the event the absorbing company or the company resulting from the cross-border merger has its registered address in Greece, the cross-border merger agreement is executed in the form of a notarial deed, to which a statutory declaration is attached attesting that creditors did not express any objection to the merger or that any objection was resolved (Art. 11(1) Greek Law on Cross-border Mergers).

26. The cross-border merger is completed when the Decision of the Minister of Development approving the merger is recorded in the General Commercial Register maintained within the General Secretariat of Commerce of the Ministry of Development and the relevant announcement is published by the Department of Public Limited Liability Companies and Credit within the General Secretariat of Commerce of the Ministry of Development in the Greek Government Gazette. When the Decision of the Minister of Development approving the merger is recorded in the General Commercial Register, the Department of Public Limited Liability Companies and Credit must notify, without delay, the relevant registries of the Member States in whose jurisdiction the other companies being merged were subject to (Art. 11(2) Greek Law on Cross-border Mergers).

When the registration of the cross-border merger is undertaken by another Member State, the Department of Public Limited Liability Companies and Credit within the General Secretariat of Commerce of the Ministry of Development deletes the Greek company being absorbed from the General Commercial Register upon notification that the decision approving the cross-border merger was registered (Art. 11(3) Greek Law on Cross-border Mergers).

27. From the date the cross-border merger has been registered, it cannot be declared void (Art. 15 Greek Law on Cross-border Mergers).

VI Minority shareholders

28. The members of the Greek company being absorbed, who did not approve the decision for the cross-border merger have the right within one month from the date the shareholders' meeting approved the cross-border merger to do the following:

(i) They have the right to file a petition with the Greek courts asking the Greek company participating in the cross-border merger to repurchase the securities or titles, on the condition that the Greek company is being absorbed or that the new company resulting from the cross-border merger has its registered office in another Member State. In this case, the provisions of Article 49a of Greek Codified Law 2190/1920 regarding Greek public limited liability companies, which provides for the right of the minority to request the repurchase of its shares by the company, apply by analogy. In order to ensure the payment of the repurchase price, the Greek courts may issue injunction or provisional measures (Art. 8(1)(a) Greek Law on Cross-border Mergers).

(ii) They have the right to claim compensation if the ratio applicable to the exchange of their securities or titles in consideration for the securities or titles in the absorbing company has been determined unjustifiably low, in accordance with the provisions of Article 77a of Greek Codified Law 2190/1920 regarding Greek public limited liability companies. In this case, the merger procedure is not postponed. The above compensation procedure is applicable in Greece only if there is a respective procedure according to the laws of the Member States of the other companies participating in the cross-border merger or if the other companies participating in the cross-border merger and which are registered in Member States that do not provide for such procedure explicitly accept in the common draft terms of the cross-border merger that the shareholders of the Greek companies being absorbed have the right to make use of the particular procedure. The decision issued according to the above procedure is binding on the company resulting from the cross-border merger and on all its members (Art. 8(1)(b) Greek Law on Cross-border Mergers).

VII Protection of creditors

29. As concerns the protection of creditors, Article 8(2) of the Greek Law on Cross-border Mergers refers to the provisions of Article 70 of Greek Codified Law 2190/1920 regarding Greek public limited liability companies and Article 54 of Law 3190/1955 regarding limited liability companies.

Regarding Greek public limited liability companies in particular, within a period of one month from the completion of the publicity formalities, the creditors of the companies to be merged, the claims of which were born before the publication and had not become due and payable on the publication date, have the right to ask for sufficient guarantees, if the financial situation of the companies to be merged renders such protection necessary and under the condition that these creditors have not already received such guarantees. Any dispute gives the right to the interested creditors to raise in writing objections against the merger. Following a petition of the company or companies to be merged, the competent court of first instance may permit the merger, despite the objections of the creditor(s), if it is ruled that the financial situation of the companies to be merged or the guarantees that have been received by or offered to these creditors do not justify their objections.

VIII Employee participation

30. The Greek Law on Cross-border Mergers, in Article 14, provides for the participation of employees in the company resulting from the cross-border merger in Greece and sets as a general rule the application of Greek law on employee participation in the event the company resulting from the cross-border merger has its registered office in Greece, providing, however, for exceptions to the extent this is necessary for the maintenance of existing rights of employees.

31. Notwithstanding the above, the rules in force concerning employee participation in Greece do not apply in the following cases:

(i) where at least one of the merging companies has, in the six months before the publication of the draft terms of the cross-border merger, an average number of employees that exceeds 500 and is operating under an employee participation system within the meaning of Article 2 of Greek Presidential Decree 91/2006 (which harmonised the Directive on European Companies), or

(ii) where Greek law does not provide for (a) at least the same level of employee participation as operated in the relevant merging companies, measured by reference to the proportion of employee representatives amongst the members of the administrative or supervisory organ or their committees or of the management group which covers the profit units of the company, subject to employee representation, or (b) employees of the establishments of the company resulting from the cross-border merger that are situated in other Member States the same entitlement to exercise participation rights as is enjoyed by those employees employed in Greece.

32. In the cases referred to in no. 31 above, the participation of employees in the company resulting from the cross-border merger and their involvement in the definition of such rights is regulated by the relevant provisions of the Regulation on European Companies (EC 2157/2001) and the Directive on European Companies (2001/86/EC), as harmonised by Greek law.

33. According to the Greek Law on Cross-border Mergers:

(i) the relevant organs of the merging companies have the right to choose without any prior negotiation to be directly subject to the standard rules for participation and to abide by those rules from the date of registration; and

(ii) the special negotiating body has the right to decide, by a majority of two-thirds of its members representing at least two-thirds of the employees, including the votes of members representing employees in at least two different Member States, not to open negotiations or to terminate negotiations already opened and to rely on the rules on participation in force in Greece.

34. When the company resulting from the cross-border merger operates under an employee participation system, the company is obliged to take measures to ensure that employees' participation rights are protected in the event of subsequent domestic mergers for a period of three years after the cross-border merger has taken effect.

Companies established in Greece and falling under the provisions of the Greek Law on Cross-border Mergers are obliged to notify the number of their employees and the number of their representatives in writing to the Ministry of Labour and Social Protection (Department of Social Inspection) within a period of three months from the completion of the merger.

IX Tax treatment

35. Greek Law 2578/1998, as subsequently amended by Law 3517/2006, brought relevant Greek tax legislation in line with the Merger Tax Directive (2009/133/EC) of 19 October 2009.

36. In accordance with Article 1 and 2 of Greek Law 2578/1998, the relevant tax provisions regarding cross-border mergers of the law apply when the following conditions apply cumulatively:

(i) a cross-border merger takes place, as defined in Greek Law 2578/1998 (Art. 2(a) Merger Tax Directive), whose conceptual term is in line with that in the Greek Law on Cross-border Mergers;

(ii) the merger takes place between companies that have their tax residence in different Member States of the European Union (under the terms of national legislation and double taxation agreements) and are subject to the taxes set out in Article 3(c) of the Merger Tax Directive;

(iii) the merger takes place between companies that have the legal form set out in Annex A of the Greek Law 2578/1998 (see also Annex (g) of the Merger Tax Directive); for companies under Greek law: public limited liability company and private limited liability companies known as 'ανώνυμη εταιρεία' and 'εταιρεία περιορισμένης ευθύνης (Ε.Π.Ε.)' respectively; and

(iv) the merger results in the transfer of assets and liabilities that (a) are situated in Greece, (b) give rise to a permanent establishment of the acquiring company or that are connected to an existing permanent establishment in Greece and (c) contribute to generating income subject to Greek income tax. The term 'permanent establishment' is defined in accordance with Article 100 of the Greek Income Tax Code and the relevant provisions of double taxation agreements.

37. In the event of a cross-border merger as defined above, the capital gain resulting from the absorption of a Greek company or a permanent establishment of a foreign company in Greece by a company from an EU Member State is not subject to Greek income tax at the time of the merger (tax deferral) according to Article 3 of Greek Law 2578/1998. Notwithstanding the above exemption, if the Greek company being absorbed by virtue of a cross-border merger has a permanent establishment (e.g. branch) in another EU Member State, the transfer of the permanent establishment due to the cross-border merger is subject to Greek capital gains tax, in which case a tax credit is given for the capital gains tax that would have been paid in the respective EU Member State where the permanent establishment is situated.

38. The aforementioned income tax deferral ceases to exist and the EU company that absorbed the Greek company or the permanent establishment of a foreign company in Greece is subject to Greek income tax for the capital gain arising from the cross-border merger in the following cases:

(i) the permanent establishment in Greece of the EU company that absorbed the Greek company or the permanent establishment of a foreign company in Greece ceases to exist;

(ii) the capital gain is taken outside or exported out of Greece;

(iii) the capital gain is credited in the accounts of the EU company that absorbed the Greek company or the permanent establishment of a foreign company in Greece; and

(iv) assets acquired by virtue of the cross-border merger are transferred outside Greece by the EU company that absorbed the Greek company or the permanent establishment of a foreign company in Greece.

39. In addition to the aforementioned tax deferral of the capital gains tax resulting from the absorption of a Greek company or a permanent establishment of a foreign company in Greece by a company from an EU Member State, Greek Law 2578/1998 also provides for the following tax treatment.

Tax reserves recorded in the books of the Greek company or the permanent establishment of a foreign company in Greece being absorbed are not subject to tax at the time of the cross-border merger, on the condition that they are transferred and recorded as is in special accounts in the books of the permanent establishment resulting from the cross-border merger.

The permanent establishment in Greece resulting from the cross-border merger can continue to use the tax losses recorded in the books of the Greek company or the permanent establishment of a foreign company in Greece being absorbed, on the condition that this is permissible according to Greek incentive legislation for domestic mergers. According to current legislation, such benefit is not applicable.

The permanent establishment in Greece resulting from the cross-border merger can continue to depreciate the assets acquired from the Greek company or the permanent establishment of a foreign company in Greece being absorbed under the same terms and conditions.

All tax benefits and incentives granted to the Greek company or the permanent establishment of a foreign company in Greece continue to exist in the name of the permanent establishment in Greece resulting from the cross-border merger.

The following acts and transactions are exempt from Greek tax, stamp duty and duties in favour of the Greek State:

(i) the merger agreement;
(ii) the contribution and transfer of assets and liabilities from the companies being absorbed to the permanent establishment resulting from the cross-border merger;
(iii) the decisions of the companies participating in the cross-border merger and any other decision or act required for the completion of the cross-border merger;
(iv) the publication of decisions in the Greek Government Gazette;
(v) the transfer of real estate from the Greek company or the permanent establishment of a foreign company in Greece being absorbed on the condition that the real estate will be used by the permanent establishment resulting from the cross-border merger for at least five years from the merger.

40. Any capital gain arising for the members or shareholders of the companies being absorbed from the issue of titles or securities in the absorbing company in exchange for titles or securities in the companies being absorbed, due to a cross-border merger, is not subject to Greek income tax. This tax exemption is granted under the following conditions:

(i) the member/shareholder acquiring titles or securities in the absorbing company does not confer on such titles or securities a tax value higher than that which the titles or securities he/she exchanged them for had before the cross-border merger;

(ii) a cash payment was not paid to the members/shareholders whose company was absorbed. In the latter case, the cash payment is subject to Greek income tax.

41. If the cross-border merger has as its principal objective or as one of its principal objectives tax evasion or tax avoidance, any tax benefits provided by virtue of Greek law 2578/1998 cease to apply from the date of the merger.

22

Ireland

MARGARET STACK, JENNIFER MCCARTHY, MICHAEL GREENE
A&L Goodbody

I Introduction

1. The Cross-border Merger Directive has been implemented in Ireland by Statutory Instrument No. 157 of 2008, European Communities (Cross-border Mergers) Regulations 2008 (the Regulations). The Regulations were given effect on27 May 2008.

II Scope

2. Subject to the exemptions listed below, the Regulations facilitate the cross-border merger of any 'Irish company', with a limited liability company or companies in other European Economic Area Member States. An 'Irish company'

is defined as a limited liability company (other than a company limited by guarantee). An 'Irish company' also includes unregistered companies to which Section 377(1) of the Irish Companies Act 1963 applies. However, in practice there is only one such Irish entity, the Governor and Company of the Bank of Ireland. Unlimited liability companies cannot avail of the cross-border merger procedure under the Regulations.

III Cash payment

3. In a merger by acquisition or a merger by formation of a new company, the shareholders of the transferor company or companies transfer all of the assets and liabilities of that company to another limited liability company in another European Economic Area Member State ('the successor company'). In exchange for those assets and liabilities, the shareholders of the transferor company or companies will receive shares or securities in the successor company, which can also be accompanied by a cash payment.[1] Article 2 of the Cross-border Merger Directive allows for a cash payment of up to 10 per cent of the nominal value of the shares or securities in the transferor company to be made to the shareholders of the transferor company. However, Article 3 allows European Economic Area Member States to exceed this threshold and allow for larger cash payments as consideration for the cross-border merger. The Regulations (as indicated at Regulation 5(2)(c)) anticipate that a cash payment may be made as consideration but do not apply any limit to the value of such a cash payment.

IV Legal consequences of the merger and enforceability

4. The principle consequence of a cross-border merger is that all the assets and liabilities of the merging companies are transferred to a successor company by operation of law. The merging companies (with the exception of the successor company where no new company is established) are dissolved without going into liquidation. The shareholders of the merging companies which have ceased to exist become shareholders in the successor company.

5. In the case of an Irish successor company, it is obliged, in consequence of the cross-border merger, to make any cash payment to the shareholders of the transferor company as required under the common draft terms. In the case of a merger by acquisition[2] or a merger by the formation of a new company, where no application has been made by minority shareholders for a cash payment

1 Where the transferor company is the wholly owned subsidiary of the successor company, no consideration is issued.

2 A merger where all of the assets and liabilities of a merging company or companies are transferred to another merging company (the successor company) and the transferor company or companies are dissolved without going into liquidation.

in lieu of shares in the successor company, all remaining shareholders of the transferor companies become shareholders of the Irish successor company.

6. Any legal proceedings that are pending by or against any transferor company shall be continued against the Irish successor company. Also, the rights and obligations arising from the contracts (including contracts of employment) of the transferor company are transferred to the Irish successor company and reference made to the transferor company in any contract, agreement or instrument shall be construed as if the Irish successor company had been a party thereto instead of the transferor company. An offer or invitation to treat made by the transferor company shall be construed as being made by the Irish successor company.

7. An Irish successor company must also comply with all filing requirements and any other special formalities as required by law (including the law of another European Economic Area Member State) for the transfer of the assets and liabilities of the transferor company to be effective in relation to other persons (Regulation 19(2) of the Regulations).

8. Regulation 21 of the Regulations disapplies certain provisions of Irish company law, which facilitate cross-border mergers involving Irish companies:

(i) Sections 30 and 31 of the Irish Companies (Amendment) Act 1983, which requires the production of an expert's report before an Irish public limited company may allot shares in exchange for non-cash consideration;
(ii) Section 149(5) of the Irish Companies Act 1963, which restricts a holding company from treating any pre-acquisition profits of any subsidiary acquired by it as profits of its own;
(iii) Section 41(1) of the Irish Companies Act 1983, which restricts the right of an Irish company to purchase any of its own shares.

9. Where there is an Irish successor company, the Irish High Court Order specifying the date on which the cross-border merger is to have effect shall constitute evidence of the effectiveness of the cross-border merger to all third parties. A cross-border merger that has taken effect by an Order of the Irish High Court cannot be declared null and void.

V Procedure

1 Draft terms of cross-border merger

10. Common draft terms shall be drawn up in writing by each of the merging companies and adopted by the board of directors of each Irish merging company, under Regulation 5 of the Regulations.

11. The common draft terms should include the information described in no. 18 of Chapter 1 of the first volume of this book. The common draft terms may also

include such additional terms as are not inconsistent with the Regulations. The common draft terms shall not provide for any shares in the successor company to be exchanged for shares in a transferor company held either by the successor company itself or its nominee on its behalf, or by the transferor company itself or a nominee on its behalf.

12. Each Irish merging company must deliver the common draft terms to the Irish Registrar of Companies (the Registrar) for registration. A notice in the prescribed form (Form CBM1) must also be delivered to the Registrar containing the following details about each merging company:

(i) its name and registered office;
(ii) its legal form and the law by which it is governed;
(iii) in the case of an Irish company, its registered number;
(iv) in the case of a European Economic Area Member State company, the particulars of the national register in which that company's file is kept and its registration number;
(v) the arrangements made for the exercise of the rights of creditors and minority shareholders of the merging companies; and
(vi) the address at which full information on these arrangements may be obtained free of charge.

13. At least one month before the general meeting of the shareholders to approve the cross-border merger, notice of delivery of the common draft terms and Form CBM1 must be published by each Irish merging company in the Irish Companies Registration Office Gazette and in at least two national daily newspapers in Ireland. The notice shall include the date of delivery of the documentation, a statement that the common draft terms are available for inspection in the Irish merging company's registered office and a statement that copies may be obtained from the Registrar.

14. The common draft terms also need to be made available for inspection by the shareholders and employees' representatives (or the employees themselves where there are no representatives) at the registered office of each Irish merging company for one month (for at least two hours a day) immediately preceding the general meeting of that company to approve the cross-border merger.

2 Directors' explanatory report

15. Under Regulation 6 of the Regulations, the directors of each Irish merging company shall prepare a report for the shareholders and the employees' representatives (or the employees themselves where there are no representatives) explaining the implications of the cross-border merger for the shareholders, the creditors and the employees of the company. The report shall also state the legal and economic grounds for the common draft terms of merger. As stated above in the case of the common draft terms, the directors' explanatory report

needs to be made available for inspection by the shareholders and employees' representatives (or the employees themselves where there are no representatives) at the registered office of each Irish merging company for one month (for at least two hours a day) immediately preceding the general meeting of that company to approve the cross-border merger.

3 Expert's report

16. A report shall be prepared by a 'suitably qualified' expert on the common draft terms. The expert can be appointed by either the directors of each Irish merging company, by the Irish High Court (on the application of all the merging companies), or by a competent authority of another European Economic Area Member State pursuant to Article 8 of the Cross-border Merger Directive. An expert is considered to be 'suitably qualified' under the Regulations if he or she is eligible for appointment as an auditor under the Irish Companies Act 1990. If an expert engaged by an Irish merging company or appointed by the Irish High Court ceases to be 'suitably qualified', he or she should immediately cease to hold office and give notice in writing to that company or the Irish High Court (as appropriate) within fourteen days. A person who carries on the functions of an expert after ceasing to be 'suitably qualified' is guilty of an offence under the Regulations.

17. The chosen expert cannot be, or have been within twelve months of the date of the common draft terms, an officer or employee of the Irish merging company, a parent, spouse, brother, sister or child of an officer of the Irish merging company (unless with the leave of the court), or a person who is a partner, or in the employment of, an officer or employee of the Irish merging company.

In relation to each Irish merging company, an expert's report is not required in the following circumstances:

(i) where the cross-border merger is a 'merger by absorption';[3]
(ii) where the cross-border merger is a merger in which the successor company holds 90 per cent or more (but not all) of the shares or other securities carrying the right to vote at general meetings of each transferor company; or
(iii) where every shareholder of every merging company agrees that such a report is not necessary.

18. The expert's report shall contain the following information:

(i) the method used to arrive at the proposed exchange ratio;

3 Under the Regulations, a merger by absorption is a merger where a wholly owned subsidiary company transfers all of its assets and liabilities to its parent company, and is then dissolved without going into liquidation.

(ii) whether, in the expert's opinion, the exchange ratio is fair and reasonable;
(iii) whether, in the expert's opinion, the method(s) used is adequate;
(iv) an indication of the values arrived at in using the method(s);
(v) an opinion on the relative importance of each method in determining the value; and
(vi) any special valuation difficulties which have arisen.

Where an Irish merging company fails to supply information when requested by an expert, that company and every officer in default will be guilty of an offence under the Regulations. Likewise, if an Irish merging company knowingly or recklessly makes a statement that is misleading, false or deceptive, that company and every officer in default will be guilty of an offence under the Regulations.

19. Again, the expert's report must be made available for inspection by the shareholders and employees' representatives (or the employees themselves where there are no representatives) at the registered office of each Irish merging company for one month (for at least two hours a day) immediately preceding the general meeting of that company.

4 Shareholders' meeting

20. The common draft terms of the cross-border merger must be approved by special resolution passed at a general meeting of any Irish merging company under Regulation 10 of the Regulations. That special resolution cannot be passed earlier than one month after the publication of the common draft terms, as described above in no. 13 of this chapter.

21. Approval by the shareholders of the common draft terms may be made subject to a number of conditions:

(i) ratification of the arrangements for 'employee participation';
(ii) an order of a competent authority in another European Economic Area Member State amending the share exchange ratio or compensation to minority shareholders;
(iii) merger control approval from the Irish Competition Authority, the European Commission, or under the law of any other jurisdiction; or
(iv) any other regulatory approval.

22. Where the cross-border merger involves an Irish transferor company, the directors of that company must inform the general meeting to approve the cross-border merger of any material change in the assets and liabilities of the Irish transferor company between the date of the common draft terms and the date of the general meeting. Likewise, the directors of the successor company shall inform the general meeting of that company of all changes that they have been informed of (if any) from the directors of the transferor company.

23. The Regulations create an anomaly in Irish law as they also allow for the special resolution of the shareholders of an Irish merging company approving the cross-border merger to be passed by way of a written resolution in accordance with Section 141(8) of the Irish Companies Act 1963. Therefore if the Irish merging company's Articles of Association allow it to pass resolutions in writing, it should not be necessary to hold a general meeting. However, the Regulations require a general meeting to be convened (pursuant to Article 9(2)) and for certain information to be provided to the shareholders at that general meeting (as described above in no. 22). It is difficult to see how an Irish merging company could satisfy the requirements of the Regulations without holding a general meeting.

24. Shareholder approval of the common draft terms is not required where the procedure is a merger by absorption (as described above at footnote 3). Also, shareholder approval of the common draft terms is not required where the procedure is a merger by acquisition (as described above at footnote 2) provided that certain conditions are met – the publication of notices, display of documentation and provision of copy documentation on request.

Where the annual accounts of any merging company relate to a financial year that ended more than six months before the date of the common draft terms then that company will have to prepare an accounting statement in the format of the last annual balance sheet.

The exemption from the requirement to get shareholder approval does not apply if any shareholders of the successor company holding 5 per cent or more of the voting shares exercises its or their right(s) to requisition a general meeting to consider the common draft terms.

5 Pre-merger certificate

25. The Irish High Court is the designated competent authority under the Regulations. If it is satisfied that an Irish merging company has properly completed the pre-merger requirements (as described in nos. 10 and 24 above), it shall issue a certificate to that effect in accordance with the Regulations. The form of the pre-merger certificate is as prescribed under the Rules of the Superior Courts (Order 75) 2010. The Rules of the Superior Courts (Order 75) 2010 also sets out the proofs which must be verified by affidavit before the Irish High Court will issue an Irish merging company with a pre-merger certificate. This pre-merger certificate is conclusive evidence that the pre-merger requirements have been properly completed.

6 Effect of the decision

26. Where the successor company is an Irish merging company, the Irish High Court must scrutinise the legality of, and approve the completion of, the cross-border merger. An application is made jointly by all the merging companies to the Irish High Court for an Order approving the completion of the cross-border

merger. The Irish High Court can grant such an Order where it is satisfied that the following conditions have been met:

(i) the successor company must be an Irish company;
(ii) pre-merger certificates showing compliance with the pre-merger requirements must be issued in relation to each merging company;
(iii) the application for the Irish High Court Order must be made within six months of the issue of each pre-merger certificate;
(iv) the common draft terms must be unchanged from those approved by the shareholders of the merging companies;
(v) any arrangements for 'employee participation' in the successor company must be determined; and
(vi) provisions must be made for creditors of any of the merging companies who would otherwise be unfairly prejudiced by the cross-border merger.

27. The Irish High Court specifies the effective date of the cross-border merger and the Order is made. The merging companies (other than the successor company) are dissolved by this Order.

VI Minority shareholders

28. Where the majority of votes cast at the general meeting of a transferor company are in favour of the cross-border merger, minority shareholders may apply to the Irish successor company to acquire their shares in the merging company for cash. A minority shareholder is a shareholder who voted against the special resolution or, where the Irish successor company holds 90 per cent or more of the shares in the transferor company, any other shareholder. They must apply to the Irish successor company to acquire their shares within fifteen days of the date of the general meeting of the transferor company approving the cross-border merger. If the Irish successor company holds 90 per cent or more of the shares in the transferor company, the fifteen days runs from the date of the publication of notice of delivery of the common draft terms. The Irish successor company shall purchase the shares at a price determined in accordance with the share exchange ratio as set out in the common draft terms.

29. Before an Order can be made by the Irish High Court approving the completion of the cross-border merger, measures must be put in place to comply with any requests for the purchase of shares of minority shareholders. The application to the Irish High Court for approval must be accompanied by a statement detailing the number and class of each minority shareholder who has requested that their shares be bought.

VII Creditors' protection

30. Creditors with a debt or claim at the time of publication of the notice of the delivery of the common draft terms to the Registrar (as described under no. 13

above) have a right to be heard at the application to the Irish High Court for an Order approving the completion of the cross-border merger.

31. As stated previously, provision must be made for creditors of any of the merging companies who have established to the satisfaction of the Irish High Court that they would otherwise be unfairly prejudiced by the cross-border merger. Under Rule 26(2)(c) of the Rules of the Superior Courts (Order 75) 2010, for the purpose of establishing the creditors of an Irish merging company entitled to be heard in accordance with Regulation 15 of the Regulations, the Irish High Court can make an order for an inquiry as to the debts or claims against that company and for the proceedings to be taken for settling a list of creditors. If any creditors of any of the Irish merging companies establishes to the satisfaction of the Irish High Court that they would otherwise be unfairly prejudiced by the cross-border merger, measures have to be put in place to protect such creditors before the Irish High Court can make an order approving the completion of the cross-border merger. Until such provision is made, the Irish High Court cannot make an Order approving the completion of the cross-border merger.

VIII Rules applicable to employee participation

1 Employee participation in companies established in Ireland resulting from a cross-border merger

32. Pursuant to Regulation 23(2) of the Regulations, an Irish successor company will be subject to the rules on employee participation in force in Ireland. Currently, Irish law does not provide for any mandatory rules on employee participation. 'Employee participation' means the right to elect some of the members of the company's supervisory or administrative organ, or the right to recommend and/or oppose the appointment of some or all of the members of a company's supervisory or administrative organ.

Notwithstanding that there are no mandatory rules on employee participation in force in Ireland, there are three circumstances in which employee participation rules shall be imported into an Irish successor company. Those are:

(i) where at least one of the merging companies has, in the six months prior to the publication of the common draft terms, more than 500 employees *and* operates a system of employee participation as described above; or
(ii) where as a matter of Irish law, there is no legal right for employees of the successor company to enjoy at least the same level of employee participation rights that existed in any of the merging companies before the cross-border merger; or
(iii) where as a matter of Irish law, there is no legal right for employees of the branches of the successor company in other European Economic

Area Member States to enjoy at least the same level of 'employee participation' rights as the Irish-based employees of the successor company enjoy.

In all of these scenarios, the participation of employees in the Irish successor company is regulated under Regulations 24–44 of the Regulations and Article 12(2), (3) and (4) of Council Regulation (EC No. 2157/2001) on the statute for a European company (SE), which was given effect by the European Communities (European Public Limited Liability Company) Regulations 2007 (S.I. No. 21 of 2007).

33. Due to the Irish transposition of the Cross-border Merger Directive, the Regulations create an anomaly. As soon as possible after the publication of the common draft terms, the management or administrative organ of each Irish merging company must take the necessary steps to start negotiations with employees' representatives on arrangements for the involvement of those employees in the Irish successor company. This requirement appears to apply irrespective of whether a system of employee participation had previously been enjoyed by employees of the merging companies. Therefore, it would appear that the Regulations create rights of involvement for employees in an Irish successor company even where a system of 'employee participation' was not operated in any of the merging companies prior to the cross-border merger. This goes beyond the requirements of the Cross-border Merger Directive, which oblige negotiations to be commenced *only where* 'employee participation' existed in one of the merging companies prior to the cross-border merger.

34. Merging companies can either unilaterally adopt the standard rules for employee involvement as are set out in Schedule 1 (the Standard Rules) of the Regulations or agree to set up a Special Negotiating Body (however the existence of these alternatives highlight an anomaly in the Regulations – no. 35 below refers). A Special Negotiating Body is created under the Regulations to which the employees of the merging companies elect representatives (proportional representation depending on the number and location of the employees). The Special Negotiating Body negotiates with the administrative organs of the merging companies to determine what involvement the employees of the merging companies will have in the successor company. The terms of the agreement are drawn up and adopted by the members of the Special Negotiating Body and the employees whom they represent. The Special Negotiating Body and the administrative organs of the merging companies must reach agreement within six months. This deadline can be extended to twelve months by agreement of the parties.

35. As pointed out above, the Standard Rules will apply where the parties decide to apply the Standard Rules without opening any negotiations (Regulation 35(5) of the Regulations). However, the Standard Rules may also apply where the time period within which the Special Negotiating Body and the

administrative organs of the merging companies were to reach agreement has elapsed (Regulation 35(1) of the Regulations).The Standard Rules set out specific rules of employee consultation. When the Standard Rules apply, a representative body of employees must be set up. The representative body is composed of employees of the successor company, elected by the employees' representatives or, in the absence thereof, by the employees themselves. The members of the representative body must be elected or appointed in proportion to the number of employees employed in each European Economic Area Member State by the merging companies. The Standard Rules provide that the election or appointment of members of the representative body must be carried out in accordance with a procedure agreed by the Special Negotiating Body. This leads to an anomaly in the Regulations, as the Standard Rules are supposed to act as an alternative to the setting up of a Special Negotiating Body i.e. the Standard Rules are designed to by-pass the requirement to set up a Special Negotiating Body and lay down standard rules for employee involvement instead. However, technically, the requirement for a procedure to be agreed by the 'Special Negotiating Body' suggests that such a body has to be established, even where the Standard Rules apply.

2 Protection of employee representatives

36. Members of the Special Negotiating Body, representative body or employees' representatives on the board of the successor company must not be penalised for their participation, by dismissal, pursuant to the Irish Unfair Dismissals Acts 1977 to 2007, unfavourable changes to conditions of employment (including selection for redundancy) or any other action prejudicial to their employment. Schedule 2 to the Regulations contains a special right for employees' representatives to complain to an Irish Rights Commissioner if any such penalising action takes place.

IX Tax

37. The Merger Tax Directive (2009/133/EC) of 19 October 2009 was implemented in part only into Irish tax law. As Irish legislation did not have concepts such as mergers by absorption it did not implement those parts of the Merger Tax Directive dealing with mergers. The Irish legislation implementing the Merger Tax Directive (Part 21 of the Taxes Consolidation Act 1997 (the Act)) addresses transfers of assets only. Exchanges of shares were already dealt with under domestic tax legislation.

38. Even though Irish company law now provides for cross-border mergers to take place as a result of the implementation of the Regulations, Irish tax law has not been amended to specifically address mergers. The Irish Revenue Commissioners are apparently satisfied that Irish tax legislation is sufficient to achieve tax neutrality in the case of a transfer of assets pursuant to a

cross-border merger. This is because at the time of implementing the original Directive into Irish law a general 'sweep up' provision was inserted in the legislation (see no. 44 of this chapter).

39. While there is no specific relief available under Irish tax law, there are reliefs which may be available under the general provisions of Irish tax law which could still be utilised in a cross-border merger scenario. Where there are no reliefs available under general provisions then the fallback position to preserve the tax neutrality of the transaction is to apply to the Irish Revenue Commissioners as noted in no. 44. This assumes the transaction is of a type to which the Merger Tax Directive applies.

1 General tax relief provisions

A Capital gains tax (CGT)

40. CGT may arise on any gain made on disposal of an asset:

(i) where assets are transferred by an Irish company as part of a cross-border merger;
(ii) where a non-Irish transferor is transferring Irish land or buildings or shares deriving the greater part of their value from Irish land or buildings; or
(iii) where a non-Irish transferor transfers assets used for a trade carried out by its Irish branch or agency.

CGT relief is available under general Irish tax provisions in respect of the following:

(i) the transfer of a business, as part of a scheme of reconstruction or amalgamation, where the transferor receives no consideration for the assets other than the assumption of the liabilities of the business being transferred; or
(ii) the transfer of assets intra-group where one company is a 75 per cent subsidiary of the other or both are 75 per cent subsidiaries of a third company.

In both instances, in a cross-border context, for relief to apply the assets transferred must be used in Ireland by a branch of the transferee or, for example, be transferred from an Irish branch for continued use in Ireland.

In the event that neither of these reliefs applies, relief may still be available under Part 21 of the Act (see below).

Where a business is transferred as part of a reconstruction or amalgamation and consideration shares in the transferee company issue not to the transferor company but to its shareholders, and their shares in the transferor company are not retained, the shareholders are treated as holding their new shares (in the transferee company) as if they were still holding their old shares (in the transferor company). No CGT arises by reason of the exchange.

B Corporate tax

41. In the context of a cross-border merger, where an Irish transferor company is being dissolved, the Irish transferor company will have ceased trading for Irish corporate tax purposes. The successor company is deemed to have commenced a new trade. Provided the same persons own 75 per cent of the trade transferred at any time within two years after the transfer, and at any time in the year before the transfer, and the trade being transferred continues to be carried on in Ireland certain reliefs apply.

Unused trading losses (if any) can be transferred to the successor company for set off against profits of the same trade. Additionally, where capital allowances have been claimed on the assets being transferred relief is available such that no balancing allowance or balancing charge arises, i.e. the assets transfer at their tax written down value.

C Stamp duty

42. Irish stamp duty may arise on the transfer of assets if the document effecting the transfer is executed in Ireland, or if it relates to Irish situate property, or any matter or thing to be done in Ireland.

However, relief from stamp duty may be available, subject to certain conditions:

(i) where the transferor and transferee are within a 90 per cent association (in terms of issued share capital, rights to dividends and rights to assets on a liquidation) and do not cease to be associated for two years after the transfer, or
(ii) where the transfer is made pursuant to a scheme of reconstruction or amalgamation.

In the first scenario the dissolution of an Irish transferor company will mean a clawback of stamp duty relieved. However, it is likely that the Irish Revenue Commissioners would grant the relief by way of concession. They have done previously where an Irish transferor company is liquidated and assets transferred remain within the group.

Aside from the potential availability of reliefs under general Irish tax provisions it is also arguable that stamp duty does not apply as the transfer occurs by operation of law under the mergers regime rather than pursuant to a conveyance on sale. The Irish Revenue Commissioners recognised this previously in the context of the transfer of Irish property following the dissolution of a foreign company by operation of law or administrative act.

D Part 21 of the Act – CGT

43. Where the general CGT reliefs cannot be applied to a cross-border merger, relief is still available under the provisions implementing the Directive into Irish law where:

(i) a trade is transferred in return for shares being issued in the transferee company to the transferor and the trade continues to be carried out in Ireland (unlikely to occur as the transferor is dissolved); or

(ii) where the assets are transferred to a 100 per cent parent company which uses the assets in a trade carried out in Ireland.

E The 'sweep up' provision

44. Where a transaction comes within the ambit of the Directive and Irish tax legislation does not deal with it, the Irish Revenue Commissioners may, upon written application, give such relief as appears to them to be 'just and reasonable' for the purposes of giving effect to that Directive.

23
Italy

FRANCESCO GIANNI, MARCO ZACCAGNINI
Gianni, Origoni, Grippo & Partners

I Introduction

1. Legislative decree no. 108 of 30 May 2008 (the 'Decree'), published in the Official Gazette no. 140 of 17 June 2008, regulates mergers among Italian companies and companies incorporated under the law of a Member State (hereinafter referred to as cross-border mergers).

The Decree implements the Cross-border Merger Directive, which, considering the need for cooperation and consolidation among companies incorporated under the law of different EU Member States, as well as the legislative and administrative difficulties that the same may face in spite of operating in the single market, sets forth provisions aimed at facilitating the carrying-out of cross-border mergers among various types of companies.

II Scope

2. The Decree applies to (i) cross-border mergers among Italian companies and companies incorporated under the law of another EU Member State, the registered office, principal place of business or headquarters of which are in the EU territory; (ii) cross-border mergers where any of the participating entities or the entity resulting from the merger are not corporate entities or are

companies having their registered office, principal place of business or headquarters outside the EU territory, as long as the applicable law of each of the other EU companies provides for the application of the Cross-border Merger Directive.

On the other hand, the Decree shall not apply to the so-called 'international' mergers, i.e. mergers involving an Italian company and companies incorporated under the law of countries other than Member States.

In defining the concept of 'companies', Article 1 of the Decree refers to the provisions of the Italian civil code as well as to Article 1 of the First Company Law Directive (68/151/EC) and also mentions the European Company and the European Cooperative Company.

Moreover, since the Member States might amend their corporate laws, and the amendments might involve the creation of new types of companies not included in such definition, the Decree also contains a provision that describes the main features of the entities that shall be considered as 'companies' for the purpose of the Decree. In particular, reference is made to companies having their own capital, legal personality, and separate assets which alone serve to cover their liabilities as well as being subject, under their applicable national law, to the provisions of the First Company Law Directive in order to protect the interests of shareholders/quota holders and third parties governing it.

III Applicable law

3. In accordance with the Cross-border Merger Directive, each company taking part in a cross-border merger shall comply with the provisions and formalities of the national law to which it is subject. In addition, consistently with the Cross-border Merger Directive, the Decree provides that, in case of conflict among the laws applicable to the involved companies, the law of the jurisdiction of the surviving company shall prevail. As far as Italian law is concerned, the Decree supplements, with respect to cross-border mergers, the applicable Italian law, i.e., the provisions set forth by the Italian civil code.

Namely, the Decree regulates: (i) the conditions relating to the cross-border mergers; (ii) the withdrawal right of the shareholders/quotaholders of Italian companies; (iii) the merger plan; (iv) the publication in the Official Gazette of the information relating to the merger; (v) the report to be drafted by the managing body; (vi) the report to be drafted by the expert; (vii) the resolution of the shareholders'/quotaholders' meeting approving the merger; (viii) the preliminary certification relating to the merger; (ix) the merger deed; (x) the examination by the notary on the lawfulness of the merger; (xi) the registration with the competent Register of Enterprises; (xii) the effectiveness of the merger and the consequences thereof; (xiii) the voidness of the merger; (xiv) the case of simplified formalities; and (xv) the employees' participation rights.

IV Conditions and withdrawal rights

4. In accordance with the Decree and the Cross-border Merger Directive, cross-border mergers shall only be possible among types of companies which may be merged under the national law of their respective Member States. This is to avoid – in case the national law of one of the merging companies prohibits heterogeneous mergers among certain types of companies – such prohibition being eluded by means of cross-border mergers.

Moreover, since the Cross-border Merger Directive empowers the Member States to protect the rights of the minority shareholders/quotaholders that oppose cross-border mergers, Article 5 of the Decree allows the same to withdraw from the company in the event that the company resulting fm the merger is subject to the law of another EU Member State (i.e., is not based in Italy). Such provision is consistent with Articles 2437 and 2473 of the Italian civil code, which grants a withdrawal right to the (dissenting, abstaining or absent) shareholders/quotaholders also in the event of transformation of the company or transfer of the registered office of the company abroad.

V Merger plan and publication in the Official Gazette

5. The merger plan shall comply with all the provisions set forth by Article 2501-*ter* of the Italian civil code, with some adjustments to the latter introduced by the Decree, which consist of further information to be included in the document, such as, by way of example: (i) the name and applicable law of the company resulting from the merger; (ii) the particular benefits, if any, proposed in favour of the directors and the members of the auditing bodies of the companies taking part in the merger, as well as in favour of the experts; (iii) information on the procedures relating to the involvement of the employees in the definition of their participation rights in the company resulting from the merger, if any; (iv) the likely consequences of the cross-border merger on employment level; (v) the starting date on which the merger becomes effective or the criteria for the determination of same.

The merger plan shall be published in the Official Gazette at least thirty days prior to the date of the shareholders'/quotaholders' meeting called in order to resolve on the same.

VI Report of the managing body and report of the expert

6. In addition to the content provided by the Italian civil code, the report of the managing body shall illustrate the consequences of the cross-border merger on the shareholders/quotaholders, creditors and employees.

Moreover, the Decree governs the information rights of the employees' representatives, as well as the possibility granted to same of drafting an opinion to be enclosed to the report of the managing body.

With respect to the report of the expert, the Decree integrates the provisions of the Italian civil code by providing that the expert shall be selected among the auditors or auditing firms enrolled in the register held with the Ministry of Justice. Furthermore, the Decree provides that a single report from one expert can be used for all the companies involved in the cross-border merger, provided that such report shall contain, in addition to the information required by Italian law, also the further information, if any, required by the law which the companies participating in the merger are subject to.

VII Resolution upon the merger and registration

7. The new rules amend the procedure provided for the adoption of the resolution on the merger, i.e., the approval of the merger plan.

First of all, the shareholders'/quotaholders' meeting may provide that the effectiveness of the approval of the merger plan be subject to a subsequent shareholders'/quotaholders' meeting resolution concerning the participation rights of the employees in the management of the company resulting from the merger.

Thereafter, upon request of the Italian company participating in the cross-border merger, a notary shall issue a preliminary certificate attesting that the formalities and activities carried out in order to implement the merger comply with Italian law.

8. In case the company resulting from the merger is an Italian company, the deed of merger shall be drafted by a notary while, in case the company resulting from the merger is incorporated under the law of another Member State, the deed of merger shall be drafted by either a notary or other competent governmental authority, as applicable.

A second evaluation is carried out by the notary on the lawfulness of the cross-border merger and, thereafter, the deed of merger is filed with the relevant Register of Enterprises.

VIII The effectiveness of the merger and its consequences

9. In accordance with the Cross-border Merger Directive, the law of the Member State which the company resulting from the cross-border merger is subject to shall determine the date on which the cross-border merger takes effect. Therefore, the Decree provides that in the event that the company is incorporated under Italian law, the merger shall be effective upon the registration of the deed of merger with the relevant Register of Enterprises.

On the other hand, in case the company resulting from the merger is not incorporated under Italian law, reference shall be made to the law under which such company is incorporated.

In order to regulate the effects of the cross-border merger, the Decree refers once again to the relevant provisions of the Italian civil code, according to which, by way of example, the company resulting from the merger assumes the rights and obligations of the incorporated companies.

Moreover, the Decree provides that the Italian company resulting from the merger shall comply with the formalities that may be provided by the law to which one of the companies participating in the merger is subject, in relation to the effectiveness vis-à-vis third parties of the transfer of certain assets, rights and obligations.

Finally, the Decree provides for the impossibility of declaring null and void a cross-border merger implemented in compliance with the provisions of the same Decree, without prejudice, however, to the right to compensation for damages to which the shareholders/quota holders or third parties damaged by the cross-border merger may be entitled.

IX Simplified formalities and participation rights of the employees

10. In case of intra-group mergers where the incorporating company holds 90% or 100% of the capital of the incorporated company, the Decree sets forth a simplified procedure.

Moreover, the Decree regulates in detail the participation of the employees and their involvement in the definition of their participation rights in the company resulting from the merger.

X Applicability

11. The Decree shall be applicable to all the cases in which the merger plan is approved following the entering into force of the Decree.

24

Latvia

MARIS BRIZGO, RAYMOND L. SLAIDINS
LAWIN Klavins & Slaidins
JOHN JA BURKE
Kazakhstan Institute of Management, Economics and Strategic Research

I Introduction

1. The Cross-border Merger Directive required Member States to implement the Directive by 15 December 2007. While the Republic of Latvia failed to meet that deadline, the delay in implementation was not of substantial duration. On 6 March 2008, the Parliament adopted amendments to the Law on the Register of Enterprises of the Republic of Latvia and on 24 April 2008 amended the Commercial Law to incorporate the legal framework enabling cross-border mergers between companies within the European Economic Area (EEA). The Parliament further amended the Commercial Law, precisely Chapter XIX, on 28 May 2008 to establish a specific legal facility to govern cross-border mergers: 'Special Provisions Related to Cross-Border Mergers'.

2. The Cross-border Merger Directive enables limited liability companies registered in different Member States of the EEA to merge and continue activity as a simple company of the Member State where the surviving company is established. In Latvia, the amended Law on the Register of Enterprises of the Republic of Latvia created a legal basis for the Register of Enterprises to register a cross-border merger when the surviving company is resident in Latvia, or, 'if the acquiring company is registered in another member

state, to carry out a legality check of the merger and to issue a pre-merger certificate' (Art. 4[3] Law on the Register of Enterprises of the Republic of Latvia). Amendments to the Commercial Law established the procedural framework.

3. Cross-border mergers in Latvia also may be covered by the following legal acts: (i) Financial Instruments Market Law, (ii) Civil Law, (iii) Competition Law and (iv) Law on Credit Institutions. Articles 5 and 7 of the Cross-border Merger Directive are implemented by Articles 335[1] and 380 to 387 of the Commercial Law.

II Scope of the new rules

4. The new rules apply to the following capital companies established under Latvian jurisdiction: private limited liability companies (*sabiedrība ar ierobežotu atbildību*, SIA) and public limited liability companies (*akciju sabiedrība*, AS). Latvia applies the Cross-border Merger Directive to Member States of the European Economic Area (EEA) (Art. 335[1](2) Commercial Law). If the merger involves investment management companies, credit institutions or insurance companies, approval from the Financial and Capital Market Commission is required under certain conditions.

5. According to the Law on European Companies, the rules of the Commercial Law applicable to public limited liability companies also should be applied to European Companies (SE). Therefore the cross-border merger rules of the Commercial Law extend to the European Company.

6. The cross-border merger rules of the Commercial Law do not apply to cooperative societies established under the Law on Cooperative Societies.

7. The Cross-border Merger Directive does not apply to cross-border mergers involving a company that solicits capital from the public to establish a collective investment scheme, operating under the principle of risk spreading and redemption of shares on demand. These entities are referred to as Undertakings in Collective Investment Schemes (UCITS).[1] The Law on Investment Management Companies, various Rules of the Financial Capital and Market Commission and Regulations of the European Commission are applicable to UCITS.

8. The Commercial Law states that a cross-border merger is a merger of two or more capital companies where at least one of the companies is registered in Latvia and the other capital companies are established in another Member

1 Commercial Law, Art. 335[1](3); any company that redeems units at the request of the shareholder or whose market value of units corresponds to the value of its Net Asset Value is excluded from the cross-border merger rules.

State of the EEA (Art. 335[1](1) and (2) Commercial Law). It means that cross-border merger may cover a private limited liability company, public limited liability company and European Company registered in Latvia, on the one hand, and a limited liability company, registered in other EEA Member States, established as a limited liability company according to the law of the relevant EEA Member State, on the other.

9. Article 335[1] of the Commercial Law clarifies that, if the acquiring company is registered outside Latvia, then the capital company registered in Latvia observes the requirements of the extant law related to the decision-making process of the merger and the protection of creditors, shareholders and employees of that company.

10. According to the Insolvency Law, if the court declares insolvency proceedings against the company, then operation of the administrative institutions of the company is suspended and the executive board and shareholders may not adopt any decisions anymore. From the declaration of the insolvency proceedings only the insolvency administrator appointed by the court may adopt decisions on behalf of the insolvent company. However, the administrator does not have authority to decide on merger within insolvency proceedings. The Insolvency Law provides that the insolvent company may take part in a merger if the meeting of creditors has approved a rehabilitation of the insolvent company and the merger was provided by a rehabilitation plan. The decision-making power that, under the Commercial Law, belongs to shareholders is vested in the meeting of creditors of the insolvent company unless otherwise provided by the rehabilitation plan.

III Definition of a merger

11. The Latvian Commercial Law states that a merger is a transaction in which the acquired company ceases to exist without going into liquidation and its assets and liabilities are transferred to the acquiring company. Cross-border mergers may take the form of two structures: consolidation and acquisition.

12. Acquisition is the process whereby the acquired company transfers its assets and liabilities to the acquiring company without the acquired company going into dissolution. Consolidation is the process whereby two or more separate companies form a third company and transfer all their assets and liabilities to the newly formed company and the original companies cease to exist without dissolution.

13. In each case, that of acquisition or consolidation, the acquired company or companies transfers all its assets and liabilities to the acquiring company, and the shareholders of the acquired company or companies become shareholders of the acquiring company according to provisions and conditions of a cross-border merger agreement.

14. In the case of an SIA (private limited liability company), a cash payment to the shareholders of the acquired company is not limited. Besides, in the case of an AS (public limited liability company), the cash payment may not exceed 10 per cent of the nominal value of the shares of the acquiring company.

15. In a merger of at least two EEA public limited liability companies, the acquiring company has the option to elect the corporate form of a European Company (SE). The minimum share capital of an SE is EUR 120,000. The legal seat is transferable to other countries without winding up the company, and re-establishing the SE in the destination forum. Latvian law provides for employee participation rights and consultation.

16. A merger of at least two EEA limited liability companies which, according to the national law of the relevant EEA Member State, is covered by the Directive where one of the companies is a public limited liability company or a private limited liability company, may result in the formation of an SIA (private limited liability company) with a minimum capital requirement of LVL 2,000 (EUR 3,850) or an AS (public limited liability company) with a minimum capital of LVL 25,000 (EUR 35,550). These companies lack the option of transferring their legal seat without liquidation. Employee participation, information and consultation requirements depend on the type of merger.

17. Latvian legislation recognises a merger of a subsidiary into a parent undertaking under Article 385 of the Commercial Law. In such case, shareholders of the acquired company are neither required to review a cross-border agreement nor adopt a decision regarding a merger. It is sufficient if the shareholders of the acquiring company adopt the decision.

18. If one of the assets that is transferred to the acquiring company due to a merger is real property, a record concerning change of owners should be registered at the Land Register. Generally, in case of the alienation of the real property and transfer of the title, a state fee for registration of the change of owners in the amount of 2 per cent based upon the purchase price or cadastral value, whichever is higher, shall be payable to the state budget. However, as was established by recent case law of the Supreme Court of Latvia,[2] in case of consolidation and acquisition of companies, the transfer of the title of real property to the acquiring company shall not be regarded as alienation and the state fee is not paid for registration of the change of owners at the Land Register.

19. If the acquiring company is not registered under jurisdiction of Latvia, then certain restrictions may apply with regard to transfer of title of the real property, e.g. foreign companies may not own the land in state border areas etc.

2 Decision No. SKC-869 of 22 November 2006 of the Civil Law Department of Senate of the Supreme Court of Latvia.

IV Legal consequences of cross-border merger

20. Acquisition means the 'acquiring company' absorbs the 'acquired company' and the 'acquired company' ceases to exist without going into liquidation (Art. 335(2) Commercial Law). Shareholders of the 'acquired company' become shareholders of the 'acquiring company'.

21. Alternatively, in case of consolidation, shareholders of the 'acquired companies' become shareholders of the newly established 'acquiring company' (Art. 335(3) Commercial Law). The 'acquired companies' that are consolidated cease to exist.

22. If the acquiring company is registered in the Republic of Latvia, the cross-border merger is effective when the respective record is registered with the commercial register and the merger is announced in the official gazette, the *Latvijas Vēstnesis* (*Latvian Herald*) (Arts. 349(5) and 387 Commercial Law).

23. If the acquired company is registered in the Republic of Latvia, the Latvian company observes all Commercial Law norms regarding the decision-making process and protection of creditors, shareholders and employees. When the Member State of the acquiring company does not provide for the protections set forth in Article 382 of the Commercial Law regarding minority shareholders the Latvian company may apply provisions of the Latvian Commercial Law provided the shareholders of the acquiring company consent to this procedure.

24. When the merger is completed, if the acquired company was organised under the Laws of Latvia, the acquired company is deleted from the commercial register under Article 386 of the Commercial Law.

V Procedure

25. The Register of Enterprises (*Uzņēmumu Reģistrs*) (www.ur.gov.lv) is the government-appointed organisation responsible for review and scrutiny of the legality of the cross-border merger. The Financial and Capital Market Commission (*Finanšu un Kapitāla tirgus komisija*) (www.fktk.lv) is involved, and approval required, when under certain conditions, the merger implicates investment management companies, credit institutions or insurance companies, and the Latvian Competition Council (*Konkurences padome*) (www.kp.gov.lv) is involved, and approval required, when the combined turnover of the merger participants in the previous year was not less than LVL 25 million (EUR 36 million), or market concentration may exceed 40 per cent.

26. In all cases, the company governed by the Laws of Latvia, whether it is the acquiring company or the acquired company, submits to the Register of Enterprises a notification regarding merger together with a draft cross-border merger agreement.

27. The draft terms of the cross-border merger agreement shall contain the following data:

(i) the firm names, registered addresses and registration numbers of all the companies involved in the cross-border merger;
(ii) the companies' capital shares (stocks) exchange coefficient and the amount of premium (if such is provided for);
(iii) the division of the capital shares (stocks) among the shareholders of the acquiring company;
(iv) the provisions for the transfer of the capital shares (stocks) of the acquiring company to the shareholders of the acquired company or companies;
(v) the time from which the capital shares (stocks) transferred give a right to receive dividends or a profit share from the acquiring company and any provisions affecting this time (if such is provided for);
(vi) the rights granted by the acquiring company to stockholders of the acquired company who own preference stock, and debenture holders, who own convertible debentures;
(vii) rights which the acquiring company grants to the members of supervisory and executive bodies of the acquired company, as well as the controller of the company;
(viii) the day from which the transactions of the acquired company shall be included in the accounting of the acquiring company and shall be regarded as transactions of the acquiring company;
(ix) the consequences of the cross-border merger for the employees of the acquired company;
(x) the activities to be conducted in the cross-border merger process and the time periods for conducting them;
(xi) the types of companies engaged in the cross-border merger and, if applicable, the type of the newly established company;
(xii) information on the valuation of the transferred assets and liabilities to the acquiring company; and
(xiii) the report on the company's commercial activities, which serves as the basis for the cross-border merger rules.

28. If all shares of the acquired company are held by the acquiring company, it is allowed to omit from the draft cross-border merger agreement data under nos. (ii) and (v) above.

29. The notice of the proposed cross-border merger agreement must be published in the official gazette, the *Latvian Herald*.

30. Unless all shareholders of all merging companies have not decided otherwise, the board must prepare a merger report, which should contain and clarify the following issues:

(i) provisions of the cross-border merger agreement;

(ii) legal and economic aspects of the cross-border merger;
(iii) share (stock) exchange ratio and amount of cash payment (if provided);
(iv) methods for calculation of share (stock) exchange ratio, the amount of cash payment, and any problems of applying these methods;
(v) information on how the cross-border merger would influence shareholders and creditors of the merging companies.

31. The Commercial Law provides that the acquiring company and the acquired company may draft a common merger report (Art. 339(2) Commercial Law).

32. It is a mandatory requirement that the auditor inspects the draft cross-border merger agreement unless all shareholders of all merging companies decide otherwise. The merging companies must grant full access for the auditor to documents necessary for carrying out of the inspection.

33. If the acquiring company owns all shares of the acquired company, then the auditor is not required to inspect the draft cross-border merger agreement.

34. The board must inform the shareholders of major changes in the condition of the acquired or acquiring company until the end of the term of the authorisation of the board or commencement of the merger.

35. Shareholders, or their representatives, have rights to:

(i) review the draft cross-border merger agreement and the merger report not later than one month prior to the date scheduled to ratify the agreement at the shareholders' meeting;
(ii) review the mandatory opinion of the auditor's inspection;
(iii) review the annual reports of all merging companies for the last three financial years;
(iv) review the report of the company's commercial activities prepared at least three months before submission of the notification to the Register of Enterprises;
(v) receive copies or excerpts of the documents mentioned above;
(vi) submit questions to the board of directors at the shareholders' meeting, concerning the draft cross-border merger agreement, merger report, legal and economic aspects of the cross-border merger and other information about merging companies, as well as to receive explanations of the board;
(vii) vote on shareholders' resolutions related to the proposed merger under Article 343(1) of the Commercial Law.

36. Creditors, or their representatives, have the following rights:

(i) all known creditors must be informed about the planned merger during fifteen days after the decision is passed approving the cross-border merger;
(ii) a notice in the official gazette, the *Latvian Herald* must be published giving creditors at least a one month term for submission of their claims;

(iii) claims of the creditors of the acquired company must be secured if they are submitted within the deadline;
(iv) claims of the creditors of the acquiring company must be secured only if they may prove that the cross-border merger endangers satisfaction of their claims.

37. The shareholders' meeting, the primary governing body under Latvian legislation, approves or disapproves the merger. In the case of private limited liability companies (SIA), at least two-thirds of the votes of the present shareholders should be cast in favour of the decision approving the merger. However, in case of public limited liability companies (AS), the number of votes in favour of the merger should be three-quarters. If the articles of association provide for a higher rate of votes, then this rate should be applied instead.

VI Merger application

38. Articles 383(2) and 384 of the Commercial Law govern the content of the merger application. The acquired company and the acquiring company, if it is registered in Latvia, are obliged to submit the application to the Register of Enterprises. The purpose of the application of the acquired company is to obtain a pre-merger certificate in order to complete the merger in other EEA Member States where the acquiring company is registered.

Alternatively, the acquiring company submits the merger application to the Registrar of Enterprises in order to finish the cross-border merger.

39. Any merging company registered in Latvia is required to attach to the merger application the following documents:

(i) merger agreement or its certified copy;
(ii) extract of the minutes and the decision on merger;
(iii) list of the shareholders who voted against the merger (if any);
(iv) merger approval (if required under applicable legislation);
(v) merger report (if required under applicable legislation);
(vi) opinion of the auditor (if required under applicable legislation);
(vii) closing financial account of the acquired company (only in case of acquisition);
(viii) articles of association of the acquiring company (only in case of consolidation); and
(ix) certification that the claims of creditors, submitted timely within the three-month period, have been secured or satisfied, that the decision on merger has not been disputed in court and that no relevant action is pending and unsatisfied.

40. If the acquiring company is registered in Latvia or is intended to be registered in Latvia, it should attach the following extra documents:

(i) list of the members of the board of directors of the acquiring company and notarised sample signatures (if a new acquiring company is formed as a result of the merger); and
(ii) list of supervisory council members of the acquiring company (if a new acquiring company is formed as a result of the merger and if the acquiring company is to have a supervisory council);
(iii) the document issued by the registrar of the other EEA Member State certifying that the acquired company has fulfilled all requirements in order to complete the cross-border merger (document may not be more than six months old).

41. The merger application is submitted to the Registrar of Enterprises and the latter verifies whether all mandatory requirements have been satisfied.[3]

42. The acquired company is deleted from the Latvian commercial register after the Registrar of Enterprises receives relevant information from the commercial register of the other EEA Member State.

43. The cross-border merger is effective when the acquiring company is recorded in the commercial register of the respective country.

VII Employee participation

44. In accordance with the Latvian Labour Law, in case of cross-border merger all rights and obligations of the acquired company resulting from the employment relationship effective at the time of the merger shall pass over to the acquiring company. The Latvian Labour Law states that the employees shall automatically go over to the acquiring company. It means that all employment contracts in effect at the time of the cross-border merger shall be automatically transferred to the acquiring company.

45. Based on the provisions of the Latvian Labour Law, consent of the employees to the cross-border merger is not required, since the merger is carried out automatically. However, in order to observe the rights of a person to freely choose the place of work, the Labour Law provides for the obligations of the employer to inform employees regarding the merger.

46. Both the acquired company and the acquiring company have an obligation to inform the employee representatives of the terms of the merger agreement. If there is no elected employee representative (e.g. trade union representative or employees' elected trustee person) then all employees shall be informed.

47. The acquiring company shall give written notice to its employees at least one month before the cross-border merger starts to have a direct impact on the working conditions and the terms and conditions of employment of its employees.

3 Law on the Register of Enterprises of the Republic of Latvia, Art. 4^3.

48. The acquired company shall give written notice to its employees at least one month prior to the cross-border merger.

49. Both the acquired and the acquiring company have an obligation to provide information regarding (i) the date of the merger; (ii) the reasons for the merger; (iii) legal, economic and social effects of the merger; and (iv) measures that will be taken in respect to the employees.

50. The acquired company shall inform the acquiring company regarding all rights and obligations which will pass over to the acquiring company. Failure to comply with the obligation does not affect the transfer of the rights and obligations and the claims of the employees against the acquiring company in relation to these rights and obligations.

51. The Latvian Labour Law does not set any special information procedure and therefore the information can be carried out either by giving to each employee an information letter, or by convening a meeting of the employees where the employees are then informed regarding the planned cross-border merger, or in other acceptable manner to ensure the provision of information to all employees.

VIII Protection of minority shareholders

52. Shareholders of the acquired company who did not agree to the cross-border merger are entitled, within two months from the time when the merger comes into effect, to request the acquiring company to redeem their shares for money (compensation).

53. The amount of compensation shall be equal to the amount which the shareholder would have acquired by dividing the property of the acquired company in the case of liquidation if it took place at the time when the decision on cross-border merger was taken.

54. From the effective date of the merger, the acquiring company shall pay the interest set by law on any compensation not paid out in the amount provided for and within the time period.

55. If shareholders of the acquired company, who do not agree with the merger, do not request compensation, they may alienate their shares within a period of two months, irrespective of any restrictions provided for in the decision, the articles of association or law.

IX Tax treatment

56. The Latvian tax laws contain general provisions applicable to cross-border mergers allowing for tax neutrality of such events (Art. 6^2 and 6^3 of the Law on Company Income Tax).

57. When a taxpayer is wound up without dissolution, the taxpayer files a tax return within one month after confirming its closing balance.

58. Losses are tax deductible assuming transfer pricing rules are followed. However, losses from receivables are not tax deductible.

59. Tax losses may be carried forward for a period of eight years.

60. Transactions in shares and securities are VAT exempt.

X Conclusion

61. The Latvian implementation of the Cross-border Merger Directive achieves the primary objectives of the Cross-border Merger Directive as set forth in the recitals and in the articles of the Cross-border Merger Directive. It is not a verbatim transposition of the Directive; rather it is integrated into the existing Commercial Law, but contains specialised provisions for cross-border mergers in Articles 380 through 387. A cross-border merger in Latvia may trigger the application of collateral legislation.

25

Lithuania

IRMANTAS NORKUS, EVA SUDUIKO
Raidla Lejins & Norcous

I Introduction

1. The Cross-border Merger Directive has been implemented in Lithuania by the Law on Cross-border Mergers of Limited Liability Companies of the Republic of Lithuania (No. X-1367 of 13 December 2007) (the 'Law on Cross-border Mergers') and the Law on Employee Participation in a Company after Cross-border Merger of Limited Liability Companies of the Republic of Lithuania (No. X-1607 of 17 June 2008) (the 'Law on Employee Participation').

2. In addition to the rules established in the Law on Cross-border Mergers, the provisions applicable to domestic mergers and established in the Law on Companies of the Republic of Lithuania (No. VIII-1835 of 13 July 2000) (the 'Law on Companies') apply to the companies participating in the cross-border mergers and companies resulting from such mergers, unless the Law on Cross-border Mergers provides otherwise (Art. 1(2) Law on Cross-border Mergers).

II Scope

3. The rules established in the Law on Cross-border Mergers apply to cross-border mergers of undertakings whose legal form according to the laws of the Republic of Lithuania is a public limited liability company (*akcinė bendrovė, AB*) or a private limited liability company (*uždaroji akcinė bendrovė, UAB*) with undertakings (i) formed in accordance with the law of a Member State, (ii) having a legal form corresponding to their legal form and (iii) having a registered office, central administration or principal place of business within the European Economic Area (Art. 1(1) Law on Cross-border Mergers).

4. The Law on Cross-border Mergers does not apply to cross-border mergers where at least one of the merging companies is a management company or collective investment undertaking (these companies may take the form of either a public or private limited liability company) operating under the Law on Collective Investment Undertakings of the Republic of Lithuania (No. IX-1709 of 4 July 2003) (Art. 1(3) Law on Cross-border Mergers).

III Cash payment

5. The general rule established in the Law on Cross-border Mergers provides that in case of a cross-border merger the cash payment may not exceed 10 per cent of the nominal value or, in the absence thereof, the accounting par value of the shares of the company resulting from the cross-border merger (Art. 10(3) Law on Cross-border Mergers). However, this rule does not apply where the national law applicable to at least one merging company or company resulting from the cross-border merger allows cash payments exceeding the said threshold (Art. 10(4) Law on Cross-border Mergers).

IV Legal consequences of a merger and enforceability

6. The Law on Cross-border Mergers sets out the same legal consequences of a cross-border merger as those specified in the Cross-border Merger Directive. In particular, under the Law on Cross-border Mergers a cross-border merger has the following consequences:

(i) the companies participating in the merger (except for the surviving company if no new company is incorporated) cease to exist (Art. 2(4) Law on Cross-border Mergers);

(ii) all assets and liabilities are transferred to the company resulting from the cross-border merger (Art. 10(1) Law on Cross-border Mergers);

(iii) the shareholders of the companies that cease to exist become shareholders of the company resulting from the cross-border merger (Art. 10(2) Law on Cross-border Mergers);

(iv) the rights and obligations resulting from employment contracts or employment relations are transferred to the company resulting from the cross-border merger (Art. 10(7) Law on Cross-border Mergers).

Where the laws of the Member States require the completion of special formalities before the transfer of certain assets, rights and obligations by the merging companies becomes effective against third parties, those formalities have to be fulfilled by the company resulting from the cross-border merger (Art. 10(1) Law on Cross-border Mergers).

7. If the company resulting from the cross-border merger is subject to the law of the Republic of Lithuania, the cross-border merger enters into effect after the scrutiny of the legality of the cross-border merger by a notary and making relevant registration entries with the Register of Legal Persons of the Republic of Lithuania (the 'Register of Legal Persons') (see nos. 27–29 of this chapter).

The Register of Legal Persons must ensure the publication of information on the completion of the cross-border mergers in accordance with the procedures set in the regulations of the said register (Art. 9(4) Law on Cross-border Mergers).

Further, in case Lithuanian laws apply to the company resulting from the cross-border merger, the Register of Legal Persons has to ensure the submission of information on the completion of the cross-border merger to the appropriate registers of the Member States to which documents of the merging companies have been submitted (Art. 9(5) Law on Cross-border Mergers).

As from completion of the cross-border merger, such merger cannot be declared null and void by a court (Art. 9(3) Law on Cross-border Mergers).

V Procedures

1 Draft terms of a cross-border merger

8. Under the Law on Cross-border Mergers, the board of directors (or chief executive officer if the board is not formed) of each merging company has the duty to prepare mutual draft terms of the cross-border merger (Art. 3(1) Law on Cross-border Mergers).

The content of such draft terms of the cross-border merger is set in the Law on Cross-Border Mergers. In addition to the information described in Chapter 1, no. 19 of this book, the draft terms of the cross-border merger should explicitly state the method of merger, i.e. merger into a new company or merger by absorption (Art. 3(1) Law on Cross-border Mergers).

9. Article 11 of the Law on Cross-Border Mergers provides for a simplified version of the draft terms of a cross-border merger in case the wholly owned subsidiary is merged with its parent company. In such case, the information listed in Chapter 1, no. 39 of the first volume of this book can be omitted.

10. The articles of association of the company resulting from the cross-border merger have to be prepared together with the draft terms of the cross-border merger and are held to be an inseparable part thereof until the completion of the merger. If the laws of the Republic of Lithuania are applied to the surviving company, the content of such articles of association is regulated by the Law on Companies (Art. 3(2) Law on Cross-border Mergers).

11. Each of the companies participating in the merger has to make a public notice informing about the prepared draft terms of the cross-border merger three times in the source specified in the articles of association with intervals of at least thirty days or make such public notice once forty days before the general meeting of shareholders scheduled to approve the draft terms, accompanied by an individual written notice to each creditor of the companies (Art. 6(1) Law on Cross-border Mergers).

The content of such notice (both public and individual) is regulated by the Law on Companies. Such notice should include (i) the main information on merging companies and company resulting from the merger (name, company code, registered address, etc.); (ii) the method of merger; (iii) information on which of the companies will cease to exist and which will continue to exist after the merger; (iv) the date from which the rights, obligations and contracts are transferred to the company resulting from the merger; and (v) information on where and when interested persons may familiarise themselves with the draft terms of the merger and the articles of association of the company resulting from the merger (Art. 65(1) Law on Companies).

12. No later than on the first day of public notice about the prepared draft terms of the cross-border merger, the draft terms, the articles of association of the company resulting from the merger, the auditor's report and the management report have to be submitted to the Register of Legal Persons, which then makes all such documents available to the public (Art. 6(3) Law on Cross-border Mergers).

13. The members of management of the companies participating in the merger who prepared the draft terms of the cross-border merger are liable for any losses that may be incurred by the shareholders of such companies as a result of their actions (Art. 69(6) Law on Companies).

2 Management report

14. The board of directors (or chief executive officer if the board is not formed) of each of the companies participating in the merger has to produce a

management report on the cross-border merger to the shareholders. Such report has to (i) indicate the purpose of the merger; (ii) explain the terms of the merger; (iii) explain and justify the legal and economic aspects of the merger; and (iv) explain the implications of the merger for shareholders, creditors and employees of the company (Art. 5(1) Law on Cross-border Mergers).

15. If the opinion on the merger of the employees' representatives of the relevant merging company is presented at least thirty days before the date of the general meeting of shareholders called to approve the draft terms of the cross-border merger, such opinion should be attached to the management report (Art. 5(3) Law on Cross-border Mergers).

16. The board of directors (or chief executive officer if the board is not formed) has to ensure that the management report is made available to the shareholders, creditors, representatives of the employees and the employees themselves no later than forty days prior to the general meeting of shareholders called to approve the draft terms of the cross-border merger (Art. 5(2) Law on Cross-border Mergers).

As mentioned above (see no. 12 of this chapter), the management report has to be submitted to the Register of Legal Persons no later than on the first day of the public announcement about the prepared draft terms of the cross-border merger (Art. 6(3) Law on Cross-border Mergers).

3 Auditor's report

17. The draft terms of a cross-border merger have to be examined by independent experts – the audit firms appointed by each of the merging companies (Art. 4(1) Law on Cross-border Mergers). Alternatively, the merging companies have an option to apply to the competent institution (in Lithuania, the Register of Legal Persons) for appointment of one independent expert for all merging companies which will prepare one joint report for all shareholders (Art. 4(2) Law on Cross-border Mergers).

The draft terms of a cross-border merger need not be examined by independent experts and the respective report need not be prepared where all the shareholders of all the merging companies so agree or the wholly owned company is merged into its parent (Arts. 4(7) and 11(1) Law on Cross-border Mergers). Furthermore, if the laws of the jurisdictions of the companies participating in the merger do not provide otherwise, the auditor's report is not required when the acquiring company owns at least 90 per cent of the shares in the company being acquired (Art. 11(2) Law on Cross-border Mergers).

18. The auditor's report should inter alia cover (i) the conclusions whether the shares exchange ratio is fair and reasonable; (ii) the methods used to determine the shares exchange ratio and conclusions on the appropriateness of these methods and their impact on the determination of the value of shares;

and (iii) the description of difficulties encountered during such evaluation (Art. 63(3) Law on Companies).

19. The board of directors (or the chief executive officer if the board is not formed) of each of the merging companies has to ensure that the auditor's report is made available to the shareholders, creditors, representatives of the employees and the employees themselves not later than forty days before the date of the general meeting of shareholders called to approve the draft terms of the cross-border merger (Art. 4(6) Law on Cross-border Mergers).

As mentioned above (see no. 12 of this chapter), the auditor's report has to be submitted to the Register of Legal Persons no later than on the first day of the public announcement about the prepared draft terms of the cross-border merger (Art. 6(3) Law on Cross-border Mergers).

20. According to Article 69(6) of the Law on Companies, auditors of the merging companies that prepared the auditor's report are liable for any losses that may be incurred by the shareholders of such companies as a result of their actions.

4 General meeting of shareholders

A Information for shareholders

21. Lithuanian laws do not contain any special rules on the notification to be made to the shareholders of the merging companies about the prepared draft terms of the cross-border merger, the auditor's report and the management report. Thus, the shareholders usually learn about the aforementioned documents from the public notification as discussed above under no. 11 of this chapter. Further, the shareholders may become aware of the prepared draft terms from the announcement about convocation of the general meeting of shareholders called to approve the draft terms of the cross-border merger. Such announcement should be made not later than twenty-one days prior to the scheduled date of the general meeting of shareholders (Art. 26(4) Law on Companies).

22. The above-mentioned documents (i.e. the draft terms of merger, auditor's report and management report) should also be made available at least thirty days before the general meeting of shareholders called to approve the draft terms of the merger at the premises of the merging companies. In addition to these documents, the company should also make available the annual accounts for the last three financial years of each merging company. If the draft terms of the merger are dated more than six months after the end of the last financial year of at least one of the merging companies, the interim accounts dated no earlier than three months prior to the date of the draft terms of the merger must also be made available at the company's premises (Art. 65(2) Law on Companies). At the request of a shareholder, the company must submit copies of the documents referred to above free of charge (Art. 65(3) Law on Companies).

In addition, the management of the merging company must notify the shareholders and the management of other merging companies (which must in turn inform their shareholders) of the material changes in the assets, rights and obligations during the period from the preparation of the draft terms of the merger to the general meeting of shareholders called to approve them (Art. 65(4) Law on Companies).

B Shareholders' approval

23. In order to implement a cross-border merger, the draft terms of the cross-border merger as well as the articles of association of the company resulting from the merger have to be approved by the shareholders of each company (Art. 7(1) Law on Cross-border Mergers), except for a wholly owned subsidiary merged into its parent company (Art. 11(1) Law on Cross-border Mergers). Such decision should be recorded in a simple written form and need not be notarised.

24. The general meeting of shareholders is held valid if attended by the shareholders who hold shares carrying not less than 50 per cent of all votes. If this quorum is not met, a second meeting can be called, which may take decisions regardless of the number of votes represented (Art. 27(1) Law on Companies).

The draft terms of a cross-border merger must be approved by a special majority of two-thirds of the votes present or represented (Art. 28(1) Law on Companies). The articles of association of the merging company may provide for a larger majority.

Where the company has different classes of shares, the decision to approve the draft terms of the merger has to be adopted by a separate vote by each class of shareholders (as well as the holders of non-voting shares) (Art. 62(1) Law on Companies).

25. The general meeting of the merging company may reserve the right to make implementation of the cross-border merger conditional on express ratification by it of the rules on the participation of employees in the company resulting from the merger (Art. 7(4) Law on Cross-border Mergers).

26. The decision of the general meeting of shareholders on the approval of the cross-border merger has to be submitted to the Register of Legal Persons within five days from adoption thereof (Art. 7(5) Law on Cross-border Mergers).

5 Pre-merger certificate

27. If Lithuanian laws apply to the company resulting from the cross-border merger, the merger is deemed completed from the date of registration of (i) the newly founded company with the Register of Legal Persons or (ii) the articles of association of the surviving company with the Register of Legal Persons (Art. 9(1) Law on Cross-border Mergers). Any such registration is subject to the mandatory pre-merger verification by the notary.

28. The notary confirms the authenticity of the documents to be submitted to the Register of Legal Persons and verifies the conformity of the articles of association and other incorporation documents with the requirements of legal acts (Art. 26 Law on Notary of the Republic of Lithuania (No. I-2882 of 15 September 1992)). After the notary's verification, the articles of association and other documents are submitted to the Register of Legal Persons for registration.

6 Effect of the decision

29. As mentioned above under no. 27 of this chapter, if the company resulting from the cross-border merger is subject to the law of the Republic of Lithuania, the cross-border merger is deemed completed from the date of registration of (i) the new company formed after the cross-border merger or (ii) the amended articles of association of the company resulting from the cross-border merger.

Such registration has to be carried out by the Register of Legal Persons no earlier than within ten days after the completion of the scrutiny of the legality of the cross-border merger by a notary as described under no. 28 of this chapter (Art. 9(2) Law on Cross-border Mergers).

The completion of a cross-border merger has the consequences described under no. 6 of this chapter.

As from the completion date of a cross-border merger, the merger cannot be declared null and void by a court (Art. 9(3) Law on Cross-border Mergers).

VI Minority shareholders

30. As was mentioned under no. 24 of this chapter, the shareholders' decision to approve the terms of the cross-border merger is adopted by qualified majority vote and unanimous support is not required. Lithuanian law does not provide for any special remedies or protection mechanism for minority shareholders who oppose the merger. Thus, even if the shareholder does not support the merger, the shareholders' shares in the merged company are exchanged for the shares in the surviving or new company.

VII Protection of creditors

31. The Law on Companies establishes an obligation of the company participating in the merger to provide additional security to every creditor (including the bondholders) who requests such security, provided that the creditor's rights arose and did not expire before the publication of the terms of the merger (Art. 66(1) Law on Companies). However, the company may refrain from providing additional security if the creditors' claims are adequately secured by pledge, mortgage, surety or guarantee. Disputes regarding additional security are settled by a court (Art. 66(3) Law on Companies).

The creditors have the right to submit their claims from the first day of publication of the terms of the merger until the day of the general meeting of shareholders called to adopt the decision to merge the companies (see no. 11 of this chapter for more information about publication of the terms of the merger).

According to Article 2.101 of the Civil Code, in case the company does not perform its obligation to provide additional security, the creditor has the right to request termination of the contract or performance of obligations before the expiry of the contract as well as compensation of damages.

VIII Rules applicable to employee participation

32. As mentioned under no. 1 of this chapter, as regards employee participation, the Cross-border Merger Directive has been implemented in Lithuania by the Law on Employee Participation.

1 Employee participation in companies resulting from the cross-border mergers established in Lithuania

33. According to the Law on Employee Participation, in the companies resulting from the cross-border mergers established in Lithuania, employee participation is possible if:

(i) at least one of the merging companies has (six months before publication of the draft terms of the cross-border merger) an average number of employees that exceeds 500 and a system of employee participation; or
(ii) the employees of at least one of the merging companies constitute part of representatives in the administration or supervision body of the merging company (Art. 4(1) Law on Employee Participation).

2 Special negotiating body ('SNB')

34. The management or administrative bodies of the merging companies have to either make arrangements for the establishment of a special negotiating body ('SNB') or decide to apply standard rules of employee participation provided in the Law on Employee Participation (Art. 5(1)).

The purpose of the SNB is to negotiate employee participation conditions in the company resulting from the cross-border merger with the management bodies of the merging companies.

35. The Law on Employee Participation establishes specific rules for the appointment of Lithuanian members of the SNB.

The general rule is that the SNB members are appointed by the employee representatives (labour union or works council) of the Lithuanian participating companies. If the number of the Lithuanian participating companies is more than one, the SNB members have to be appointed by the common consent of the employee representatives of all participating Lithuanian companies (Art. 11(1) Law on Employee Participation).

In the absence of employee representatives in a merging Lithuanian company, the employees have the right to elect their representatives to the SNB directly. In such case the management or administrative bodies of the participating company have to convene the general meeting of employees, which would elect the SNB members by secret ballot. The same election procedure applies if the employee representatives fail to appoint the SNB members within thirty days after receiving the draft terms of the cross-border merger. In the latter case the general meeting of employees may be convened by any employee representative (Art. 11(2) Law on Employee Participation).

If the number of participating Lithuanian companies is more than one and the employee representatives of these companies fail to appoint the SNB members within thirty days after receiving the draft terms of the cross-border merger, or there are no employee representatives in at least one of the participating Lithuanian companies, the SNB members are elected by secret ballot at the general conference of the delegates of participating companies' employees (one delegate for every ten company's employees) (Art. 11(3) Law on Employee Participation).

3 Protection of employee representatives

36. The SNB members as well as employee representatives sitting in the administrative or supervisory bodies of the company resulting from the cross-border merger that are employed in Lithuania have the same level of protection as employee representatives in the territory of Lithuania and enjoy the same rights and protection as employee representatives in Lithuania, in particular, as concerns (i) participation in the meetings, (ii) payment of salary, (iii) prohibition on being dismissed from work without permission of the employee representative body (where they were elected by secret ballot at the general conference of the delegates of participating companies' employees, such consent is given by the State Labour Inspectorate (Art. 8 Law on Employees Participation)).

IX Tax treatment

37. Lithuania has transposed the provisions relating to cross-border mergers of the Merger Tax Directive into the Law on Corporate Income Tax of the Republic of Lithuania (No. IX-675 of 20 December 2001) (the 'Law on Corporate Income Tax').

38. The Law on Corporate Income Tax provides for tax free mergers between Lithuanian companies, between two foreign companies, and between a foreign company and a Lithuanian company. In order for a foreign company to qualify for the application of the tax neutral regime it has to be tax resident in one of the Member States, must have the corporate form established in the Annex to

the Merger Tax Directive and has to be a payer of taxes outlined in Article 3(c) of the Merger Tax Directive.

39. The Law on Corporate Income Tax provides for the following types of mergers, which can qualify as tax-free:

(i) one or more companies (the 'transferring companies') are merged into another existing company (the 'receiving company') and at the time of the merger all the assets, rights and obligations of the transferring companies are transferred to the receiving company, and the shareholders of the transferring companies in exchange for the shares held in the transferring companies receive shares issued by the receiving company; where during the exchange the difference between the price of the shares of the transferring companies and the shares of the receiving company is covered by a cash payment, it shall not exceed 10 per cent of the nominal value of the shares, or in the absence of the nominal value it shall not exceed 10 per cent of their accounting par value;
(ii) one or more companies (the 'transferring companies') are merged into a new company (the 'receiving company') and at the time of the merger all the assets, rights and obligations of the transferring companies are transferred to the receiving company, and the shareholders of the transferring companies in exchange for the shares held in the transferring companies receive shares issued by the receiving company; where during the exchange the difference between the price of the shares of the transferring companies and the shares of the receiving company is covered by a cash payment, it shall not exceed 10 per cent of the nominal value of the shares, or in the absence of the nominal value it shall not exceed 10 per cent of their accounting par value;
(iii) a company (the 'transferring company') transfers all its assets, rights and obligations to another company (the 'receiving company') which controls 100 per cent of the authorised capital (100 per cent of the shares representing its capital) of the transferring company (Art. 41(2) Law on Corporate Income Tax).

Noteworthy, the above mergers qualify as tax-free only if after the merger the receiving company pursues its activities in Lithuania on the basis of the assets, rights and obligations of the transferring company (Art. 41(3) Law on Corporate Income Tax).

40. Tax neutrality on the shareholders' level in case of the merger satisfying the above conditions is received by way of exempting any differences in share prices from the corporate income tax.

In accordance with Article 42(1) of the Law on Corporate Income Tax, where the shareholders of the transferring company receive shares of the receiving company in exchange for the shares held in the transferring company, an increase in the value of the said shares shall not be treated as income of such shareholders. In this case, the acquisition price of the new shares of the receiving entity received by the shareholders shall be the acquisition price of the shares in the transferring company before the transfer was effected.

However, where monetary settlement was made, such amounts are considered to be taxable income of the shareholders. In accordance with Article 12(15) of the Law on Corporate Income Tax, such income earned by a Lithuanian taxpayer would be tax exempt if such tax payer had held more than 25 per cent of shares in the transferring company for a period longer than three years.

41. On the transferring companies' level, an increase in the value of the assets transferred to the receiving company is not treated as income of the transferring company and is not taxed at the moment of the transfer (Art. 42 Law on Corporate Income Tax). However, the receiving company should continue calculation of depreciation of such assets according to the rules applied by the transferring company before the transfer was effected. Depreciation is calculated using the same method.

In case a Lithuanian company receives long-term assets from a foreign company, the Lithuanian company shall at its own discretion determine the period for depreciating the received long-term assets. Such period should be set in accordance with the Law on Corporate Income Tax and shall be reduced by the number of months that the foreign company had used the assets.

42. In general, losses from the operating activities can be carried forward for an unlimited period provided the company continues the activities due to which such losses were incurred, and losses incurred as a result of transferring securities or derivatives can be carried forward for the period of five years (Art. 30(4) Law on Corporate Income Tax).

As concerns transfer of losses in case of mergers, Article 43 of the Law on Corporate Income Tax allows transfer of unused losses of the transferring company to the receiving company if the receiving company continues carrying out the activities taken over or a part thereof for a period not shorter than three years. In case a Lithuanian company is merged into a foreign company, the losses transferred to such foreign company can be carried forward by the permanent establishment of the foreign company continuing received activities in Lithuania. The losses can be carried forward starting with the tax period during which the merger was concluded and the activities of the transferring company and any losses related thereto were transferred to the receiving company.

The requirement to carry out the transferred activities for the three year period is a necessary criterion in order for the exemption to be applicable. In case such activities are suspended before the period of three years elapses, the receiving company is obliged to recalculate the profits of the relevant tax periods and pay the residual tax amounts. However, in case the receiving company ceases performance of the transferred activities later than after three years, the losses related to the transferred activities will not be carried forward starting with the tax period when the transferred activities are suspended.

In addition, only losses from operating activities may be transferred to the receiving company. Losses resulting from the disposal of securities and derivative financial instruments may be transferred only by financial institutions.

26

Luxembourg

MARGARETHA WILKENHUYSEN, LOUISA SILCOX
NautaDutilh

I Introduction

1. The Grand Duchy of Luxembourg was one of the very first countries to be provided with rules on mergers with the law of 7 September 1987. Such mergers were however limited to domestic mergers between Luxembourg public limited liability companies (*société anonyme*). Two years after having partially implemented the Cross-border Merger Directive by two laws dated 23 March 2007 (the 'Merger Laws') allowing the absorption of a foreign company by a Luxembourg company, the Luxembourg Parliament has fully implemented the Cross-border Merger Directive by the law of 10 June 2009 (the 'Law') into the Luxembourg law on commercial companies of 10 August 1915 (the 'Company Law').

II Scope

2. The scope of the Law is broader than the Cross-border Merger Directive itself. The Law permits mergers between a Luxembourg company with legal personality, i.e., commercial companies: public limited-liability companies (*société anonyme*) (SA), partnerships limited by shares (*société en commandite par actions*) (SCA) and European companies (SE), in addition to cooperatives (*société cooperative*), private limited-liability companies (*société à responsabilité limitée*) (SARL) and European cooperative societies (SCE), civil companies and economic groupings (*groupement d'intéret économique*).

3. The Law does not limit its scope to mergers with entities in the European Union but enlarges it to third countries where such cross-border merger is not prohibited by the law of such third country.

4. The Law (Art. 257(2) of the Company Law) also allows explicitly a company which has been declared bankrupt to participate in a cross-border merger. The same applies to companies which are under composition (*concordat préventif de faillite*) proceedings or controlled management (*gestion contrôlée*) and suspension of payments (*sursis de paiement*).

5. Furthermore the Company Law also provides that for operations which are assimilated to mergers, namely where one or more companies enter into liquidation procedures and transfer their assets and liabilities to another company in return for the issuance of shares to the members of the absorbed company, the provisions relating to simplified mergers shall apply. Such an issuance may take place with or without a cash balance.

6. The Luxembourg Company Law has further authorised the application of a simplified procedure to mergers when the cash balance exceeds 10 per cent of

the nominal value of the shares issued in return for the assets and liabilities of the acquired company.

7. Finally the Luxembourg Company Law (Arts. 285 ff.) on Divisions (*scissions*) also allows divisions involving foreign companies.

III Types of merger

In general the Company Law sets forth two possible types of merger (Art. 258 of the Company Law).

1 Merger by acquisition (Art. 259 of the Company Law)

8. Merger by acquisition (Art. 259 of the Company Law) is the operation whereby one or more companies, following their dissolutions without liquidation, transfer to another pre-existing company all their assets and liabilities in exchange for the issue to the members of the company or companies being acquired of shares or corporate units in the acquiring company and a cash payment, if any, not exceeding 10 per cent of the nominal value of the shares or corporate units so issued or, in the absence of a nominal value, of their accounting par value.

9. Such a merger can also take place where one or more of the companies being acquired are in liquidation, provided that those companies have not yet begun to distribute their assets to their members.

10. The Law (Art. 259(3)) also provides that where a European Company (SE) is formed by way of a merger by acquisition, the acquiring company shall take the form of a European Company when the merger takes place.

2 Merger by incorporation of a new company (Art. 260 of the Company Law)

11. Merger by incorporation of a new company is the operation whereby several companies transfer all their assets and liabilities in exchange for the issue to their members of share or corporate units of a new company to be incorporated (Art. 260 Company Law). The rule regarding the European Company is also applicable.

IV Procedure

1 Draft terms of the merger

12. Among other things and in addition to the information required for domestic mergers (Art. 261 of the Company Law), the common draft merger terms, drawn up in writing by the administrative and management bodies of the merging companies, shall include, inter alia: the articles of the acquiring company, the impact of the cross-border merger on employment, the information relating to the valuation of the assets and liabilities which are transferred to the

absorbing company and the dates of the merging companies' accounts used to establish the merger.

2 Publication of the draft terms of the merger

13. The common draft terms of merger shall be published in the National Gazette of each of the Member States concerned (Art. 262 of the Company Law), at least one month before the date of the general meeting convened to decide on the common draft terms of merger. The publication shall include in addition to the information required for domestic mergers the following information (Art. 262(2) of the Company Law): name, form and registered offices of the merging companies, register of commerce and companies and registration number and information on special protection for creditors.

3 Management report

14. A report must be drawn up by the management or the board of the merging companies and must be made available one month before the date of the general meeting which is to decide on the merger (Art. 265 of the Company Law). The report must detail the consequences of the cross-border merger on the shareholders, creditors and employees. In case of cross-border mergers, such report shall be made available to the employees' representatives or where there are no such representatives, to the employees themselves (Art. 265 of the Company Law). If the management or administrative body of any of the merging companies receives, in good time, an opinion from the representative of their employees, that opinion shall be appended to the report.

4 Independent expert's report

15. The common draft terms of merger must be subject to an examination and a written report to the members (Art. 266 of the Company Law). An independent expert must be chosen among the *réviseurs d'entreprises* but it is possible to require that the report be drawn up by one or more experts for all the merging companies. In such case, the appointment shall be made, at the joint request of the merging companies, by the presiding judge of the chamber of the *Tribunal d'Arrondissement* dealing with commercial matters, in the district in which the registered office of the acquiring company is located, sitting as in urgency matters. In the report, the expert must state whether the share exchange ratio is or is not fair and reasonable. Neither an examination of the common draft terms by an independent expert nor the independent expert's report are required if all of the shareholders of each of the merging companies have so agreed.

16. In case of a cross-border merger, such expert's report must be available one month before the date of the general meeting called to decide on the common draft merger terms.

5 Shareholders' right to inspect

17. Every member of the merging companies (Art. 267 of the Company Law) is entitled to inspect the following documents at the registered office at least one month before the date of the general meeting called to decide on the common draft terms of merger: the common draft terms of merger, the annual accounts and the annual reports of the merging companies for the last three financial years, the report of the management and administrative bodies of the merging companies.

6 Approval by the general meetings

18. The merger requires the approval of the general meetings of each of the merging companies and, where appropriate, of the holders of securities other than shares or corporate units, after examination of the report of the management and of the report of the independent expert. Such decision requires that the conditions as to the quorum and majority laid down for the amendment of the articles are fulfilled.

19. A *société à responsabilité limitée*, a *société cooperative* or an economic interest grouping can only acquire another company or economic interest grouping if the shareholders or members of such other companies fulfil the conditions to become a shareholder or member (Art. 267*bis* of the Company Law). In a *société cooperative*, each member has the right to resign at any time without having to satisfy any other conditions.

20. The consent of all members is required in acquiring companies, and if the companies being acquired are *sociétés en nom collectif*, or *sociétés coopératives*, the partners of which have an unlimited and joint liability, civil companies or economic interest groupings.

21. Except in the case where the consent of all members is required, the approval of the merger by the general meeting of the acquiring company is not necessary if (i) the publication described above ('publication of draft terms of mergers') is made on behalf of the acquiring company, at least one month before the date of the general meeting of the company or companies being acquired convened to decide on the common draft terms of merger, (ii) all the members of the acquiring company are entitled, at least one month before the date indicated above to examine at the registered office of the company the documents indicated above ('rights of the shareholders to inspect') and (iii) one or more members of the acquiring company holding at least 5 per cent of the shares or corporate units in the subscribed capital are entitled up to the day following the holding of the general meeting of the company being acquired to require the convening of a general meeting of the acquiring company to decide whether to approve the merger.

7 Minutes of the general meetings

22. The minutes of the general meeting deciding upon the merger shall be drawn up in the form of a notarial deed. The same applies to common draft terms of merger where the merger need not be approved by the general meetings of all merging companies.

23. For cross-border mergers, a Luxembourg notary must examine the legality of the cross-border merger and deliver a certificate confirming the compliance of the pre-merger acts and formalities for the part of the procedure relating to the company governed by Luxembourg law.

24. In addition, each participating company must send to the Luxembourg notary responsible for attesting to the completion of the merger for the surviving company the pre-merger certificate mentioned above, within six months from issuance of this certificate by the notary or other authority designated under local law (for a foreign company participating in the merger), together with the approved terms of cross-border merger (Art. 271(2) Company Law).

25. If the law of the state to which a merging company is subject provides for a procedure to scrutinise and amend the ratio applicable to the exchange of securities or corporate units, or a procedure to compensate minority members without preventing the registration of the cross-border merger, such procedure shall only apply if the other merging companies, situated in a state that does not provide for such procedure, explicitly accept when approving the draft terms of the cross-border merger. The members of that merging company have recourse to such a procedure to be initiated before the authority having jurisdiction over that merging company. In such cases, the notary may issue the certificate referred to above even if such a procedure has commenced. The certificate must, however, indicate that the procedure is pending. The decision in the procedure shall be binding on the company resulting from the cross-border merger and all its members.

V Rights of creditors

1 Ordinary creditors

26. Under Article 268(1) of the Company Law, creditors of the merging companies, whose claims pre-date the date of the publication of the deeds recording the merger, may apply within two months of that publication to the presiding judge of the chamber of the Luxembourg court dealing with commercial matters in the district in which the registered office of the debtor company is located and sitting as urgency matters, to obtain adequate safeguard of collateral for any matured or unmatured debts, where the merger would make such protection necessary. The president of the court shall reject the application if the creditor is already in possession of adequate safeguards or if such safeguards are

unnecessary, having regards to the assets and liabilities of the company after the merger. The debtor company may cause the application to be turned down by paying the creditor, even if it is a term debt. If the safeguards are not provided within the time limit prescribed, the debt shall immediately fall due. The Company Law (Art. 268(2) and (3)) also provides for specific rules if the company being acquired or the acquiring company is a *société en nom collectif, société en commandite par actions société en commandite simple* or *société cooperative.*

2 Bondholders

27. The rules described in the above paragraph shall apply to the holders of bonds of the merging companies, unless the merger has been approved by a meeting of the bondholders or by the bondholders individually.

3 Securities holders

28. The holders of securities other than shares or corporate units to which special rights are attached must be given rights in the acquiring company, at least equivalent to those they possessed in the acquired company. This shall not be the case if the alteration to those rights was approved by a meeting of the holders of such securities. In the event of failure to convene such meeting or if such meeting refuses to accept the proposed alteration, the securities concerned shall be repurchased at a price corresponding to their valuation in the terms of the merger.

VI Entry into force

29. In accordance with Article 272 of the Company Law, the merger shall take effect when concurring decisions of the companies involved shall have been adopted. In accordance with Article 273 the merger shall have no effect vis-à-vis third parties until after the publication of the minutes of the general meeting which is to decide on the merger. By derogation to these Articles 272 and 273 of the Company Law, in case of absorption by a Luxembourg company of a foreign-law-governed company, the merger only becomes effective and opposable towards third parties after the publication of the minutes of the general meeting that is to decide on the merger.

VII Consequences of the merger

30. Upon such completion of the merger, further to Article 274 of the Company Law, all of the elements of the acquired company are transferred to the acquiring company. This is termed the 'universal transfer' ('*transfert universel*') whereupon all elements, assets and liabilities of the acquired company are directly transferred to the acquiring company's capital and are immediately

enforceable against both the acquiring and the acquired companies, as well as vis-à-vis third parties. The transfer is automatic and direct, bypassing shareholder(s) of the acquired company. The universal transfer also includes all rights and obligations relating to employment contracts with the acquired company, as further explained under Section XI. The second consequence is that all the shareholder(s) of the acquired company automatically become shareholder(s) of the acquiring company in the proportions set out under the share exchange ratio. The third consequence is that upon the completion of the merger, the acquired company ceases to exist, without any further liquidation or other winding-up measures required. This also entails the cancellation of the shares of the company being acquired as held by or on behalf of either of the merging companies.

31. The above effects all take place simultaneously and *ipso jure* upon the completion of the merger, and without necessitating any specific mention in either the merger report or the shareholders' decisions of the acquired or the acquiring company.

32. However, it is to be noted that the transfer of certain assets require specific measures (such as the change of ownership of real property or certain intellectual property rights), as outlined by Article 274(2) of the Company Law. As long as such specific measures have not yet been taken after the merger by the acquiring company (further to the acquired company ceasing to exist), the transfer of property is not enforceable against third parties. Such is the case if the acquired company owned buildings, patents or trademarks, for example, whereby the acquiring company is required to proceed to the registration of its ownership, in conformity with the specific rules relating to the transfer of property for each of the domains. To cover any potential difficulty in relation to the transfer of any specific ownership, in practice the minutes of the shareholders' resolutions will expressly refer to the transfer of ownership of any such specific good or right.

33. In case of cross-border mergers, the rights and obligations of the merging companies arising from contracts of employment or from employment relationships and existing on the date on which the cross-border merger takes effect are transferred to the acquiring party at the date on which the cross-border merger takes effect.

VIII Actions against the management

34. Article 275 of the Company Law provides that shareholders of the acquired company may take individual liability action against the members of its managing body. Such proceedings would aim to obtain indemnification for any damage that the shareholder(s) prove to have suffered due to the misconduct of the directors in either the preparation stages or the conduct of the merger. Any

liability so invoked will be joint and several for the members of the management bodies. Each director has the possibility of excusing her/himself from all liability upon proving that no misconduct may be personally attributed to her/himself.

35. Such liability may be invoked in the event of the managing body omitting to mention the corporate object of each merging company, or any of the information required under Article 261 of the Company Law as set out under section IV of this chapter, in the draft cross-border merger report. Their liability may also be engaged for failure to submit the report to the employee representatives, or to the employees themselves, at least one month before the general meeting to decide upon the merger. However, the omission of any detail in the draft merger report, although giving rise to potential criminal fines, is insufficient grounds to allow the merger to be avoided.

36. Such liability proceedings may also be introduced by the shareholder(s) of the acquired company against the administrative body and the experts in the discharge of their duties, jointly with the managing body or individually.

37. The above provisions only apply to the organs and experts intervening on behalf of the acquired company however. The liability of the acquiring company may be engaged under the general provisions of Article 59 of the Company Law, i.e. jointly and severally liable both towards the company and towards third parties for violation of the company's articles of association or for violation of the Company Law, and towards the shareholders and the company for misconduct in the management of the company's affairs. In accordance with general law, they may discharge themselves from liability upon proving that no misconduct may be directly attributed to them and that they had reported any such violation to the first general meeting following them having acquired knowledge of said violation.

IX Avoidance of the merger

38. Upon completion, the cross-border merger may only be avoided under strict and limited circumstances (Art. 276 of the Company Law). The Company Law requires that the avoidance be ordered by a court decision on the grounds of the absence of either the absence of a notarised act or upon the decisions of the general meetings of either of the merging companies being declared void. Article 276 further states that in derogation to the provisions on national mergers, upon completion of a cross-border merger, whereby a Luxembourg company acquires a foreign law governed company, an action for avoidance by a third party may not be ordered. It is interesting to note that neither reasons of public interest nor incorrect proceedings relating to the merger project prepared by the management body are permitted as grounds to avoid the merger.

X 'Simplified' mergers

39. The Merger Laws introduced a subsection III to Section XIV of the Company Law, relating to 'simplified mergers'. A merger is so defined when the acquiring company obtains all the shares, or other securities conferring voting rights, in the company to be acquired. In the event of a national merger, the Law permits the merger to take place without the administrative steps and provisions outlined under section IV of this chapter (notably without a management report, or the approval by the general meeting of the acquiring company). However, in the event of a cross-border merger, the Luxembourg legislator's quest for legal security is apparent, as even in the event of the merger of a subsidiary with its parent company, the management report is still required and still to be made available to the employees, containing the consequences of the merger on their employment, as well as to the shareholders as under Article 267(1)d). Article 279(2) further removes the necessity for the decisions of the general meeting of shareholders in the event of a cross-border merger.

40. The above merger simplification procedures are not, however, reserved to parent companies and their subsidiaries. The Merger Law introduces a second paragraph to Article 281 of the Company Law, whereby in the event of a cross-border merger carried out by a company holding 90 per cent or more of the shares or other securities carrying voting rights, the report by an independent expert shall only be required in the event that it is required by the national law of either of the companies.

XI Employee participation

41. The general principle relating to employee participation, as outlined under the Cross-border Merger Directive, requires the national legislation of the new company to continue to enforce employees' rights, including those of employees' participation rights relating to the merger of their company.

1 Employee participation in the merger process

42. The Merger Laws provide an entire new section to the Luxembourg Labour Code,[1] as regards the level of employee participation within the framework of a merger process, and will be applicable to cross-border mergers. The new section implements the SE Regulation (EC 2157/2001), extending the requirements for a European Company to all companies and requiring that (i) special provisions be set, especially in the field of employee involvement and (ii) in all Luxembourg public limited companies employing over 1,000 employees, and in all Luxembourg public limited liability companies in which the participation

1 Luxembourg Labour Code Book IV, Title II, Chapter VI, Section 4 'Employee participation in case of cross-border merger'.

of the Luxembourg state is over 25 per cent, at least three employee representatives be appointed to the managing body. In the event the conditions are not fulfilled in the framework of a cross-border merger, then Article 23 of the SE Regulation would be applied, thus requiring specific employee involvement in relation to the requirements of the SE Directive (EC 2001/86), which sets out the specific requirements as to the involvement of employees.

43. In practice, once the managing body of each of the merging companies has drawn up its detailed written report upon the merger, the Merger Laws specify that in the event of a cross-border merger, such a report will be made available to the members and representatives of the employees. In the event that there are no such employee representatives (such as in a company employing fewer than fifteen employees), the report is to be made available to the employees themselves, no less than one month before the shareholders' general meeting to decide upon the terms of the draft terms of the merger. Failure to do so will engage criminal fines on behalf of the managing board.

44. Furthermore, the Merger Laws specifically permit the general meetings of each of the merging companies to reserve the right to condition the implementation of the cross-border merger upon its express ratification of arrangements relating to the employees' participation in the newly formed company.

2 Employee participation in the newly formed company

45. In addition and pursuant to the cross-border merger, the newly created company will be required to take adequate measures to ensure employees' participation rights during the initial three years following the completion of the merger. 'Employee participation' in such a sense does not entail active participation in everyday managerial decisions, which remain reserved for the management board, but rather entails participation in the supervising and strategic development of the new company. The means of participation are varied. It may be decided that the employees form an actual part of the managing or administrative body, or that the employees may be represented by an independent and separate body. The option remains open to the managing body and the employees of the founder companies to choose a different form of participation, as long as the level and information remain at at least the same level as under that of a separate body.

46. Further outlining the importance accorded to employee participation, the Luxembourg Labour Code specifically protects employee representatives from dismissal and imposes their mission as to 'safeguard and defend the employees interests in all work related areas [...]', a broad role which in practice covers nearly every scope of employment, including that of mergers. The Company Law further specifically requires employee representatives to be provided with sufficient office space as well as financial and material resources to be able to correctly fulfil their duties.

47. In the event that no satisfactory arrangement is found, the standard rules set out in the Annex to the SE Directive are applicable. Such rules include the right for employees to elect, appoint, recommend or oppose the composition of a specific board representing the employees.

3 The extensive scope of employee participation under Luxembourg law

48. The Luxembourg legislator extends the scope of the Merger Laws far beyond that of the framework fixed by the Directive, as under the Merger Laws, the obligations and means of employee participation in cross-border mergers is extended to cross-border mergers with companies outside of the European Union and even if the new company to be formed will be situated outside of the European Union.

49. However, despite extensive employee protection and involvement the question remains raised as to the system of employee participation in a company formed other than as a public limited liability company (*société anonyme*), which remains a legal vacuum under Luxembourg law.

XII Other procedures assimilated to mergers

50. The Company Law also provides for operations which are assimilated to mergers, namely, where one or more companies enter into liquidation procedures and transfer their assets and liabilities to another company in return for the issuance of shares to the members of the absorbed company, the provisions relating to simplified mergers shall apply. Such an issuance may take place with or without a cash balance. The Luxembourg Company law has further authorised the application of simplified procedure to mergers when the cash balance exceeds 10 per cent of the nominal value of the shares issued in return for the assets and liabilities of the acquired company.

51. The third assimilated procedure relates to company divisions and was further completed by the Merger Law. The Merger Law defines company divisions by acquisition as the procedure whereby following the dissolution without liquidation of a company, the said company transfers all of its assets and liabilities to another company with or without issue of new shares and cash payment not exceeding 10 per cent of the nominal value of the shares allocated. Division by incorporation of a new company follows the same principle, except the assets and liabilities of the dividing company are transferred to a company to be incorporated. The procedure for company divisions is closely modelled on those for mergers, with the same procedural requirements, the same *ipso jure* effects and the same limited possibilities for avoiding the division for example, as well as the same requirements for employee participation.

XIII Tax treatment

52. The Merger Tax Directive has been implemented in the Income Tax Law ('ITL') by two laws of 20 December 1991 and 20 December 2001. Under these laws, cross-border (inside the European Union) and domestic mergers can potentially be achieved in a tax neutral way in compliance with the conditions of the Merger Directive. A subsequent law dated 21 December 2007 broadened the scope beyond the scope of the Merger Tax Directive by extending the regime in certain instances to companies resident in the European Economic Area that are subject to a tax corresponding to Luxembourg income tax.

53. In line with the principles laid down in the Merger Tax Directive it implemented, Luxembourg applies tax neutrality to qualifying mergers, divisions, partial divisions, transfers of assets and exchange in shares involving one or more resident Luxembourg companies (or Luxembourg permanent establishments) and one or more EU or EEA resident companies (permanent establishments).

54. The tax neutrality is achieved via a corporate income tax roll-over relief of latent capital gains existing at the time of the transfer on the condition that these gains would remain subject to future taxation in Luxembourg. For that purpose, the receiving company connects assets and liabilities to a Luxembourg permanent establishment. If the receiving company continues the original book value of the transferred assets and liabilities, it will be considered to hold such assets and liabilities from their initial acquisition date by the transferring company. Luxembourg ITL does not allow for the transfer of the carry forward losses which are forfeited.

55. Cross-border mergers that are eligible for the exemption regime are mergers of (i) Luxembourg fully taxable companies into EU resident companies as defined by Article 3 of the Merger Directive and (ii) EEA resident companies (which includes EU resident companies) into Luxembourg fully taxable companies.

1 Tax consequences at the level of the transferred company

56. For the merger to be eligible for tax neutrality at the level of the transferred company, the following cumulative conditions must be met:

(i) the entire business (i.e. all of its assets and liabilities) should be transferred as a result of and at the time of a dissolution without liquidation;

(ii) the transfer should be made in exchange for shares in the receiving company and, if applicable, a cash payment not exceeding 10 per cent of their nominal value or, in the absence of a nominal value, of their accounting par value or should result in the cancellation of a shareholding held by the acquiring company in the absorbed company; and

(iii) unrealised capital gains transferred on the operation must be subject to Luxembourg taxation in the future and the transfer is performed at accounting value.

2 Tax consequences at the level of the acquiring company

57. The acquiring company will have to continue the book values of the assets and liabilities received at the book value used by the absorbed company in its balance sheet. Under that condition, the date of acquisition of the acquired assets will for tax purposes be deemed to correspond to the date they were acquired by the absorbed company.

58. However, if the acquiring Luxembourg company previously held shares in the absorbed company, these would be deemed to have been realised at their fair market value at the time of the merger. Even though this capital gain would as a rule be taxable, an exemption would apply if the shareholding represented at least 10 per cent of the capital of the absorbed company. No minimum holding period needs to be met for this capital gains exemption to apply. Failing the participation in the absorbed company to reach the 10 per cent threshold, capital gains would also be exempt if the shareholding had an acquisition value of at least EUR 6 million and was held for at least twelve months prior to the merger.

3 Tax consequences at the level of the shareholder(s) of the transferred company

59. The shareholders of the transferred company have the option to roll over any latent gains realised upon exchange of shares in the absorbed company for shares in the absorbing company. The roll-over implies that the newly acquired shares in the absorbing company would be deemed identical to the shares they were exchanged for in terms of tax value and time of acquisition.

27

Malta

ADRIAN GABARRETTA, COLM O'CONNOR, NADIA CASSAR
Ganado & Associates

I Introduction

1. The Cross-border Merger Directive has, for the most part,[1] been implemented in Malta by virtue of subsidiary legislation, entitled the Cross-border Mergers of Limited Liability Companies Regulations (Legal Notice 415 of 2007), (the 'Company Regulations'), which entered into force on 15 December 2007.

II Scope of rules

2. There are three types of cross-border merger mechanisms contemplated by the Company Regulations (Reg. 3(4) (a), (b) and (c) Company Regulations). They may be categorised as follows:

(i) *merger by acquisition*: where one or more companies, on being dissolved without going into liquidation, transfer all their assets, rights, liabilities and obligations to another existing company in exchange for the issue to their members of securities or shares representing the capital of that company. A cash payment may also constitute part of the consideration for such type of cross-border merger (see no. 6 of this chapter);
(ii) *merger by formation*: where two or more companies, on being dissolved without going into liquidation, transfer all their assets, rights, liabilities and obligations to a newly formed company in exchange for the issue to their members of securities or shares in that newly formed company. A cash payment may also constitute part of the consideration for such type of cross-border merger (see no. 6 of this chapter); and
(iii) *merger by absorption*: where a company, on being dissolved without going into liquidation, transfers all its assets, rights, liabilities and obligations to the company holding all the securities or shares representing its capital.

3. The specific types of Maltese companies that may avail themselves of these types of cross-border merger mechanisms are public and private limited liability companies. This is in line with Article 1 of the First Company Law Directive, as referred to in the Company Regulations (Reg. 3(3)(a)).

4. However, it is to be noted that the cross-border merger mechanisms outlined above do not apply to any Maltese company the object of which is the collective investment of capital provided by the public, which operates on the principle of risk-spreading and the units of which are, at the holders' request, repurchased or redeemed, directly or indirectly, out of the assets of the company (Reg. 4(3) Company Regulations). An example of such type of corporate

1 Article 16 of the Directive, dealing with employee participation rights in cross-border mergers, has been implemented in Maltese law by virtue of subsidiary legislation, entitled the Employee Involvement (Cross-border Mergers of Limited Liability) Regulations 2008 (Legal Notice 165 of 2008).

entity operating in Malta would be a collective investment scheme, the growth of which has been especially pronounced here in recent years.

5. In addition, it is worth highlighting that any Maltese company participating in a cross-border merger is required to comply with the provisions and formalities of the Companies Act (Chapter 386 of the Laws of Malta) (the 'Act').[2] In this regard, and in line with Article 343(6) of the Act, any Maltese company that is subject to a court-ordered liquidation may not participate in a cross-border merger. Likewise, in the case of a voluntary liquidation, the same prohibition applies to a Maltese company that has started the process of distributing its assets, or for which a declaration of solvency has yet to be made (Art. 343(5) and (6) Act).

III Cash payment

6. No cash payment made in respect of a cross-border merger may exceed 10 per cent of the nominal value or, in the absence of a nominal value, the accounting par value of the shares or securities representing the capital of the company resulting from the cross-border merger (Reg. 3(4) Company Regulations). This general rule applies to both domestic and cross-border mergers (Art. 343(2) and (3) Act).

7. However, as an exception to this rule, where the laws of another Member State of a company participating in the cross-border merger allow the aforesaid cash payment to exceed 10 per cent, then this limitation on cash payment does not apply (Reg. 4(2) Company Regulations).

IV Legal consequences and enforceability of a cross-border merger

8. In circumstances where the company resulting from the cross-border merger is to be registered (or, indeed, is already registered) in Malta, the Maltese Registrar will issue a certificate of completion stating the date on which the merger shall take legal effect.

9. Once such a certificate has been issued by the Registrar, it will not be possible to subsequently declare a cross-border merger null and void (Reg. 17(4) Company Regulations).

10. From the date on which it takes effect, a cross-border merger by acquisition/absorption shall result in the following (Reg. 18(1) Company Regulations):

(i) any acquired company shall cease to exist;
(ii) all of the assets, liabilities, rights and obligations[3] of any acquired company shall be transferred, by operation of law, to the acquiring company; and

2 To the extent that the Company Regulations do not provide otherwise (Reg. 5(1)).

3 Included in the 'rights and obligations' transferring to the company resulting from the cross-border merger are those arising from contracts of employment or employment relationships.

(iii) the shareholders of any acquired company will become shareholders in the acquiring company.[4]

11. In the case of a cross-border merger by formation, the following shall occur (Reg. 18(2) Company Regulations):

(i) any merging company shall cease to exist;
(ii) all of the assets, liabilities, rights and obligations of any merging company shall be transferred, by operation of law, to the newly formed company which results from the cross-border merger; and
(iii) the shareholders of any merging company will become shareholders in the newly formed company resulting from the cross-border merger.

12. If the transfer of any assets, rights or obligations under the cross-border merger requires the completion of certain formalities in order to be effective against third parties, then the obligation to fulfil this task shall fall on the company resulting from the merger (Reg. 18(3) Company Regulations). Relevant factors to be considered here include registration in the appropriate registries of title to any transferred shares or real property.

V Procedure

1 Draft terms of cross-border merger

13. The first step for any Maltese company participating in a cross-border merger is to prepare the common draft terms of the cross-border merger. This document is to be prepared by the board of directors of the participating company and must, at a very minimum, contain the information requirements referred to in Article 5 of the Cross-border Merger Directive, which have been faithfully mirrored in the Company Regulations (Reg. 6). Note, however, that, in the case of a cross-border merger involving the absorption of a wholly owned subsidiary, that part of the draft terms dealing with share exchange ratios may be dispensed with (Reg. 19(1) Company Regulations).

14. The completed common draft terms of the cross-border merger will need to be signed by both a director and secretary of any participating Maltese company. However, the draft terms are not required to be in notarised form, as is the case in some other Member States, such as Estonia and Germany, for example (no. 8 of Chapter 11; no. 6 of Chapter 12 of the first volume of this book).

15. Once the draft terms of the cross-border merger have been delivered to the Registrar and he is satisfied that the above-mentioned requirements of the Company Regulations have been met, he is obliged to register this document – without delay. He is also obliged to publish a statement to this effect in the

4 Obviously, this will already be the case in circumstances where a parent company is absorbing a wholly owned subsidiary.

Government Gazette, or on the Registry of Companies' website. This publication must be made at least one month in advance of the general meeting of the company being held for the purposes of deciding on the approval of the cross-border merger (Reg. 7(3) Company Regulations).

16. If an interested party wishes to contest the registration by the Registrar of the common draft terms of the cross-border merger, then he may do so by way of application before the Maltese courts within one month of the publication by the Registrar of the aforementioned statement (Reg. 13(1)(a) Company Regulations). A contestation may be made on the grounds that the common draft terms of the merger have not been validly drawn up.

2 Directors' report

17. In addition to preparing the common draft terms of the cross-border merger, the board of directors of any Maltese merging company is required to draw up a report which both justifies and explains the legal and economic aspects of the proposed cross-border merger, as well as setting out its implications for members, employees and creditors.

18. The directors' report is to be made available to both members and employee representatives not less than one month before the general meeting of the company to decide on approving the cross-border merger (Reg. 8(2) Company Regulations). If there are no employee representatives in the company, then the report should be made available directly to the employees themselves. Furthermore, if an opinion on the directors' report is submitted in good time by the employees' representatives to the board of directors, then it must be appended to the report (Reg. 8(3) Company Regulations).

3 Independent expert's report

19. The next requirement imposed by the Company Regulations is for any participating Maltese company to engage an independent expert, who has been approved by the Registrar, to produce a written report on the draft common terms of the cross-border merger.

20. In drawing up any report, any independent expert shall be entitled to obtain all relevant documents and information from the company that are necessary for the proper discharge of his duties (Reg. 9(3) Company Regulations).

21. The principal aim of any expert's report is to ensure that the share exchange ratio taking place as part of the cross-border merger is both reasonable and fair. To this end, his report is required to specify the following (Reg. 9(2) Company Regulations):

(i) the method or methods used to arrive at the proposed share exchange ratio;

(ii) whether such method or methods are adequate in the case in question, indicating the values arrived at using such method, or methods, and giving an opinion on the relative importance of such method or methods in arriving at the value decided on; and
(iii) any valuation difficulties which have arisen in arriving at the proposed share exchange ratio.

22. In instances where at least one of the merging companies is Maltese, or where the company resulting from the cross-border merger is to be registered in Malta, the requirement for each company to have an independent expert acting on its behalf can be dispensed with. Instead, at the joint request of the merging companies, one or more independent experts may be appointed by the Registrar in order to draw up a written report for all the merging companies (Reg. 9(4) Company Regulations).

23. In certain instances the requirement for an independent expert's report may be dispensed with in its entirety. They are as follows (Regs. 9(5), 19(1) and 19(2) Company Regulations):

(i) where all the members of the companies participating in the cross-border merger have so agreed;
(ii) where a cross-border merger is being carried out by a company holding all the shares and securities conferring the right to vote at general meetings of the company being acquired; and
(iii) where a cross-border merger is being carried out by a company holding 90 per cent of the shares and securities conferring the right to vote at general meetings of the company being acquired.[5]

4 General meeting of shareholders

A Information for shareholders

24. The following information must be made available for inspection by any member of a Maltese merging company at least one month in advance of the date fixed for the general meeting to decide on the draft terms of the cross-border merger (Reg. 11(1) Company Regulations):

(i) the common draft terms of the cross-border merger;
(ii) the annual accounts and the annual reports of each merging company for the preceding three financial years;
(iii) an accounting statement drawn up by each merging company as at a date which shall not be earlier than the first day of the third month preceding the date of the draft terms of the merger if the latest annual accounts

5 Note: in this particular scenario minority shareholders have the right to have their shares purchased for an agreed consideration corresponding to their fair value or, in the event of disagreement, at a price determined by the Maltese courts.

relate to an accounting period which ended more than six months before that date;

(iv) the directors' report for any participating Maltese company;

(v) the independent expert's report for any participating Maltese company.

25. In addition, and in order for a general meeting of a merging Maltese company to be validly convened, the Act requires a minimum of fourteen days' notice in writing to be given to every member of the company (Art. 130 Act).[6] The notice should contain the following:[7]

(i) the text of the proposed resolution to approve the cross-border merger;

(ii) the principal purpose of the resolution; and

(iii) a statement that the resolution is an extraordinary one (such type of resolution is required to approve a cross-border merger; see section 4B).

B Shareholders' approval

26. The decision by the Maltese company to adopt the common draft terms of the cross-border merger (together with any alterations or additions necessary to the constitutional documents of the company) requires the approval of the company's members.[8] Such approval is to be given by the passing of an extraordinary resolution at a general meeting of the company.[9] Under Maltese law, an extraordinary resolution is one passed by those members holding, in the aggregate, not less than 75 per cent in nominal value of the shares represented and entitled to vote at the meeting and at least 51 per cent in nominal value of all the shares entitled to vote at the meeting (Art. 135(1)(a) Act).[10]

27. If the members of the Maltese company decide by extraordinary resolution to approve the cross-border merger, then such resolution, together with an authentic copy of any instrument giving effect thereto, must be filed for registration with the Registrar.

6 It is noted that a shorter notice period may be given, provided that it is consented to by all the members entitled to attend and vote at the meeting (Art. 130 Act). Furthermore, a company's Articles may provide for a longer notice period.

7 A. Muscat, *Principles of Maltese Company Law*, Malta University Press, 2007, 1073.

8 The only exception to this rule is where the acquiring company is Maltese and the conditions of the Company Regulations relating to the publication and inspection of the draft common terms of merger have been fulfilled (Art. 345(6) Act). However, even here, if one or more shareholders in the acquiring company holding at least 5 per cent of the voting share capital request a general meeting of the company to approve the cross-border merger then this request must be acceded to.

9 If there is more than one class of shareholder in the Maltese merging company whose rights are affected by the merger, then each such class shall be subject to a separate vote on the merger.

10 Note: if one (but not both) of the aforesaid majorities is achieved, another meeting may be convened within thirty days to take another vote on the resolution. The procedure for passing a shareholders' extraordinary resolution at such subsequent meeting is less onerous (Art. 135(b) Act).

28. On receipt of these documents, if the Registrar is satisfied that the requirements of the Company Regulations have been met, he is obliged to publish a statement in the Gazette or on the Registry of Companies website (Reg. 12(1) Company Regulations). He is also obliged to promptly publish a notice of the aforesaid registration in a daily newspaper circulating wholly, or mainly, in Malta.

29. Any interested party who wishes to contest the validity of the members' extraordinary resolution must do so within three months of the publication of the aforementioned Registrar's statement (Reg. 13(1)(a)). Such contestation is required to be made by way of application to the Registrar before the Maltese courts and will be on the grounds that the purported members' extraordinary resolution is void or voidable.

30. If the application made by the interested party is allowed by the Maltese courts and it is found that there is a defect liable to render the contemplated cross-border merger defective, then the Company Regulations state that the Maltese courts shall grant the relevant companies a period of time in which to remedy the situation – provided, of course, that it is capable of remedy (Reg. 13(1)(b) Company Regulations).

5 Pre-merger certificate

31. Once the Maltese Registrar is satisfied that a Maltese merging company has complied with and completed the necessary pre-merger acts and formalities, then he shall issue a pre-merger certificate conclusively attesting to this fact (Reg. 14 Company Regulations).

32. It is to be noted that the pre-merger certificate may only be issued by the Registrar after three months have elapsed since the Registrar's publication in a daily newspaper of, *inter alia*, the fact that the cross-border merger has been approved by the Maltese merging company (Reg. 14 Company Regulations).

33. It is also to be noted that, if any objections or contestations have been made by the relevant person(s) by way of application under the Company Regulations, then the pre-merger certificate may only be issued by the Registrar once the final judgement rejecting such application has been made. Obviously, if any such application is allowed, then the Registrar will not be in a position to issue a pre-merger certificate (Reg. 14 Company Regulations).

6 Effects of the decision

34. Once the Registrar has issued the pre-merger certificate, it will form an integral part of the legal perfection of any cross-border merger.

35. In instances where the company resulting from the merger is registered (or to be registered) in Malta, then the Registrar will require the pre-merger

certificate of any Maltese company participating in the merger. The Registrar will also require the pre-merger certificate issued by the relevant authority of the Member State to which any foreign merging company is subject (Reg. 17(2) Company Regulations). Such certificates should be submitted to the Registrar within six months of their issue together with copies of the duly approved common draft terms of the cross-border merger of each company involved in the merger (Reg. 17(2) Company Regulations).

36. It will then be the task of the Maltese Registrar to conclusively determine the legal validity of the cross-border merger. To do this, he must ensure that those elements of procedure necessary for the proper completion of the cross-border merger have been satisfied. In particular, he will be required to ensure that all the merging companies have approved common and identical terms of merger and, where appropriate, that employee participation requirements have been determined (Reg. 17(1) Company Regulations). He will also be concerned with ensuring that any applicable fees have been paid.

37. If the Registrar is satisfied that all the necessary pre-completion elements of the cross-border merger have been fulfilled, then he will proceed to issue a certificate to this effect (Reg. 17(3) Company Regulations). The certificate shall, *inter alia*, include the name and registration number of the company resulting from the cross-border merger, as well as the effective date of the merger.

VI Minority shareholders

38. The decision of the Maltese merging company to approve the cross-border merger by way of an extraordinary resolution of its members in general meeting is binding – even on those members who opposed such approval. However, notwithstanding this fact, any members who dissented against the cross-border merger may be entitled to request the redemption of their shares on such terms as may be agreed (Reg. 10(3) Company Regulations). For the sake of good order and evidential purposes, any member objecting to the cross-border merger should have his objection recorded in the minutes of the relevant company meeting.

39. If it is not possible for the dissenting members, or the company, to reach an agreement on the terms of redemption of the relevant members' shares, then an application may be filed by either party to the Maltese courts to determine the matter (Reg. 10(3) Company Regulations). Such application must be filed within three months of the publication by the Registrar of the common draft terms of the cross-border merger.

40. It is to be noted that, where any other merging company is situated in a Member State that does not allow for such a share redemption procedure, the right of the members of the Maltese company to have their shares redeemed under this scheme is contingent on the explicit acceptance of any participating foreign

merging company (Reg. 10(3) Company Regulations). Such approval should be made by any foreign merging company when it is deciding to adopt the common draft terms of the cross-border merger.

VII Protection of creditors

41. Creditors of any Maltese company participating in a cross-border merger may object to the merger by way of application to the Maltese Courts (Reg. 13(2) Company Regulations). In order to be valid, any such application must be made by a creditor within the period of three months following the Registrar's publication of the Maltese company's decision to approve the cross-border merger. Furthermore, it is important to highlight that a creditor's application to the Maltese courts may only be made if the debt owed to the creditor existed prior to the aforementioned publication by the Registrar.

42. If, by virtue of such application, a creditor is able to show good cause as to why the cross-border merger should not take effect, then the objection to the merger may be upheld by the Maltese courts. Alternatively, the Maltese courts may allow the cross-border merger to proceed, on the condition that sufficient security is given to safeguard the debt owed to the creditor (Reg. 13(2) Company Regulations).

43. Debenture holders in any Maltese participating company may also object to a cross-border merger in the same manner. However, the right of any debenture holder to avail itself of this particular remedy is subject to the company's debenture holders not having already approved the cross-border merger, either individually or in a special meeting convened for this purpose (Reg. 13(2) Company Regulations).

VIII Employee participation

1 General

44. Article 16 of the Cross-border Merger Directive, dealing with employee participation rights in cross-border mergers, has been implemented in Maltese law by virtue of subsidiary legislation, entitled the Employee Involvement (Cross-border Mergers of Limited Liability) Regulations 2008, (Legal Notice 165 of 2008), (the 'Employee Regulations'). The Employee Regulations gained legal force in Malta on 1 July 2008.

45. It is important to note that the Employee Regulations do not create an *ad hoc* procedure for employee participation in cross-border mergers. On the contrary, reference is made in the Employee Regulations to the employee participation procedures for a Societas Europaea which are contained in the Employee Involvement (European Company) Regulations 2004 (Legal Notice 452 of 2004), (the 'European Employee Regulations'). Certain provisions of the

European Employee Regulations are to apply *mutatis mutandis* to employee participation in cross-border mergers (Reg. 7(3) Employee Regulations). This approach is somewhat unsatisfactory, although it mirrors the approach taken in the Cross-border Merger Directive itself (Art. 16) (no. 6 of Chapter 1 of the first volume of this book).

46. Maltese law does not provide for mandatory employee participation in the management of companies. However, where the company resulting from the cross-border merger is to be registered in Malta, then Maltese rules in this regard will be set aside where any of the scenarios outlined in Article 16(2) of the Cross-border Merger Directive (as faithfully transposed into domestic law) apply (Reg. 7 Employee Regulations).

2 Appointment of members to special negotiating body ('SNB')

47. If the Maltese rules concerning employee participation are set aside, then an SNB must be established in order to negotiate employee representation in the Maltese registered company which will result from the cross-border merger. The management of the respective companies participating in the cross-border merger will bear responsibility for setting up the SNB and this should be done as soon as possible after the publication of the draft common terms of merger (Reg. 7(3) Employee Regulations and Reg. 3(1) European Employee Regulations).

48. The Maltese participating company's representative(s) to the SNB are to be selected by means of a ballot (or ballots, as the case may be) of the company's employees (Reg. 13 Employee Regulations and Reg. 5(1) European Employee Regulations). Candidate representatives may be either employees of the company or, where the management of the Maltese participating company permits, a representative of a trade union who is not an employee of the company.

49. In terms of the proper conduct of the ballot, an independent ballot supervisor shall be appointed by the management of the Maltese participating company in order to ensure that a fair and efficient election is held (Reg. 7(3) Employee Regulations and Reg. 5(e) European Employee Regulations).

50. It will be the duty of the ballot supervisor to formally publish the results of the ballot held to appoint the members of the SNB. The SNB shall be considered to have been established on the date of publication by the ballot supervisor of the results of the ballot (Reg. 7(3) Employee Regulations and Reg. 5(5) European Employee Regulations).

3 Protection of employee representatives

51. The members of the SNB shall, in the exercise of their functions, enjoy protections and guarantees in line with those afforded to employee representatives

in the Employment and Industrial Relations Act 2002 (Reg. 13 Employee Regulations and Reg. 13(1) European Employee Regulations). In particular, the members shall have the right to paid time off work for the performance of their duties, including attendance at meetings of the SNB (Reg. 13 Employee Regulations and Reg. 13(2) European Employee Regulations).

IX Tax treatment

1 General

52. Mergers can give rise to prohibitive tax implications at two different levels: (i) at the level of the merging companies and (ii) at the level of merging companies' shareholders. These tax consequences can be mitigated by various tax exemptions or tax deferral provisions applicable under Maltese laws.

53. The Merger Tax Directive has been implemented into Maltese laws by Legal Notice 238 of 2003 (as amended by Legal Notice 59 of 2006). Thus in the circumstances to which the Merger Tax Directive applies tax neutrality is achieved for the merging company and its shareholders.

2 Taxation at the level of the merging entities

54. If a Maltese merging company transfers all its assets and liabilities to an EU receiving company in return for the issue of new shares by the EU receiving company to the Maltese company's shareholders, the transfer of the assets/liabilities can take place at tax book value without the realisation of any hidden reserves in the assets/liabilities. This applies provided that the transferred assets/liabilities continue to remain attached to a permanent establishment ('PE') of the receiving company in Malta. This rule has the effect of preserving Malta's taxation rights in respect of the PE profits and denying any step-up in the value of assets. Capital allowances thus continue to be available in respect of the tax book value (rather than at the assets' current market value).

3 Taxation at the level of the shareholders

55. In case of a merger involving the Maltese disappearing company, the shareholders of the said Maltese company carry over the original tax base of their old shares into the shares of the EU receiving company. An interesting aspect of this rule is that, unless the shareholders are Maltese persons, Malta will lose its right to tax the hidden capital gains arising to the shareholders since in case of the eventual sale of shares in the EU receiving company there will be no link with Malta for Malta to be able to exercise its taxation rights.

56. In case of a merger involving a Maltese surviving company, the merger will in principle not trigger any tax implications for the existing shareholders since

they would not be disposing of their shares. The issue of shares to the new shareholders will also not give rise to any income tax implications. However, anti-dilution provisions were introduced into Maltese legislation, with effect from 2010, targeting situations where the market value of shares held by a person in a company is reduced as a result of a change in the issued share capital. However these anti-abuse provisions will, amongst others, not apply where the surviving company does not own, directly or indirectly, immovable property situated in Malta and it can be shown that the change is effected for bona fide commercial reasons and does not form part of a tax-avoidance scheme.

4 Losses

57. The Merger Tax Directive also provides that if in a purely local scenario Maltese tax law would have allowed the transfer of losses from the transferor company to the transferee company, then the losses of the transferor company are available against the PE's profits. Maltese tax laws are silent as to whether losses of the absorbed company can be utilised against the profits of the new merged entity and the Revenue practice in previous years has been to disallow such losses and unabsorbed capital allowances. Nevertheless from a legal perspective this approach is debatable since the merged entity will be assuming all assets and liabilities of the dying entity.

5 Cross-border mergers outside the scope of the Merger Tax Directive

58. The scope of the Merger Tax Directive is, however, limited as it tries to balance both the interests of the parties involved in the merger as well as the taxation rights of the state in which the transferring company is situated. In the circumstances not covered by the Merger Tax Directive, purely Maltese tax considerations will apply.

6 Inbound mergers

59. As already mentioned above in case of inbound mergers it is a moot point whether losses or unabsorbed capital allowances can be used by the new merged entity. However, a new rule has been introduced in case of inbound mergers resulting from a cross-border merger pursuant to the Directive where none of the assets owned by the company on the day of merger were owned by any merging company which was resident or domiciled in Malta. In such case the law allows the resulting entity to elect for a step-up in the value of the assets situated outside Malta. This rule should thus allow capital allowances to be taken at the stepped-up value. Furthermore, in case of any transfer of assets that are chargeable assets for capital gains purposes, only the capital gain accruing from the point in time the merged entity is resident in Malta will be taken into consideration.

7 Outbound mergers

60. Transfers of assets and liabilities, in case of an outbound merger, should not trigger any tax on capital gains if either:

(i) the merger does not produce any change in the individual direct or indirect beneficial owners of the companies involved and in the value held by each such ultimate beneficial owner (in such case the law provides for a no-loss-no-gain situation); or
(ii) the conditions for an intra-group transfer are satisfied (in which case the law also provides for tax deferral); or
(iii) in case of assets constituting a participating holding for Maltese tax purposes (in which instance the law provides for an exemption).

61. In respect of the shareholders of the Maltese company being absorbed, there should be no capital gains tax implications if either:

(i) the merger does not produce any change in the individual direct or indirect beneficial owners of the companies involved and in the value held by each such ultimate beneficial owner; or
(ii) the said shareholders are not resident in Malta, the Maltese company does not own directly or indirectly immovable property in Malta and the beneficial owner of the gain is not owned and controlled by, directly or indirectly, nor acts on behalf of, individuals who are ordinarily resident and domiciled in Malta.

8 Stamp duty

62. Immovable property and marketable securities are chargeable assets for stamp duty purposes. Thus a merger may potentially give rise to stamp duty liability. However stamp duty is avoided in cases where:

(i) the transfer documents are executed outside Malta and not made use of in Malta; or
(ii) the conditions applicable for the exemption in respect of the restructuring of companies are satisfied.

28

Portugal

MARGARIDA BARROCAS, MARCELO ALVES,[1]
MARIANA FERREIRA[2]
Barrocas Advogados

1 Section IX – tax treatment.
2 Section VIII – employee participation.

I Introduction

1. The Cross-border Merger Directive was implemented in Portugal by Law no. 19/2009 of 12 May 2009. This law has set a new regime applicable to cross-border mergers involving companies with registered seat in Portugal, which has included also the amendment of the Portuguese Companies' Code (hereinafter referred to as the 'CC') and Commercial Registry Code. The new regime is applicable to the companies with registered seat in Portugal, which participate in a cross-border merger process and, on a subsidiary basis, the general rules governing domestic mergers.

II Scope of the new rules

2. The CC (Art. 117-A), following the Cross-border Merger Directive, defines as cross-border mergers within the EU mergers involving companies incorporated in accordance with the legislation of a Member State of the European Economic Area (EAA) whose registered office, central headquarters or principal place of business is located within the EAA, where at least (i) two of the companies involved in the merger are subject to the legislation of different Member States and (ii) one of the companies involved in the merger is subject to Portuguese legislation, i.e. has its registered seat in Portugal.

3. The following companies, which are subject to Portuguese law, may take part in a cross-border merger within the EU: public companies by shares (*sociedades anónimas*) and private limited liability companies (*sociedades por quotas*).

4. The *sociedades em nome colectivo* and the *sociedades em comandita simples* may not participate in a cross-border merger.

III Cash payment

5. In domestic mergers, the cash compensation to which the shareholders may be entitled as a result of the merger may not exceed 10 per cent of the nominal value of the shares or participations received in exchange (Art. 97-5 CC) – where there are no specific different regulations derived from the entering into force of the law, the provisions related to domestic mergers are applicable on a subsidiary basis.

IV Legal consequences and enforceability of a cross-border merger

6. Pursuant to a cross-border merger, two or more companies become a single company by the block transfer of their assets and liabilities and the allocation to the shareholders of the companies subject to dissolution of shares or participations in the resulting entity or company, which may be newly formed or

consist of one of the merging companies. Cross-border mergers have the same effects as domestic mergers:

(i) the incorporated companies are dissolved or in case of creation of a new entity all merged companies are dissolved and all assets and liabilities of the companies subject to dissolution are transferred to the company resulting from the merger (the incorporating company or new company);
(ii) the shareholders of the companies subject to dissolution become shareholders of the company resulting from the merger (the incorporating company or new company).

V Procedure

1 Draft terms of cross-border merger

7. The directors of each of the companies involved in the merger shall prepare, jointly, the draft terms of cross-border merger (Art. 98-1 CC). The draft terms of cross-border merger shall be without force or effect unless approved by the general shareholders' meetings of all companies involved in the merger (Art. 117-F CC).

The draft terms of cross-border merger shall contain at least the following elements (apart from any other that might be necessary or convenient for a total understanding of the operation at stake) – (Arts. 98-1 CC and 117 CC):

(i) the type, motives, conditions and purposes of the merger for each and all companies involved in the merger;
(ii) the type, corporate name, registered seat, share capital, number of registration with the commercial registry of each one of the companies involved in the merger as well as the corporate name and registered seat of the company which results from the merger;
(iii) the corporate share that any of the companies may have in the share capital of any of the others;
(iv) the balance sheet of each one of the companies involved in the merger, in which is included, among other elements, the amounts of the assets and liabilities to be transferred to the incorporating company or the new company, as the case may be;
(v) the parts, shares or quotas to be attributed to the shareholders of the company to be incorporated or the companies to be merged (as the case may be) and, if applicable, the amounts in cash which are to be attributed to the same shareholders. The exchange ratio of the corporate shares must also be specified;
(vi) the modification project to be introduced in the company's contract of the incorporating company or the contract's project of the new company;
(vii) the protection measures to be applied to the rights of third parties, which are not shareholders, to participate in the company's profits;

(viii) the types of protection measures applicable to the creditors' rights;
(ix) the date as from which the operations of the incorporated company or the companies to be merged (as the case may be) are to be considered, from an accounting point of view, as performed on behalf of the incorporating or the new company (as the case may be);
(x) the rights guaranteed by the incorporating company or the new company (as the case may be) to shareholders, of the incorporated company or the companies to be merged (as the case may be), which hold any special rights;
(xi) any special advantages granted to the experts who intervene in the merger or the members of the administration or supervisory bodies of the companies which participate in the merger;
(xii) regarding the mergers in which the incorporating company or the new company (as the case may be) is a public company by shares (*sociedade anónima*), the modalities of delivery of the shares of those companies and the date as from which those shares grant any rights to profits as well as the different types of those rights;
(xiii) the rules applicable to the shares' (or other representative securities of the share capital of the company which result from the merger) transfer;
(xiv) the date of closure of the accounts of the companies which participate in the merger, which are used to define the conditions which ground the cross-border merger;
(xv) if applicable, the information about the procedures pursuant to which are established the provisions relating to the employees' intervention in the definition of their participation rights in the company which result from the cross-border merger;
(xvi) the foreseeable effects of the merger in the labour sector.

In the event of a takeover merger where the surviving company directly or indirectly holds all shares or participations in the share capital of the company or companies taken over, the legal regime provided for the exchange of corporate shares, the reports of the experts of the taken over company and the shareholders of the taken over company is not applicable and the shareholders do not become shareholders of the surviving company. Furthermore, in these cases, the approval of the draft terms of cross-border merger by the taken over companies' general shareholders' meetings is not mandatory and, under certain conditions, the approval of the draft terms of cross-border merger by the surviving company's general shareholders' meeting can also be exempted (Art. 117-I CC).

8. A pre-merger certificate for each one of the companies participating in the merger (with registered seat in Portugal) must be issued by the relevant Commercial Registry Office (before the merger is carried out), which attests that all acts and formalities which are prior to the merger were duly observed. Furthermore, in order for this certificate to be issued, also the draft terms of

cross-border merger must already be duly registered and published as well as the reports of the companies' corporate bodies and experts where applicable.

2 Management board

9. The management board of each company involved in the merger shall draft, jointly, the draft terms of cross-border merger, which apart from having to include all data referred in no. 7 of this chapter, must also include, or in an attachment to it, the evaluation criteria used by the management board as well as the grounds of the corporate shares' exchange ratio (Art. 98-3 CC).

10. As from the date of publication of the draft terms of cross-border merger's registry, there must be made available for consultation (and to take any copies without any charge) to the shareholders, employee representatives or, in the absence thereof, to the employees themselves, as well as to the companies' creditors, at the registered seat of each of the companies involved in the merger, the following documents (Art 101-1 CC):

(i) draft terms of cross-border merger;
(ii) report and opinions issued by the company's bodies and experts;
(iii) accounts, reports of the management bodies, reports and opinions of the supervisory bodies and decisions issued by the shareholders' general meetings on those accounts, in relation to the last three corporate years.

Where the management board receives, up to the date scheduled for the meeting of the shareholders' general meeting, an opinion issued by the employee representatives, this opinion shall be attached to the reports prepared by the company's bodies and experts (Art. 101-2 CC).

3 Expert's report on the draft terms of cross-border merger

11. The management body of each company involved in the merger that has a supervisory board must communicate to the latter the draft terms of cross-border merger and its attachments, for it to issue an opinion on them (Art. 99-1 CC).

If there is no supervisory board, the management body of each company involved in the merger must present the draft terms of cross-border merger to an official accountant or an official accountants' company which is independent from all companies which intervene in the merger (Art. 99-2 CC).

If all companies which participate in the merger decide to submit the draft terms of cross-border merger to a single official accountant or a single official accountants' company, this can be done as per Art. 117 D-2 and 3 of the CC.

12. The experts' reports must contain a grounded opinion on the adequacy and reasonableness of the corporate shares' exchange ratio and must, at least, indicate: (i) the methods used to set the proposed exchange ratio; (ii) the grounds for application of those methods, what values such methods result in, the relative

importance that was attributed to them in the determination of the proposed values and any special valuation difficulties (Art. 99-4 CC).

The experts may obtain any information and documents believed to be necessary from the companies involved in the merger, and perform any examinations deemed indispensable (Art. 99-5 CC).

13. The expert's report on the draft terms of cross-border merger, as contained in Article 99-2 of the CC (as referred in no. 11 above) and the expert's opinion, as contained in Article 99-4 of the CC (as referred in no. 12 above) shall not be necessary if all shareholders and the holders of any other titles with voting rights of all the companies involved in the cross-border merger decide to exempt those obligations (Art. 99-6 CC).

14. The reports issued by the experts relating to the draft terms of cross-border merger are among the documents to be made available to the shareholders, employee representatives and corporate creditors at the time of calling the general shareholders' meeting to approve the cross-border merger (Arts. 100-3 and 101-1 CC).

4 Merger balance sheet

15. Each company involved in the merger may deem its last approved balance sheet to be its merger balance sheet, provided that such balance sheet should have been closed within the term of six months prior to the date of the draft terms of cross-border merger. In alternative, the merger balance sheet may be a balance which is reported to a date that must not be prior to the first day of the third month before the date of the draft terms of cross-border merger (Art 98-2 CC).

The balance sheet of each company involved in the merger must contain, among other elements, the value of the assets and liabilities to be transferred to the incorporating company or the new company (Art. 98-1-d CC).

16. The companies' accounts, for the last three business years, are among the documents to be made available to shareholders, corporate creditors and employee representatives as from the date of publication of the registry of the draft terms of cross-border merger (Art. 101-1-c CC).

5 General meeting of shareholders

A Information for shareholders

17. Upon the publication of the registration of the draft terms of cross-border merger and as from the calling of the shareholders' meetings of the companies to which approval of the cross-border merger is submitted, the following documents must be made available to their shareholders, corporate creditors and employee representatives, for examination thereof at the registered office of the relevant company (Arts. 100-3 and 101-1 CC):

(i) the draft terms of cross-border merger;
(ii) report and opinions issued by the company's bodies and experts;
(iii) accounts, reports of the management bodies, reports and opinions of the supervisory bodies and decisions issued by the shareholders' general meetings on those accounts, in relation to the last three corporate years.

Shareholders, corporate creditors and employee representatives may request the delivery, free of charge, of a copy of those documents.

18. After the draft terms of cross-border merger are registered the shareholders' meetings are called, which shall take place at least one month after publication of the meeting's call. Other forms of communication to the shareholders are also accepted. The calling of the meeting must mention that the draft terms of cross-border merger and documentation therein attached can be consulted at the registered office of each company (Art. 100-2-6 CC).

19. Once the general meeting of shareholders has started, the management board must state expressly if, as from the preparation of the draft terms of cross-border merger, any relevant modification to the factual elements in which they were grounded occurred and, in affirmative case, which modifications to the draft are necessary to introduce. In this latter case, the meeting must decide if the merger procedure shall be renewed or if it carries on with the original proposal's discussion (Art. 102-1 and 2 CC).

B Shareholders' approval

20. The merger must be approved by the general shareholders meeting of each company involved, strictly complying with the draft terms of cross-border merger. Notwithstanding the foregoing, takeover mergers where the surviving company holds, directly or indirectly, all shares or participations in the share capital of the company or companies taken over shall not require the approval of the merger by the general shareholders' meetings of the companies taken over (Art. 117-I.3 CC).

Where the merger takes place by creating a new company, the merger resolution must include the provisions legally required to incorporate it.

21. Unless the by-laws should provide for a higher quorum or majority, approval of the cross-border merger by a Portuguese company shall require the same quorum as the one established for changing the by-laws.

For public companies by shares (*sociedades anónimas*): (i) in the first call, the presence of shareholders is legally required, in person or by proxy, representing at least a third of the company's share capital and the favourable vote of two-thirds of the voting capital (Arts. 117-B, 117-F.2, 103-1, 85-2, 383-2 and 386-3 CC); and (ii) in the second call, the Portuguese law demands the favourable vote of two-thirds of the voting capital present at the general meeting, in person or by proxy (Arts. 85-2, 103-1, 117-B, 117-F.2, 383-3 and 386-3 CC).

For private limited liability companies (*sociedades por quotas*): the favourable vote of at least three quarters of the votes corresponding to participations in the share capital (Arts. 117-B, 117-F.2, 103-1, 85-2, 265-1 and 265-3. CC) is required.

22. The merger can only be registered after obtaining the consent of the shareholders who have become prejudiced by the operation due to (i) an increasing of their obligations, (ii) a disregard of their special rights or (iii) a change in the proportion of the shares held, as set forth in the merger's draft.

23. If any of the companies involved in the merger has different types of shares, the merger resolution needs also the approval at special meetings to be performed among shareholders of each share's category.

24. Upon approval thereof, the merger resolution shall be registered at the Commercial Registry Office and published at the official website of the Portuguese Government http://publicacoes.mj.pt.

6 Pre-merger certificate

25. A pre-merger certificate, for each one of the companies participating in the merger (with registered seat in Portugal) must be issued by the relevant Commercial Registry Office (before the merger is carried out), which attests that all acts and formalities prior to the merger were duly observed. Furthermore, in order for this certificate to be issued, also the draft terms of cross-border merger must already be duly registered and published as well as the reports of the companies' corporate bodies and experts where applicable.

26. Where the company resulting from the merger has its registered seat in Portugal, the Portuguese Commercial Registrar shall supervise the legality of the cross-border merger by attesting the following elements: (i) approval of the draft terms of cross-border merger in the same terms by the companies involved in the merger,(ii) fixation of the employee participation provisions, where necessary, in accordance with the applicable legal provisions. For such purposes, each of the companies involved in the merger shall forward to the relevant Commercial Registrar the draft terms of cross-border merger approved by its general shareholders' meeting and the certificate mentioned in Article 10 of the Cross-border Merger Directive (see no. 25 above) within six months of the date of issuance thereof (Art. 117-G CC).

7 Effects of the cross-border merger

27. Where the company resulting from the merger is subject to Portuguese law, the merger shall be effective upon registration of the new company or, as the case may be, upon registration of the takeover with the competent Commercial Registry (Art. 117-H CC). Upon registration thereof, the incorporated companies or all merged companies, as the case may be, are extinguished and all their

rights and obligations are transmitted to the incorporating or new company, as the case may be. Furthermore, the shareholders of the extinguished companies become shareholders of the incorporating or new company, as the case may be (Art. 112 CC).

VI Shareholders' right to be discharged

28. Once approved, the cross-border merger shall be binding on all shareholders of the Portuguese companies involved, even if they have voted against the merger resolution. Notwithstanding the foregoing, a shareholder that has voted against the merger may, if the law or the company's contract so allows, and within one month counting as from the date of the resolution, require that the company acquires or determines the acquisition of its corporate share or, in alternative, the shareholder may alienate its corporate share pursuant to the company's contract (Art. 105 CC).

VII Protection of creditors

29. Within one month following the date of publication of the project's registry the creditors of the participating companies, whose credits existed prior to that publication, may issue a judicial opposition to the merger as long as they have requested to the company the satisfaction of their credits or the offering of a guarantee at least fifteen days before and their request was not accepted (Art. 101-A CC).

30. A judicial opposition shall prevent the definitive registration of the merger with the commercial registry until any of the following facts occur:

(i) it is decided as not proceeding by the court;
(ii) the opponent has waived its opposition;
(iii) the company has paid to the opponent or rendered the guarantee awarded by the court or concluded by agreement;
(iv) the opponent has agreed on the registration; or
(v) the amount owed to the opponent is held on deposit.

VIII Employee participation

31. Employee participation rights, unlike the remaining provisions of the Cross-border Merger Directive, were not included in the CC. Conversely, these provisions were implemented by the Law 19/2009 of 12 May 2009 (Arts. 39 to 45). In fact, the Portuguese CC merely refers to employee participation rights as provided by law.

32. Employee participation rights are, in general, acknowledged by Portuguese law. However, with regard to companies resulting from a cross-border merger

(as provided in the CC) and with registered seat in Portugal or with a subsidiary or representation in Portugal, employee participation rights are determined under Law 19/2009 of 12 May 2009 (except for procedural matters such as the voting of representatives and certain matters regarding the resources available for the employee representatives, to which the rules governing the company of origin of the representative apply).

The regulation governing employee participation, as implemented by Law 19/2009 of 12 May 2009 shall apply to companies resulting from the cross-border merger with registered office, subsidiary or representation in Portugal in the following cases: where at least one of the companies involved in the merger, during the six months prior to the publication of the draft terms of cross-border merger, employs an average number of employees greater than 500 and is managed with employee participation and/or the general Portuguese rules on employee participation rights do not provide for the same entitlement to exercise participation rights as is enjoyed under the special provisions of Law 19/2009 of 12 May 2009.

33. Employee participation rights are the result of a negotiation between the special negotiation body and those involved in the merger.

Law 19/2009 of 12 May 2009 provides for two distinctive procedures regarding employee participation rights – one of which results from the negotiation of the special negotiation body and the other which is residual and applies when the competent company bodies so determine, when the parties do not reach an agreement within six months of negotiations (which can be extended by another period of six months) and the competent body of each company agrees to apply the residual procedure or when an employee participation system applies before the merger in one of the companies involved, affecting at least one-third (1/3) of the total number of employees of all companies involved, or when such a system applies to a lower proportion and the special negotiation body so resolves.

34. As a general rule, the members of the special negotiation body shall be elected in accordance with the respective domestic legislation, in proportion to the number of employees employed in each Member State by the companies involved in the merger and their affected subsidiaries and workplaces, at a rate of one position for each 10 per cent or fraction thereof of the total number of employees in all Member States. However, considering that under this rule it may occur that a Member State (i.e., the companies of a Member State) does not have a representative, Law 19/2009 of 12 May 2009 provides for measures to correct this rule.

35. The subsidiary provisions concerning employee participation referred to above comprise the right of the employees of the company resulting from the merger to elect, designate, recommend or object to the designation of a number of members of the company's management or supervision body equal to the

highest proportion then in force in the companies involved in the merger prior to registration thereof.

IX Tax treatment

1 Implementation of the Merger Tax Directive in Portugal

36. The current tax provisions relating to cross-border mergers are set forth in the Merger Tax Directive (Council Directive 2009/133/EC of 19 October 2009).

37. This special tax regime has not yet been duly transposed to Portuguese internal rules, being the tax regime applicable to mergers currently regulated in Subsection IV of Section VI of Chapter III of the Portuguese Corporate Income Tax Code, approved by Decree-law no. 442-A/88 of 30 November 1988, after last amendment introduced by the governmental budget for 2010, the Law no. 3-B/2010 of 28 April 2010 (*Código do Imposto sobre o Rendimento das Pessoas Colectivas*) (the 'IRC Law').

38. The objective of the Merger Tax Directive and of the IRC Law is to neutralise those tax costs which may represent an obstacle to corporate restructuring transactions such as mergers, divisions, partial divisions, transfers of assets and exchanges of shares, which are regarded as necessary and beneficial for the domestic and EU economy. Such objective is achieved by allowing for the deferral of the tax due on capital gains which arise in connection with the restructuring transaction at the level of the companies involved.

39. The corporate documentation supporting the restructuring transaction must expressly include the option by the taxpayers involved for the application of the tax neutrality regime to the restructuring transaction. Additionally, such option must be notified to the Portuguese tax authorities in the annual declaration of tax and accounting information (i.e. no prior authorisation by the Portuguese tax authorities is required in order to enjoy the benefits of the tax neutrality regime).

40. Finally, the IRC Law contains an anti-avoidance provision in accordance with which the tax neutrality system will not be applicable if the main purpose of the corporate restructuring transaction is tax avoidance. In particular, the tax neutrality regime will not be applicable when the restructuring transaction is not based upon favourable commercial reasons such as the reorganisation or rationalisation of the activities of the companies involved. It also will not be applicable when one or more of the merged companies do not have their aggregated income subject to the general tax regime under the IRC Code.

2 Definition of merger under the IRC Law

41. In accordance with the Merger Tax Directive, the IRC Law defines a merger as an operation whereby:

(i) one or more entities transfer all their assets and liabilities to another existing entity in exchange for the issue to their shareholders of securities representing the capital of that other company and, if applicable, a cash payment not exceeding 10 per cent of the nominal value, or in the absence of a nominal value, of the accounting par value of those securities;

(ii) two or more entities transfer all their assets and liabilities to a new entity that they form, in exchange for the issue to their shareholders of securities representing the capital of that new entity and, if applicable, a cash payment not exceeding 10 per cent of the nominal value, or in the absence of a nominal value, of the accounting par value of those securities; or

(iii) an entity transfers all its assets and liabilities to the company holding all the securities representing 100 per cent of its capital.

3 Taxation of the income generated on the merger

42. A merger, division or partial division shall not give rise to any taxation of capital gains calculated by reference to the difference between the real values of the assets and liabilities transferred and their values for tax purposes.

43. With regard to taxation of members of merged or demerged companies, it is accepted not to assess capital losses or gains realised as a result of a merger or demerger if, in relation to the new corporate rights, the value by which the former were inscribed is maintained. However, this does not preclude such company members from being taxed on the amounts in cash, which may be attributed to them by reason of such merger or demerger.

4 Tax losses

44. The receiving company may be allowed to take over the losses of the transferring company which had not yet been exhausted for tax purposes. For this purpose a specific authorisation from the Minister of Finance should be obtained until the end of the month that follows the request to register the merger in the Commercial Registry. The authorisation from the Minister of Finance is subject to the demonstration that the merger is valid for economic reasons.

5 Tax value and acquisition date of the acquired assets and rights as well as of the securities issued to the shareholders of the transferring entity

45. Generally speaking, the assets and rights acquired by the acquiring company as a consequence of the merger will maintain for tax purposes the same value and acquisition date that they had in the transferring entity.

Similarly, the securities representing the capital of the acquiring entities allotted to the shareholders of the transferring entity will maintain for tax purposes the value and acquisition date of the securities transferred by said shareholders.

6 Indirect taxation consequences of the merger

46. The transfer of immovable property as a result of the merger or demerger is subject to municipal tax on real estate transfer (*Imposto Municipal sobre Transmissão Onerosa de Imóveis* – IMT), which is levied on the taxable net wealth of the real estate of all immovable property belonging to merged or demerged companies that is transferred to the fixed assets of those companies resulting from a merger or demerger, or on the amount shown in the fixed assets of the companies, if higher, according to the Municipal Tax on Real Estate Transfer Code (*Código do Imposto Municipal sobre Transmissão de Imóveis*), approved by Decree-law no. 287/2003 of 12 November 2003, after last amendment introduced by the governmental budget for 2009, the Law no. 64-A/2008 of 31 December 2008.

47. In accordance with the Stamp Taxes Law approved by Law no. 150/99 of 11 September 1999, after last amendment introduced by the governmental budget for 2010, the Law no. 3-B/2010 of 28 April 2010 (*Código do Imposto do Selo*) mergers (as defined in the IRC Law) are exempted from taxation. Transfer of immovable assets are subject to stamp duty.

48. To enterprises that exercise directly and as their main activity an agricultural, commercial, industrial activity or supply of services and that are reorganised as a result of concentrations between undertakings or cooperation arrangements, the following tax benefits may be granted: (i) exemption from IMT in respect of immovable property not designed for housing purposes necessary for the concentration or cooperation; (ii) exemption from stamp duty in respect of transfer of the immovable property referred to in paragraph (i) or of incorporation, increase in capital or in the assets of the joint stock company necessary to concentration or cooperation; (ii) exemption from emoluments and other legal charges.

29

Republic of Slovenia

JURIJ DOLŽAN, MATIJA KNAPIČ, SAMO HERIČ
Odvetnik Jurij Dolžan, Mitja Vidmar & Igor Zemljarič

I Introduction

1. The Cross-border Merger Directive was implemented into the legal system of the Republic of Slovenia (hereinafter referred to as 'Slovenia') via amendments to the Companies Act (*Zakon o spremembah in dopolnitvah Zakona o gospodarskih družbah* or ZGD-1A), which entered into force on 31 January 2008 and was published in the Official Journal no. 10/2008 (Uradni list RS, no. 10/2008) of 30 January 2008 (hereinafter referred to as 'ZGD-1A' or the 'Amendments') and the Worker Participation in Decision-making by Cross-border Mergers of Limited Liability Companies Act (*Zakon o soodločanju delavcev pri čezmejnih združitvah kapitalskih družb*, hereinafter referred to as 'ZSDČZKD') which entered into force on 7 June 2008 and was published in the Official Journal no. 56/2008 (Uradni list RS, no. 56/2008) of 6 June 2008.

2. Provisions of ZGD-1A are integrated into the Companies Act, as amended (*Zakon o gospodarskih družbah*,[1] hereinafter referred to as 'ZGD-1') in Articles 622.a to 622.l of ZGD-1. Prior to the implementation of the Cross-border Merger Directive, ZGD-1 included provisions applicable to internal mergers. Article 622.b(2) of ZGD-1 provides that cross-border mergers shall be *mutatis mutandis* governed by the provisions applicable to internal merger, unless specific provisions applicable to cross-border mergers apply. As a result of such approach the Amendments only introduced the minimum necessary changes to implement the Cross-border Merger Directive. Before the implementation of the Cross-border Merger Directive it was not clear what would happen in a case of a merger involving companies from other states which are members of the European Economic Area, however, on the basis of the *SEVIC*[2] case, such mergers would seem to be allowed in accordance with provisions of the Cross-border Merger Directive even before its implementation.

ZSDČZKD provides for implementation of Article 16 of the Cross-border Merger Directive only. Let it be noted that the law providing for the general provisions on employee participation is the Worker Participation in Management Act (*Zakon o sodelovanju delavcev pri upravljanju*,[3] hereinafter referred to as 'ZSDU') in relation to which ZSDČZKD provisions on employee participation shall be *lex specialis*.

II Scope

3. Cross-border merger provisions of ZGD-1 shall be applicable to cross-border mergers of (i) limited liability companies defined in Article 1 of the First

1 Uradni list RS no. 42/2006 (10/2008), 68/2008 of 2 July 2008.

2 European Court of Justice, 13 December 2005, Case C-411/03.

3 ZSDU-UPB1 Uradni list RS 42/2007.

Company Law Directive (68/151/EEC) or (ii) companies with share capital and recognised legal personality that possess their own assets which alone serve to cover their obligations and are subject to national law conditions concerning protection of interests of third persons provided for by the First Company Law Directive (hereinafter referred to as 'companies').[4] In accordance with Article 622.b ZGD-1, companies with their registered seat in Slovenia (hereinafter referred to as 'Slovenian company') may be involved in a cross-border merger as:

(i) companies acquired by a company incorporated by the laws of another Member State where the acquiring company has its head office, central administration or its principal place of business or a branch in the other Member State, or
(ii) companies resulting from a merger of two or more companies formed under the law of different Member States.

Pursuant to Article 622.a of ZGD-1, the company resulting from the cross-border merger (hereinafter referred to as 'resulting company') may be either:

(i) a new company resulting from a merger of two or more companies in which the acquired companies are dissolved while all assets and liabilities from the original companies are transferred to the new company (hereinafter referred to as 'new company'), or
(ii) a company existing before the merger and to which all assets and liabilities are transferred from the acquired company.

The acquired company shall mean a company from which assets and liabilities have been transferred to the resulting company (hereinafter referred to as 'acquired company').

The acquiring company shall mean (as provided by Article 580 of ZGD-1, applicable to both internal and cross-border mergers) a company to which assets and liabilities of one or more companies being acquired shall be transferred (hereinafter referred to as 'acquiring company').

Cross-border merger provisions shall not apply to cross-border mergers involving a company the object of which is the collective investment of capital provided by the public, which operates on the principle of risk-spreading and the units of which are, at the holders' request, repurchased or redeemed, directly or indirectly, out of the assets of such company.

4. Slovenia did not opt to implement the exception for cooperative societies provided for in Article 3(2) of the Cross-border Merger Directive. It should be noted that cooperative societies in Slovenia have a special legal status and are not organised under provisions of ZGD-1.

4 Art. 622.a of ZGD-1, as amended.

5. The Slovenian legal system also provides for internal mergers of unlimited companies (Art. 639 of ZGD-1), however provisions on cross-border mergers of such companies are not provided for. Although this exceeds the scope of the Cross-border Merger Directive and the Amendments, it could be argued that in light of the *SEVIC* case, denial of cross-border merger involving an unlimited company by the competent authorities may be regarded as a breach of 'freedom to establish'.[5]

6. ZGD-1 does not address concerns regarding the protection of competition. However, mergers of companies are considered as concentration of companies in accordance with the Competition Act (*Zakon o preprečevanju omejevanja konkurence*, hereinafter referred to as 'ZPOmK-1'[6]), and thus may be prohibited if such concentrations significantly restrict effective competition on the territory of Slovenia or a significant part of its territory (Art. 11 ZPOmK-1).

The decision to allow or deny any merger shall lie with the Competition Protection Office (*Urad Republike Slovenije za varstvo konkurence*, hereinafter referred to as 'UVK'). UVK shall be informed of a (potential) merger by the involved companies, nevertheless UVK may also investigate any merger ex off. After UVK has been informed of a pending merger, it shall verify whether such a concentration is compatible with the rules of competition and shall, after the conclusion of the procedure, issue a decision as to the approval, prohibition or conditional approval of the merger (see Chapter 1 of the first volume of this book, no. 14).

UVK is an administrative body and therefore its decisions may be subject to an independent court review provided by the Administrative Dispute Act (*Zakon o upravnem sporu*,[7] hereinafter referred 'ZUS-1') and applicable to all administrative disputes.

III Remuneration of the contribution

7. In accordance with Article 580 of ZGD-1 an (internal or cross-border) merger shall result in assets of the acquired company being transferred to the Resulting Company and shareholders of the acquired company receiving shares of the resulting company.

8. The exchange ratio between shares of the resulting company and of the acquired company shall be such as to ensure that the economic position of shareholders shall not change (hereinafter referred to as 'exchange ratio'). This shall be achieved if the economic value of (former) shares of the acquired company shall be equal to the economic value of shares of the resulting company. If

5 J. Bedrač, 'Čezmejne združitve gospodarskih družb v EU – takoj?', Prava praksa, 2006/12, pp. 6–8.

6 Uradni list RS no. 36/2008 (40/2009).

7 Uradni list RS no. 105/2006 (62/2010).

the number of shares and the exchange ratio do not allow for shares to be exchanged in even numbers, the difference shall be paid in cash (hereinafter referred to as 'cash payment'). In accordance with Article 580(5) of ZGD-1 the amount of cash payment shall not exceed 10 per cent of the value of the lowest issue value of shares issued by the acquiring company. Slovenia did not opt to exceed the value of the amount which may be paid in cash in the process of transfer of assets and liabilities, available under Article 3(1) of the Cross-border Merger Directive (see Chapter 1 of the first volume of this book, no. 2).

9. Article 622.i of ZGD-1 provides for possibility of a court review of cash payment. The review shall be available to shareholders who at the general meeting of the acquired company made an objection to the merger. This right shall also be enjoyed by a shareholder who did not attend the general meeting if the shareholder was unlawfully prevented from attending the general meeting or if the general meeting was not duly/properly convened or if the matter put to the agenda of the general meeting was not duly/properly published. Procedural provisions applicable to court review of the exchange ratio (see no. 10 of this chapter) shall apply, *mutatis mutandis*, also to the court review of the cash payment (Art. 622.i and 603 of ZGD-1).

10. In accordance with provisions of Articles 605 to 615 of ZGD-1, the exchange ratio determined in the context of the relevant merger may be challenged before the acquired company by any shareholder of the acquired company.

Shareholders may also start legal procedure challenging the exchange ratio if they fulfil the following conditions: (i) they had shareholder status for the entire period from the date when the general meeting of the company in which they were shareholders adopted a resolution giving consent to the merger until the date on which the proposal for a court test of the exchange ratio was lodged; and (ii) they have not renounced the right to an additional cash payment; and (iii) their total interest in any individual company which participated in the merger accounts for at least one-hundredth of the subscribed capital of this company or the value of their total lowest emission amount reaches at least €25,000 or they together hold all the shares meeting the conditions of the first and the second indent of this.

The applicable court proceeding shall be conducted in accordance with the provisions of the law regulating the non-litigious civil procedure. In the proceedings the court may also establish facts that the participants to the proceedings have not stated and introduce evidence not presented by the participants. The court must publish on the filed notification a proposal for a court test of the exchange ratio in the Official Journal. Shareholders may file their proposal for a court test of the exchange ratio within a period of one month from the publication of the notification that the proposal has been filed. The opposing party in the proceedings for a court test of the exchange ratio shall be the acquiring company. In the proceedings at the first instance the acquiring company may propose that the court allow it to provide additional shares instead of additional cash payments.

The court may change the proposed exchange ratio and give the shareholders grounds to demand extra cash payments or extra shares. Shareholders not involved in the challenge of the exchange ratio shall also be represented in the procedure by a special joint representative, who shall be an attorney at law, a notary or an auditor. The shareholders may waive their right to challenge the exchange ratio by a written statement made in the form of a notarial record, or by an oral statement at general meeting of the involved company voting upon the merger, entered into the minutes of the general meeting. Before the ruling, the court may ask an expert settlement panel (hereinafter referred to as 'panel') to give its opinion on the exchange ratio, while the court shall be obligated to do so if any person involved in the proceedings demands the panel to be involved. The panel shall advise persons involved of the possibility of a settlement, which may result in a settlement agreement carrying the same legal consequences as a court ruling.

An appeal against the ruling with which the court decided on the exchange ratio may be filed within one month of the court ruling being delivered. An appeal may be filed by the acquiring company, any of the applicants or joint representatives. If the court has permitted the acquiring company to provide additional shares instead of additional cash payments an appeal against the ruling on the exchange ratio may also be filed by shareholders of the acquiring company whose rights are prejudiced as a result of the provision of additional shares. The time limit for responding to an appeal shall be one month.

Article 604 of ZGD-1, stipulating that approval of an internal merger shall not be challenged for reasons of inadequate exchange ratio or cash payment, applies in principle also to cross-border mergers. However in accordance with Article 622.i of ZGD-1 in a case of a cross-border merger the approval of the general meeting may be challenged for reasons of inadequate exchange ratio if companies involved in the cross-border merger are based in Member States which do not enable judicial review of the exchange ratio, unless it is expressly agreed at general meetings of such companies that:

(i) shareholders of Slovenian companies may propose a judicial review of the exchange ratio against a Slovenian company resulting from a merger, or
(ii) shareholders of an acquired Slovenian company may propose a judicial review of the exchange ratio against a company resulting from a merger with its head office in another Member State, under the same conditions and procedure as would apply in an internal merger taking place in Slovenia.

Article 622.i(3) of ZGD-1 provides that only shareholders who announced to challenge the exchange ratio at the general meeting or within a month of the general meeting may propose the legal review thereof.

IV Legal consequences and enforceability of a cross-border merger

11. As a general rule, in accordance with Article 580 of ZGD-1, a merger shall result in the acquired company being dissolved, while all assets and liabilities are transferred to the resulting company.

12. In accordance with Article 591 of ZGD-1, cross-border mergers between two or more existing companies (Art. 2(2)(a) Directive) shall have at least the following legal consequences.

All assets and liabilities of the acquired company shall be transferred to the resulting company, which shall make the resulting company a universal legal successor of the acquired company. The resulting company shall be bound by all legal relations and obligations of the acquired company, except if: (i) the acquired company is party to a bilateral contract, (ii) neither party (of the bilateral contract) has fulfilled all obligations under the contract, and (iii) the universal legal succession would result in the resulting company being bound by incompatible obligations, or the fulfilment of such obligations would result in an unfair burden for the resulting company. In such case obligations from such bilateral contract shall be altered in accordance with interest of both parties.

The acquired company shall cease to exist, whereby the acquired company shall be dissolved without being liquidated. As a result, the members of the acquired company shall become members of the resulting company (except where the members of the acquired company are not provided with shares of the resulting company).

13. Article 616 of ZGD-1 provides that in case of cross-border merger resulting in the establishment of a new company (Art. 2(2)(b) Directive), rules applicable for mergers between existing companies shall be applied *mutatis mutandis* whereby the new company shall be deemed the resulting company. Administrative organs of involved companies shall take all necessary legal requirements to establish the new company including the entry into the register of companies (hereinafter referred to as 'register').

14. The above legal consequences shall take affect after relevant changes are registered in the register (see nos. 11 and 12 of this chapter).

15. Articles 597 and 598 of ZGD-1 applicable to both internal and cross-border mergers provide, in line with Article 17 of the Cross-border Merger Directive, that after a merger has been registered by the registration court and made public, the merger may no longer be declared null. Persons who have filed a motion to declare the merger null before the merger was registered may change the motion to a demand for damages suffered as a result of registration.

V Procedure

1 Draft terms of cross-border merger

16. Implementing Article 6 of the Cross-border Merger Directive, Article 622.c of ZGD-1 regulates drawing up of common draft terms of cross-border merger[8] (hereinafter referred 'common draft terms'). Note that for internal mergers ZGD-1 provides for a similar document referred as 'merger contract' (*pogodba o pripojitvi*) and that provisions applicable to such merger contract shall be used *mutatis mutandis* for common draft terms.

17. Article 622.c of ZGD-1 provides that the common draft terms shall be drawn up by management of each of the involved companies and authenticated by a notary. It shall include at least:

(i) the legal form, name and registered office of the involved companies and those proposed for the resulting company;
(ii) the exchange ratio and/or the amount of any cash payment;
(iii) the terms for the allotment of shares representing the capital, and the amount of cash payment of the resulting company, or a statement, where applicable, that no such allotment (either cash or shares) shall be paid;
(iv) the likely repercussions of the cross-border merger on the employees of the company involved;
(v) the date from which the shares of the resulting company shall entitle the holders to a share in profits and any special conditions affecting such entitlement;
(vi) the date from which the transactions of the acquiring companies shall be treated for accounting purposes as being those of the resulting company;
(vii) the rights conferred by the resulting company on members of the acquiring companies enjoying special rights or on holders of securities other than shares representing the company's capital, or the measures proposed concerning them;
(viii) any special advantages granted to the auditors or other experts expected to be involved in the merger or to members of management, supervisory or controlling organs of the merging companies;
(ix) the draft statutes of the resulting companies;
(x) where appropriate, information on the procedures by which arrangements for the involvement of employees in the definition of their rights to participation in the resulting company are determined pursuant to Article 16 of the Cross-border Merger Directive (see no. 40 of this chapter);
(xi) information on the evaluation of the assets and liabilities which are transferred to the resulting company;

8 Let it be noted that the term used in the Amendments for Common Draft Terms is "plan" (*načrt*).

(xii) balance cut-off dates of accounting reports of involved companies which were the basis for establishing the terms of the cross-border merger.

Furthermore, common draft terms shall also include the amount of monetary compensation offered to (minority) shareholders who contested the merger at a general meeting of the acquired company or who did not have the chance to vote at the general meeting (see. no. 37 of this chapter). The common draft terms shall also include provisions applicable in case of simplified procedure for parent-subsidiary merger (see no. 35 of this chapter).

Fulfilling the requirements of the Cross-border Merger Directive on publication of common draft terms (see Chapter 1 of the first volume of this book, no. 18) provided by Article 6(2) of the Cross-border Merger Directive, Article 622.e of ZGD-1 regulates that upon convocation of the general meeting of involved companies for the purpose of approval of the cross-border merger the common draft terms shall be presented to the registration court, and shall thus be made available to the public. Information regarding the availability of the common draft terms shall be included in the invitation for the general meeting along with the information regarding: (i) the type, name and registered office of every merging company; (ii) the registration court (or body) at which the documents referred to in Article 3(2) of the First Company Law Directive are filed in respect of each involved company, and the number of the entry of the above documentation in a register held by the registration court; (iii) an indication, for each of the involved companies, of the arrangements made for the exercise of the rights of creditors and of any minority members of the involved companies and the address at which complete information on those arrangements may be obtained free of charge. In accordance with Article 297 of ZGD-1, invitation to the general meeting shall be published at least one month before the meeting. In accordance with Article 11 of ZGD-1 any disclosure of information or communications required by law shall be published in the Official Journal of RS (*Uradni list RS*).

2 Management report

18. As regulated by Article 7 of the Cross-border Merger Directive and provided by Article 622.č of ZGD-1, management of each involved company shall draw up a report intended for shareholders, explaining and justifying the legal and economic aspects of the cross-border merger and explaining the implications of the cross-border merger for shareholders, creditors and employees (hereinafter referred to as 'management report'). Additionally, in accordance with Article 582 of ZGD-1 applicable to both internal and cross-border mergers, the management report shall also include information on: (i) reasons for the merger and (ii) the content of the common draft terms especially regarding matters to be included in points (ii), (iii) and (vii) of the common draft terms. Furthermore, if any problems occurred regarding the evaluation of the value of the involved companies and if these problems affected the evaluation of

the exchange ratio, the discussion of such matters shall be included in the management report.

Article 622.č of ZGD-1 also stipulates that the management report shall be made available to the representatives of the employees or, where there are no such representatives, to the employees, at least one month before the general meeting. If management of any of the involved companies receives, in good time, such opinion from the representatives of their employees on the merger, that opinion shall be attached to the management report.

19. Article 582 of ZGD-1, applicable to both internal and cross-border mergers, allows management or administrative bodies of different merging companies to draw up a joint management report.

20. In accordance with Article 622.č(4) of ZGD-1, in cases of cross-border mergers the right to be presented with the management report may not be waived in any circumstances. Note that in the case of an internal merger, in the simplified procedure (see no. 35 of this chapter), shareholders may waive the obligation of the management report being drawn up in the form of a notary letter.

3 Auditor's report

21. Provisions implementing Article 8 of the Cross-border Merger Directive on independent expert reports may be found in Article 662.d of ZGD-1, applicable to cross-border mergers, and Article 583 of ZGD-1, applicable to both cross-border and internal mergers. The Articles mentioned provide that the common draft terms shall be checked by one or more independent experts. The experts shall be suggested by the supervisory board or, where there is no supervisory board, by management of a company and shall be appointed by a court of law (Art. 584(2) of ZGD-1) (see Chapter 1 of the first volume of this book, no. 12). The expert shall draw up a report (hereinafter referred to as 'auditor report'). The auditor report shall include an opinion of the experts on the exchange ratio and an opinion on the cash payment offered. This statement shall also: (i) indicate the method or methods used to arrive at the exchange ratio proposed; (ii) indicate reasons why this method is considered appropriate; and (iii) if more than one method was used, a note on the exchange ratio which would be appropriate on the basis of each of the methods used, the importance of each method in relation to each other and all possible problems related to each method used.

If as a result of a cross-border merger the assets and liabilities of a Slovenian company shall be transferred onto a resulting company registered in another Member State, the auditor report shall include a reference to share capital and time reserves of the merging companies (Art. 622.d(5) of ZGD-1). The auditor report need not include an opinion on the exchange ratio if the acquired company is owned by a sole owner or if all shareholders of the acquired company decide so (see no. 35 of this chapter). This decision shall only be valid if confirmed by a notary.

22. In accordance with Article 583 of ZGD-1, the same expert or experts may draw up the auditor report for more than one of the involved companies, furthermore, the merging companies may issue a joint auditor report.

23. Experts drawing up the auditor report shall be liable for damages to all involved companies and the shareholders of these companies if the auditor report fails to fulfil legal requirements for auditor reports. Provision on liability for drawing up annual reports of companies, as defined in ZGD-1 (Art. 53 ZGD-1 to 75 ZGD-1), shall be applicable *mutatis mutandis* to establish liability of authors of the auditor reports. The experts shall be liable to the amount of €150,000. Such limit of the liability for damage shall not apply if the damage was caused intentionally or by gross negligence.

4 Supervisory board report

24. Slovenian law requires an opinion of the supervisory board on the merger at this point of the procedure. Note that the Cross-border Merger Directive does not provide for such a requirement, and that the Amendments implementing the Cross-border Merger Directive into the Slovenian legal system do not include any provisions on the supervisory board's opinion. We may therefore conclude that a Slovenian company involved in a cross-border merger shall be obligated to obtain the opinion of the supervisory board, based on the rules applicable to internal mergers. However a company with its head office outside of Slovenia, shall not be required to provide such an opinion if the domestic law of the company shall not request one.

25. In accordance with Article 584 of ZGD-1, the auditor report (along with the management report) shall be presented to respective supervisory boards of each of the merging companies. Each of the supervisory boards shall prepare a written report presenting the supervisory board's opinion on the merger (hereinafter referred to as 'supervisory board report').

Should a company involved in a merger not have a supervisory board, the presentation of a supervisory board report shall not be required.

5 Shareholders' meeting

26. The requirement for the approval of the common draft terms by the general meeting defined in Article 9 of the Cross-border Merger Directive is implemented by Articles 622.e and 622.f of ZGD-1, however the majority of procedural requirements to obtain such approval shall be governed by Articles 585 and 586 of ZGD-1, applicable to both internal and cross-border mergers.

27. The common draft terms shall be voted upon by the general meeting of each of the involved companies. The approval shall require a three-quarters (3/4) majority vote of capital present at the general meeting, unless the statute of a company requires a higher majority vote. If different classes of shares

exist in a company, consent of each class of shares shall be required. The collective consent of a class shall be voted upon with a normal (>50 per cent) majority vote.

28. The general meeting shall be called upon by the management of each of the merging companies (Art. 297 of ZGD-1) at least one month in advance. In accordance with Article 586 of ZGD-1, at least one month prior to the general meeting, shareholders of each merging company shall have the possibility to examine:

(i) the common draft terms (see no. 16 of this chapter);
(ii) the annual reports of all merging companies for the past three financial years;
(iii) if the accounting date of the merger and date of balance sheet of the last annual report of each of the merging companies do not coincide, the final reports of these companies shall be completed providing data until the day of the merger,[9] provided that the reports have been audited to that date;
(iv) if the last annual report of each involved company refers to a financial year which ended more than six months prior to the merger, interim balance sheets of the company, compiled at the final day of the last quarter prior to the merger;
(v) the management report(s) (see no. 18 of this chapter);
(vi) the auditor report(s) (see no. 21 of this chapter); and
(vii) the supervisory board report(s) (see no. 24 of this chapter).

In accordance with Article 586(4) of ZGD-1, each shareholder may ask for a copy of the above documents. In accordance with Article 622.e(3) of ZGD-1 the same may be requested by any creditor of the acquired company if, as a result of the merger, the assets and liabilities of a Slovenian company shall be transferred to the resulting company registered in another Member State. These copies shall be delivered at the latest on the next working day, following request.

At the general meeting of each of the involved companies the above documents shall also be presented (Art. 586(5) and 586(6) of ZGD-1). Furthermore, management shall explain/provide its position on the merger in the form of an oral statement. Management shall also inform members of the general meeting of any significant changes noted by the management which have occurred after the common draft terms have been drawn up, whereby changes considered significant shall be changes which may affect the exchange ratio.

29. In accordance with Article 9(2) of the Cross-border Merger Directive, Article 622.f(2) of ZGD-1 enables the general meeting of the acquired company to condition its approval on a conformation that employee participation shall be ensured in the resulting company (see no. 16 of this chapter).

9 Art. 68 of ZGD-1.

6 Pre-merger certificate

A Slovenian company the acquired company

30. Article 622.k of ZGD-1, implementing Article 11 of the Cross-border Merger Directive, requires a court acting in the role of a register body, to review the legality of actions taken in the procedure of cross-border mergers. Management of a Slovenian acquired company shall request that the court enters the intention of the cross-border merger into the Register. Attached to the request shall be:

(i) the common draft terms (see no. 16 of this chapter);
(ii) minutes of the general meeting of the acquired company at which the approval for the cross-border merger was voted upon;
(iii) approval or consent of the competent state or other body, if required;
(iv) the management report of the acquired company (see no. 18 of this chapter);
(v) the auditor report (see no. 21 of this chapter);
(vi) final report of the acquired company on the cross-border merger;
(vii) proof of publication of the common draft terms;
(viii) proof that the right to challenge the exchange ratio was ensured;
(ix) proof of due protection of creditors;
(x) a statement of the management of the acquired company that no actions were taken to declare the approval of the general meeting or the procedure of convocation of the general meeting null or void, or that such actions were unsuccessful or that the shareholders waived such a right;
(xi) a statement of the management of the acquired company as to the number of shareholders who opted for monetary compensation (see no. 37 of this chapter).

Following the request of the management of the acquired company the court shall review the cross-border merger procedure. To this effect the court shall determine if all legal requirements for cross-border mergers, including provisions on the appropriate exchange ratio, are met. If the court shall be satisfied, it shall enter the intention into the Register and issue a (pre-merger) certificate, as required by Article 10 of the Cross-border Merger Directive, confirming that legal requirements of Slovenian law for a cross-border merger have been fulfilled. Article 622.k(6) of ZGD-1 provides that the resulting company shall inform the court when the legal requirements for a cross-border merger in accordance with the law of the Member State where the resulting company shall be registered have been met.

B Slovenian company the resulting company

31. Implementing provisions of Article 12 and Article 13 of the Cross-border Merger Directive, Article 622.l of ZGD-1 prescribes the procedure by which the designated court of law, acting in the role of registration body, shall register

and make public a cross-border merger if the resulting company shall be a Slovenian company.

32. Application for registration of the cross-border merger in the Register shall be submitted by management of each of the merging companies with the competent court for the resulting company (Art. 622.l(1) of ZGD-1). Let it be noted that Article 590(1) of ZGD-1 governing application in cases of internal mergers provides that the application for registration of a merger may also be submitted for a company being acquired by the management of the resulting company. It seems that this may also apply to cross-border mergers if both the resulting company and at least one of the acquired companies is a Slovenian company.

Article 622.l(2) requires the application to be supported by documentation provided for in Article 590 of ZGD-1, which shall include:

(i) a statement from the management of each of the merging companies that:
- no challenge to the decision of the general meeting approving the merger has been filed in due time, or
- filed challenges contesting the decision of the general meeting approving the merger have been declared null or have been denied with binding effect or actions have been dismissed or withdrawn, or
- all the shareholders have renounced, in the form of a notarial record, their right to contest the general meeting resolution giving consent to the merger by acquisition or to have it declared null;

(ii) if a simplified procedure is possible, a statement from the management of the acquiring company to the effect that the shareholders of the acquiring company have not exercised their right to demand that the general meeting of the acquiring company take a decision on consent for the merger by acquisition, or that they have waived that right by means of a statement drawn up in the form of a notarial record;

(iii) the common draft terms;

(iv) the minutes of the general meetings of all merging companies at which a decision was taken on the consent for the merger;

(v) the management report(s);

(vi) auditor report(s);

(vii) the supervisory board report(s);

(viii) the closing reports of the companies being acquired;

(ix) approval or consent of the competent state or other body, if required;

(x) proof that an intended merger by acquisition was duly published; and

(xi) the statements from the persons insuring cash payments if applicable.

In addition to the above Article 622.l (2) of ZGD-1 requires a submission of a pre-merger certificate from the registration body of the Member State in which the acquired company has its head office. Furthermore, in accordance with Article 622.l(3) of ZGD-1, the court shall confirm that general meetings of all involved companies have approved the same common draft terms and if employee participation negotiations have been attempted by all involved companies on the topic of employee participation in the resulting company.

33. Should the court be satisfied that the above conditions were met, it shall enter the cross-border merger into the Register. This shall be done in accordance with Article 591 of ZGD-1. The designated court shall register the merger of all involved companies simultaneously. Names and application numbers of all involved companies shall also be entered. Furthermore, the acquired company shall name a representative appointed to receive shares of the resulting company which shall be provided to the shareholders of the acquired company or the amount of cash payments offered. The cross-border merger may only be registered after the court has received notification from such a representative that the resulting company has fulfilled its obligations. In accordance with Article 622.l(4), the court shall notify the fact of registration to the registration body of the Member State competent for the acquired company.

7 Effect of the decision

34. In accordance with Article 622.b of ZGD-1 a cross-border merger shall become valid when so provided by law of the Member State applicable to the resulting company. According to Article 591 of ZGD-1, if resulting company shall be a Slovenian company, the merger shall become valid upon entering the merger into the register.

8 Simplified procedure

35. In cases of mergers governed by simplified procedure in which the resulting company holds all the shares of the acquired company (parent-subsidiary) (see no. 39 of Chapter 1 and Art. 15(1) Dir.), Article 622.c(4) of ZGD-1, applicable to cross-border mergers only, provides that in the common draft terms, (i) the exchange ratio and/or the amount of any cash payment need not be defined (ii) that the description of procedure of exchange of shares of the resulting company need not be defined, (iii) that terms for the allotment of shares representing the capital, and the amount of cash payment of the resulting company, or a statement, where applicable, that no such allotment (either cash or shares) shall be paid, need not be defines, (iv) that the date from which the shares of the resulting company shall entitle the holders to a share in profits and any special conditions affecting such entitlement need not be defined (see no. 17 of this chapter). Furthermore, management report need not provide, (v) legal and economic reasons for the merger, and (vi) legal and economic explanation of the content of the common draft terms especially regarding matters to be included in points (ii), (iii) and (vii) of the common draft terms (see no. 18 of this report). Also (vii) the auditor report need not include a statement of the experts on the exchange ratio and an opinion on the cash payment offered, as provided by Article 583(5) of ZGD-1 (see no. 21 of this report). In addition Article 622.f(1) of ZGD-1, applicable to cross-border mergers only, expressly

provides that approval of the merger by the general meeting of the acquired company shall not be required.

36. In cases of mergers in which the resulting company holds at least 90 per cent of the shares of the acquired company (see no. 40 of Chapter 1 and Art. 15(2) Dir.) Article 599 of ZGD-1, applicable to both internal and cross-border mergers, provides that the approval of the general meeting shall not be required unless (i) management of the resulting company requests the approval or (ii) unless shareholders of the resulting company controlling at least 5 per cent of share capital require an approval of the general meeting.

VI Minority shareholders

37. Implementing provisions of Article 4(2) of the Cross-border Merger Directive on the protection of minority shareholders, Article 622.g of ZGD-1 provides shareholders of a Slovenian company acquired by a company from another Member State have the right to demand monetary compensation instead of shares of the acquiring company (hereinafter referred to as 'monetary compensation').[10] Any shareholder shall be granted the right to monetary compensation if (i) the shareholder opposed the cross-border merger at the general meeting, (ii) the shareholder was unlawfully prevented from participating at the general meeting, (iii) the general meeting was not dully called upon, or (iv) the issue put to the vote at the general meeting was not duly published.

In accordance with Article 600 of ZGD-1, applicable to both internal and cross-border mergers, if the resulting company shall be a Slovenian company, minority shareholders shall be granted much the same rights as described above, but only if (i) shares of the acquired company may be traded freely, (ii) while trade of shares of the resulting company is limited by the approval of the company.

38. As required by Article 6(2)(c) of the Cross-border Merger Directive and mirrored in Article 622.c(3) of ZGD-1, publication of the common draft terms in the National Journal of the relevant Member States shall include the amount of monetary compensation offered to shareholders fulfilling the above requirements. The publication of this information shall not be needed if one person holds all shares of the acquired company or if this right is waived by all entitled participants (see no. 17 of this chapter).

VII Creditors' protection

39. As required by Article 4(2) of the Cross-border Merger Directive, the rights of creditors of companies involved in a cross-border merger shall be protected. To this effect Article 592 of ZGD-1, applicable to cross-border mergers involving

10 Note the difference between monetary compensation and cash payment (see no. 7 of this chapter).

a Slovenian company as the resulting company as well as to internal mergers, provides that creditors may request insurance of their non-matured, uncertain or conditional claims, provided that they have requested such an insurance within six months after notification of the entry of the merger to the Register (see no. 32 of this chapter). To be granted insurance, creditors have to demonstrate the probability that the fulfilment of their claims is jeopardised by the merger. Creditors who have the right of priority in bankruptcy proceedings shall not be granted this right. Upon entry of the merger into the Register creditors shall be reminded of their right.

Article 622.j of ZGD-1 furthermore provides for protection of creditors involved in a cross-border merger in which the resulting company shall be a company from another Member State. This group of creditors shall be granted much the same protection as creditors protected by Article 529 of ZGD-1. Notwithstanding the aforesaid the two following exceptions shall apply: (i) creditors need to demand special protection within one month (not six months) after publication of the common draft terms and (ii) claims of creditors are deemed to be jeopardised if the sum of share capital and time reserves of the resulting company shall be lower than sum of share capital and time reserves of the acquired company.

VIII Rules applicable to employee participation

1 Employee participation in resulting companies established in Slovenia

40. Article 16 of the Cross-border Merger Directive on employee participation was implemented into the Slovenian legal system via a separate law, ZSDČZKD (see no. 1 of this chapter), enacted for the implementation of Article 16 of the Cross-border Merger Directive only. In accordance with Article 2 of ZSDČZKD, it shall apply to (i) Slovenian companies, (ii) other companies and (iii) companies dominated by such a company and its subsidiaries (hereinafter referred to as 'affiliated companies') involved in a cross-border merger in Slovenia with registered offices in other Member States.

41. The aim of ZSDČZKD is (i) to provide the procedure by which the special negotiating body (hereinafter referred to as 'SNB') appointed to negotiate employee participation in the resulting company shall be formed, and (ii) to establish minimum standards of employee participation.

In accordance with Article 4 of ZSDČZKD, (i) general Slovenian legislation on employee participation shall be applicable to Slovenian resulting companies. However, in accordance with Article 5 of ZSDČZKD, rules provided by ZSDČZKD on employee participation shall apply if (see no. 2 of this chapter) (i) six months prior to the cross-border merger at least one of the involved companies had on average employed at least 500 people and employee participation was ensured in such a company by way of the right to elect or appoint certain members of the company's supervisory or administrative organs (hereinafter referred to as 'employee members of organs' or 'EMO') or the right to recommend and/or oppose the appointment of other (not EMO) members of the supervisory or administrative organs (hereinafter referred to as 'organs'); (ii) Slovenian legislation does not provide for at least the same level of employee participation as was ensured in involved companies, whereby the level of employee participation shall be measured with reference to the proportion of EMO or employee representatives in the management group covering the company's profit units; or (iii) Slovenian legislation does provide for at least the same level of employee participation to employees employed in a subsidiary (from Slovenia) of a resulting company registered in another Member State as would be provided to other employees employed in Slovenia (see no. 41 of Chapter 1 of the first volume of this book).

42. In accordance with Article 20 of ZSDČZKD and Article 16(3)(e) of Dir. employee participation shall be ensured in a resulting company if (16(3)(e) of Dir.):

(i) employee participation was ensured in one or more involved companies, affecting at least 30 per cent of the employees of all involved companies,
(ii) employee participation was ensured in one or more involved companies, affecting less than 30 per cent of the employees of all involved companies, and the SNB opts to ensure employee participation in the resulting company (see no. 47 of this chapter).

However, if employee participation was not ensured in any of the involved companies, the resulting company need not ensure employee participation.

2 Special negotiating body ('SNB')

A Starting negotiations

43. In accordance with Article 6 of ZSDČZKD, after publication of the common draft terms (see no. 17 of this chapter) administration of involved companies shall as soon as possible start negotiations with representatives of employees (hereinafter referred to as 'representatives'[11]) of all involved companies as to employee participation after the cross-border merger (see Chapter 2 of the first volume of this book, no. 21). To this effect the representatives or, if there are no such representatives, the employees directly, shall be informed of (i) the identity and the structure of the involved companies and affiliated companies, (ii) the number of employees in each Member State employed by the involved companies and affiliated companies, (iii) the number of representatives of the involved companies, and (iv) the number of employees involved in the decision-making process of the organs of the involved companies.

11 Note the difference between representatives and EMOs (see no. 41 of this chapter).

As a result of negotiations, a written agreement on employee participation in the resulting company (hereinafter referred to as 'the Agreement') may be concluded. However the conclusion of the Agreement shall not be a requirement for the negotiations (see no. 48 of this chapter).

B Formation of the SNB

44. To conclude the Agreement, the SNB shall be formed. In accordance with Article 7 of ZSDČZKD, the number of members of the SNB shall be such that the number of members from each Member State shall be proportional to the number of employees from each Member State compared to the persons employed by the involved companies and affiliated companies. Employees from each Member State shall appoint one member of the SNB for each 10 per cent of employees from that Member State compared to the aggregate of persons employed in the involved companies and affiliated companies; extra seats shall be available to ensure that employees of each involved company registered in any Member State which shall cease to exist as an independent legal entity shall be represented by a member of the SNB (see no. 11 of Chapter 2 of the first volume of this book). The number of extra members shall not exceed 20 per cent of members of the SNB and shall not cause double representation. Each member of the SNB shall have one vote. Members from each Member State shall represent all employees from that Member State (Art. 14 ZSDČZKD).

The number of persons employed shall be deemed to be the number of persons employed at the time of publication of the common draft terms by the involved companies in different Member States. The number shall be recalculated only if the number of employees shall change sufficiently to change the calculation of the number of members appointed to the SNB.

45. Members of the SNB from Slovenia shall be voted upon by the employee council[12] (*svet delavcev*) of each involved Slovenian company.

The employee council, representative labour unions and at least fifty employees of each involved company and affiliated company, shall have the right to appoint a candidate for membership of the SNB (Art. 10 ZSDČZKD).

46. In accordance with Article 13 of ZSDČZKD all costs of the negotiations and costs of the SNB shall be covered by the merging companies.

C Decision-making process of the SNB

47. In accordance with Article 14 of ZSDČZKD, the SNB shall make decisions with a single majority vote (>50 per cent) whereby members casting their votes shall also represent at least half of employees of the involved companies.

12 The employee council is a body, provided for by ZSDU, which may be formed in any company in Slovenia with the purpose to insure employee participation in the interest of the employees. Employee councils work parallel with labour unions.

However, in accordance with Article 15 of ZSDČZKD, a two-thirds majority vote of all members of the SNB, representing two-thirds of the employees from at least two Member States, shall be required for a decision to lower the standard of employee participation if such a decision shall affect at least 25 per cent of employees. The level of employee participation shall be deemed lowered if (i) the proportion of EMOs in the organs of the resulting company shall be lower than that of the highest proportion of EMOs in the organs or within the management group covering the company's profit units of involved companies, or if (ii) the employees shall not have the right, or shall be limited in their right, to elect, appoint, recommend or oppose any member of the organs.

A two-thirds majority vote of the SNB, representing two-thirds of employees from at least two Member States, shall also be required for a decision not to begin the negotiation or to cease negotiations before the Agreement was concluded (see no. 43 of this chapter). In such a case the legislation on employee participation of the Member State in which the resulting company shall have its registered office shall apply (Article 16 ZSDČZKD).

48. Article 11 of ZSDČZKD grants the SNB the authority to negotiate with management of involved companies the employee participation in the resulting company. The SNB shall start negotiations with administrative organs of the involved companies as soon as possible, and shall conclude the negotiations within six months. Only by a special agreement may the negotiation be prolonged, for a period not exceeding a year after formation of the SNB. If an agreement shall not be entered into within the above deadlines the negotiations shall be deemed unsuccessful. In such a case provisions of ZSDČZKD on employee participation shall apply (see no. 53 of this chapter).

49. The SNB may have expert assistance in the negotiations. Experts providing the assistance may be present in the negotiation meeting.

Notwithstanding the obligation of the merging companies to cover all costs of the SNB, the companies shall only be obliged to cover costs for one expert (see no. 46 of this chapter).

50. If merging companies have different forms of employee participation the SNB may decide upon the form of employee participation which shall be used in the resulting company in Slovenia. The SNB shall communicate this decision to management of the merging companies (Article 15 ZSDČZKD).

D The Agreement

51. In accordance with Article 18 of ZSDČZKD the Agreement shall include:

(i) provisions on the application of the Agreement,
(ii) the date on which the Agreement shall enter into force, the time period of the Agreement and the circumstances which may lead to renegotiations and the process governing such renegotiations,

(iii) the method of employee participation which shall include the number of members of organs of the resulting companies which shall be elected, appointed, recommended or opposed by the employees, and the rights of the employees.

3 Employee participation provided by ZSDČZKD

52. The provisions on employee participation proposed by ZSDČZKD, provided in Chapter 4 of ZSDČZKD, aim to ensure a minimum level of employee participation in companies involved in a cross-border merger (see no. 41 of this chapter). The provisions may also be regarded as a starting point of the negotiation process for the Agreement and as a 'safety net' on which the employees may rely in case the negotiations do not result in a satisfactory agreement.

53. In accordance with Article 19 of ZSDČZKD, the provisions of Chapter IV (included are Articles 19 to 25) shall be applicable if:

(i) both sides involved in the negotiations so agree,
(ii) the Agreement shall not be concluded within the time frame provided by ZSDČZKD (see no. 48 of this chapter) and management of the involved companies, following a decision to continue the process of registration of the cross-border merger, decide to make provisions of ZSDČZKD on employee participation applicable to the resulting company and if the decision to cease negotiations was not taken by the SNB (if such a decision was taken employee participation shall be governed by national law of the Member State in which the resulting company shall have its registered office), and if
(iii) management of involved companies decide so before the negotiations start.

54. In accordance with Article 21 of ZSDČZKD, employees of the resulting company shall have the right to elect, appoint, recommend or oppose a designated number of members of organs of the resulting company, whereby the number shall be such as to ensure that the proportion of such members of organs in the resulting company shall be equal to the highest proportion of such members of organs of the companies involved in the relevant merger.

55. Article 22 of ZSDČZKD provides that the distribution of seats in the organs of the resulting company between EMO shall be decided upon by the SNB. The distribution of seats shall ensure that the number of EMOs in the organs from each Member State shall be proportional to the number of employees from each respective Member State in the resulting company. If this should result in employees from one Member State having more than one EMO, with employees from another Member State not having an EMO at all, the seats of EMO shall be redistributed to ensure that each Member State shall have an EMO. Employees from the Member State in which the

resulting company shall have its registered office shall always be ensured one EMO.

If the organs of the resulting company shall undergo a change, the seats of EMO shall be redistributed.

56. ZSDČZKD provides in Article 24 that EMO of a Slovenian resulting company shall be voted upon or named by the employee council.

If after the merger the resulting company subsequently participates in an internal merger with a Slovenian company, employee participation shall be ensured in accordance with national law on employee participation. However, if the national law does not provide for at least the same level of employee participation as ensured by ZSDČZKD, the employee participation provision shall apply for the next three years (Art. 25 ZSDČZKD) after such subsequent merger.

4 Protection of employee representatives

57. Article 27 of ZSDČZKD provides that the representatives and EMOs in Slovenia shall be granted the same protection as provided by the part of the Employment Relationship Act (*Zakon o delovnih razmerjih*, hereinafter referred to as 'ZDR'[13]) which protects employee representatives from being dismissed and the ZSDU.

58. Article 113 of ZDR[14] provides that EMO and labour unions representatives may not be dismissed without consent of the organs of which such employee is a member, or the labour union, unless for economic reason on the side of the employer, and only if such employee was offered alternative employment but refused it or if the employer is in a procedure of dissolution. Such protection rights shall not apply where an employee is in breach of the law, collective employment contract or employment contract.

59. Article 67 of ZSDU provides that the salary of the representatives may not be lowered and that the employee representatives may not be subject to disciplinary or compensation claims, provided that the employee is not in breach of the law, collective employment contract and employment contract. Furthermore Article 67a of ZSDU provides that if the company involved is subject to a legal transfer (i.e. merger, take-over), the representatives shall keep their status if conditions for continuance of the mandate of employee representatives shall exist with the new employer as well if so provided by the law. However, if employee representatives shall lose their mandate as a result of the transfer, the (former) representatives shall remain subject to same protection for the following nine months.

13 Uradni list RS no. 42/2002 (103/2007).

14 ZDR provides for general rules on labour law of Slovenia.

IX Tax treatment

60. The Merger Tax Directive was implemented into the Slovenian legal system via the renewed Corporate Income Tax Act (*Zakon o davku od dohodkov pravnih oseb*, hereinafter referred to as 'ZDDPO-2'[15]).

The provisions of ZDDPO-2 are applicable to both cross-border and internal mergers, i.e. mergers among Slovenian tax residents. Article 48 of ZDDPO-2 provides that the definition of merger shall be the same as provided by ZGD-1.

61. Tax aspects of a cross-border merger shall be governed by provisions of ZDDPO-2 if a number of conditions provided by Articles 50 and 51 of ZDDPO-2 are fulfilled. The most important two are the following:

(i) the acquired company (the term used in ZDDPO-2 is 'transferring company' or *prenosna družba*) shall be a (tax) resident of a Member State other than Slovenia and the resulting company (the term used in ZDDPO-2 is 'receiving company' or *prevzemna družba*) shall be a resident of Slovenia, provided that after the merger the transferred assets, liabilities, reservations, reserves and losses do not form a part of a permanent establishment of the resulting company with its head office outside of Slovenia;
(ii) the resulting company is a (tax) resident of a Member State other than Slovenia and the acquired company is a resident of Slovenia or Member State other than Slovenia, provided that after the merger the transferred assets, liabilities, reservations, reserves and losses form a part of the permanent establishment of the resulting company in Slovenia.

The above conditions are set so as to determine which mergers are to be the subject of Slovenia tax legislation. In such a case individual mergers shall be carried out with the goal of tax neutral merger. As a result, if the mentioned procedure is carried out properly, no additional taxation shall be implied on the side of both the acquired and the resulting company in connection with a cross-border merger, thus making the cross-border merger tax-neutral. On the other hand, if the conditions mentioned above are not met (which should rarely be the case), tax implications are possible; however, it is even more likely that tax legislation of another Member State, rather than the tax legislation of Slovenia, shall apply.

62. Let it be noted that the above-described tax-neutral cross-border merger is such only in accordance with Slovenian legislation. Tax legislation of other Member States and its tax impact on the specific merger should also be considered.

15 Uradni list RS no. 117/2006 (56/2008, 76/2008, 5/2009, 96/2009, 43/2010).

X Conclusion

It may be concluded that Slovenian law (ZGD-1A) implementing the Cross-border Merger Directive did so by implementing the very minimum requirements of the Cross-border Merger Directive. As a result, provisions of internal mergers are the basis on which cross-border mergers may occur in the future. In fact, provisions of internal mergers shall not be followed only if the Amendments explicitly provide so. An exception to this is the implementation of Article 16 of the Cross-border Merger Directive (on employee protection), which was implemented by a special law (ZSDČZKD) detailing employee participation in companies resulting from a cross-border merger.

Until now Slovenia has implemented both the Cross-border Merger Directive, and the European Company (SE) directive. The two solutions may be considered by companies when consolidating, whereby the creation of SE may be more appropriate for bigger companies, cross-border mergers may be more appropriate for small and medium-sized companies. It should be interesting to follow the development of cross-border merger options in Slovenia, since legal entities in a small and open economy like Slovenia should make full use of provisions of the Cross-border Merger Directive. However, to our knowledge, no cross-border mergers involving Slovenian companies have taken place so far.

30

Romania

GABRIELA CACEREA
Nestor Nestor Diculescu Kingston Petersen

I Introduction

1. The Cross-border Merger Directive was implemented in Romania by way of an amendment to the Company Law No. 31/1990, through the Government Emergency Ordinance No. 52 of 21 April 2008, in force as of 30 April 2008,[1] which introduced a new section regulating cross-border mergers.

1 Official Gazette of Romania, 30 April 2008.

II Scope of the new rules

2. Pursuant to the provisions of the Company Law, the new rules regarding cross-border mergers apply to almost all companies governed by the Company Law, i.e. joint stock companies (*societate pe actiuni* – SA), partnerships limited by shares (*societate in comandita pe actiuni* – SCA), limited liability companies (*societate cu raspundere limitata* – SRL) and European Companies (*Societas Europaea* – SE). These rules are not applicable to companies limited by shares (*societate in comandita simpla* – SCS) or to general partnerships (*societate in nume colectiv* – SNC), which cannot be involved in a cross-border merger process.

In case the resulting company following the cross-border merger is a partnership limited by shares, incorporated and operating under the Romanian law, the shareholders of the absorbed company shall always be limited partners of the resulting partnership limited by shares, unless otherwise provided in the decision approving the merger project (Art. 251^2(4) of the Company Law).

3. The scope of the cross-border merger rules is also provided under the Cross-border Merger Directive, which specifies that the rules thereof are not applicable to collective investment organisms in movable assets and closed investment funds, as well as any other entities having as object of activity the collective placement of resources provided by the public which operate on the principle of risk-spreading and whose units may be, at the holder's request, purchased or redeemed, directly or indirectly, out of the company's assets (Art. 3(3) Directive). Under the Romanian law, the collective investment organisms in movable assets and closed investment funds are governed by Law No. 297 of 28 June 2004 regarding the capital market.[2]

4. As a particularity of the Romanian Company Law, Romanian companies and European Companies headquartered in Romania holding the ownership right over a land in Romania may participate in a cross-border merger in which the absorbing or newly established company is incorporated in an EU Member State only after a five-year term from Romania's accession to the EU or a seven-year term in case of agricultural land (Art. 251^2(1) Company Law).

5. Based on the Cross-border Merger Directive according to which the assets and liabilities are transferred on the date of dissolution without liquidation of the absorbed company, a company undergoing the liquidation procedure may not participate in a cross-border merger. Nevertheless, a national merger may be performed even if the dissolved company is under liquidation, provided that the distribution of proceeds among the shareholders has not yet commenced (Art. 238(4) Company Law).

2 Official Gazette of Romania, 29 June 2004.

Under the Romanian law, in case the company under liquidation is insolvent, the liquidator has the obligation to request the opening of the insolvency proceedings (Art. 270[1] Company Law).

III Cash payment

6. According to the Cross-border Merger Directive, a cash payment of more than 10 per cent of the nominal value, or of the accounting par value of those securities or shares, may be made, provided that the law of at least one of the Member States of the companies participating in the cross-border merger so allows (Art. 251[4](2) Company Law).

The Romanian law only allows cash payment to the shareholders in an absorbed company within the limit of 10 per cent of the nominal value of the shares allocated in the surviving company and does not provide for any additional cash payment to the benefit of the shareholders of the companies participating in the merger. As such, provided that the national law of the foreign company or companies involved in the process (in which a Romanian company also takes part) so stipulates, the more than 10 per cent cash payment shall be permitted to be made. Otherwise, the merger shall be governed only by the rules comprised in the Cross-border Merger Directive, as long as the cash payment does not exceed 10 per cent of the nominal value or, in the absence of the nominal value, of the accounting par value of those securities or shares (Art. 2(2) Directive).

IV Legal consequences and enforceability of a cross-border merger

7. As a result of the cross-border merger, the assets and liabilities of the companies participating in the process will be transferred without liquidation to the surviving company, producing the same legal effects as a national merger, as follows:

(i) all assets and liabilities are transferred from the absorbed company to the absorbing/newly established company;
(ii) the shareholders of the absorbed company become shareholders of the absorbing/newly established company according to the allocation rules established in the merger project;
(iii) the absorbed company, or, as the case may be, the companies forming the resulting entity, cease to exist (Art. 251[15](1) Company Law).

As further detailed in no. 27 of this chapter, once the cross-border merger has become effective, its nullity can no longer be invoked after the date of the merger (Art. 251[19](2) Company Law).

8. Under the Romanian law, the cross-border merger will produce its effects as of the following dates in case the absorbing company or the newly established company shall be in the Romanian jurisdiction:

(i) date of the registration with the Trade Registry of the company, in case of establishing a new company;
(ii) date of registration with the Trade Registry of the act amending the articles of association of the absorbing company, except for the case when, by the agreement of the parties, it is stipulated that the operation will produce its effects on a different date; in the latter case, the stipulated date cannot be (i) subsequent to the end of the current financial year of the absorbing company or of the beneficiary companies, or (ii) prior to the end of the last finalised financial year of the companies transferring their patrimony, or (iii) prior to the control of the legality of the merger performed by the tribunal, commercial department;
(iii) date of registration, in case of establishing a European company (Art. 251^{15}(2) Company Law).

In case the absorbing company or the newly established company resulting from the cross-border merger is subject to the jurisdiction of another Member State then the law of the latter shall determine the date on which the merger takes effect.

The absorbed companies' rights and obligations resulting from employment relationships existing on the date of completion of the cross-border merger are transferred to the absorbing/newly established company on the same date (Art. 251^{15}(3) Company Law).

V Procedure

1 Draft terms of cross-border merger

9. The directors or members of the directorate of the companies participating in the process prepare the draft terms of the cross-border merger (Art. 251^{5}(1) Company Law). No formalities have to be fulfilled as regards this document (e.g. notarised, authentic form). However, the notarised form is required in relation to the act amending the constitutive act in case a plot of land is transferred (as mentioned in no. 21 of this chapter).

The draft terms shall include the information mentioned in no. 19 of Chapter 1 of this book (Art. 251^{5} Company Law). In case the surviving company owns 100 per cent of the shareholding of the absorbed company/companies, the elements provided at points (ii), (iii) and (iv) of no. 19 of Chapter 1 are not applicable (Art. 251^{17} Company Law).

The directors of the absorbed company or of the companies forming the resulting company are liable to the shareholders of the respective legal entities for the faults committed while preparing and performing the merger (Art. 251^{16}(1) Company Law).

10. The common draft terms signed by the representatives of the companies participating in the merger shall be registered with the respective Trade Registry

Offices of the entities involved in the operation. The draft terms or an excerpt thereof, endorsed by the Trade Registry director/person designated by the general director of the National Trade Registry, shall be published in the Official Gazette of Romania, at the parties' expense, upon the order of the Trade Registry director/person designated by the general director of the National Trade Registry or upon the parties' request, at least thirty days before the date of the general meeting of shareholders deciding upon the cross-border merger (Art. 251^6(2) Company Law).

The merger common draft terms excerpt shall contain at least the following elements:

(i) the type, name and registered office of each company participating in the merger;
(ii) the Trade Registry Office where the draft terms and the act amending the articles of association of the resulting company were submitted;
(iii) the conditions in which the company's creditors may exercise their opposition (Art. 251^6(3) Company Law).

2 Management report

11. The management bodies of the participating companies (i.e. directors/members of the directorate) shall prepare a written report detailing the merger process and presenting its legal and economic grounds. The report shall be made available to the shareholders at least thirty days prior to the general meeting deciding on the merger, both at the company's headquarters and on the company's website, for free access of the shareholders.

The report shall also be made available to the employees' representatives or, in case such representatives have not been designated, to the employees themselves, provided that either the absorbing/newly established company is a European company or in one of the merging companies is set in place a mechanism for employees' involvement in the company's activity of the nature provided for in Article 2(k) of the SE Directive.

12. According to the Cross-border Merger Directive, the report shall also explain the implications of the cross-border merger for members, creditors and employees (Art. 7(1) Directive).

3 Auditor's report

13. Under the Romanian law, one or more experts, natural or legal persons, acting independently on behalf of each Romanian or European company established in Romania, participating in the merger, are designated by the Trade Registry director/person designated by the general director of the National Trade Registry to examine the common draft terms and to prepare a written report for the shareholders (Art. 251^8(1) Company Law).

The experts' report will mention the following elements (Art. 251^8(2) Company Law):

(i) whether the share exchange ratio is correct and reasonable;
(ii) the method/methods used for determining the exchange ratio proposed;
(iii) whether the method/methods used are adequate for the specific case;
(iv) the values resulting from applying every method;
(v) the experts' opinion regarding the importance of each method in order to determine the value finally retained;
(vi) any difficulties arisen during the performance of the evaluation.

The Trade Registry director/person designated by the general director of the National Trade Registry shall appoint one or more experts acting independently on behalf of all companies involved in the operation, at the common request of such entities, including those from another Member State (Art. 251^8(3) Company Law).

14. Neither an examination of the common draft terms of the cross-border merger by independent experts nor an expert report shall be required if all the members of each of the companies involved in the cross-border merger have so agreed (Art. 251^8(5) Company Law).

The experts' report is also not required in case the merger by absorption is performed between a parent company and a company it fully owns (Art. 251^{17} Company Law). Also, if the absorbing company is subject to the jurisdiction of a different Member State which holds 90 per cent or more of, but not the entire, share capital of the absorbed company which is subject to the Romanian jurisdiction, the absorbing company shall not have the obligation to require the preparation of the expert report unless it is required under the law of its jurisdiction (Art. 251^{18}(1) Company Law).

Each designated expert has the right to receive all relevant information/documents and also the right to perform all necessary investigations in view of drafting the report.

15. The experts drafting the report mentioned herein on behalf of the absorbed company or of the ones forming the resulting company are liable towards the shareholders of the respective legal entities for the faults committed during performance of their duties (Art. 251^{16}(2) Company Law).

4 General meeting of shareholders

A Information for shareholders

16. After taking note of the report(s) mentioned above, the general meeting of each of the companies involved in the merger shall decide upon the draft common terms, with the observance of the conditions provided for amending the articles of association and for summoning the general meeting. Such

meeting shall be held within three months of publication of the draft common terms in the Official Gazette of Romania (Art. 251[11](1) Company Law).

17. For this purpose, at least one month prior to the date when the general meeting of shareholders is held, the management bodies of the companies taking part in the merger process shall submit to the shareholders, at the company's registered office, the draft terms and the management and experts' reports.

Moreover, copies of the annual financial statements and the management reports for the last three financial years of the companies taking part in the merger process shall be made available to the shareholders. Should the last annual financial statements be prepared for a financial year ended more than six months prior to this date, the financial statements prepared no earlier than the first day of the third month previous to the date of the merger process shall be made available at the company's office.

The shareholders will be able to obtain free of charge copies of the documents enumerated above or excerpts of the same (Art. 244(2) Company Law).

B Shareholder approval

18. The general meeting of shareholders has to approve both the merger and the common draft terms. Under the Company Law, the vote requirements in relation to the general meeting of shareholders are different for joint stock companies and limited liability companies. Thus, for the validity of the approval of the cross-border merger, in joint stock companies the presence of shareholders holding at least a quarter of the total voting rights is required at the first call, and the presence of the shareholders holding at least a fifth of the total voting rights is required at subsequent calls (Arts. 251[11](1) and 115 Company Law).

The decision regarding the merger process shall be taken by the vote of a special majority of two-thirds of the voting rights held by the shareholders who are present or represented, except for the case when the articles of association provide for stricter provisions (Arts. 251[11](1) and 115 Company Law). As for limited liability companies, the Company Law stipulates that the resolutions shall be taken with unanimity of votes, except if otherwise provided by the articles of association (Art. 192 Company Law). In case the shares are of several categories, the merger shall be approved pursuant to the results of the votes on categories, exercised as provided above (Art. 251[11](2) Company Law).

In case either the absorbing or newly established company is a European company, or in one of the merging companies is set in place a mechanism for employees' involvement in the company's activity of the nature provided for in Article 2(k) of the SE Directive, the general meeting of shareholders may condition the approval of the merger upon the express confirmation by the meeting of the mechanisms of involving the employees in the activity of the absorbed/newly established company (Art. 251[11](3) Company Law).

19. When the cross-border merger triggers the enhancement of the obligations of the shareholders of one of the participating companies – Romanian legal

persons – the decision of the general meeting of shareholders has to be taken with unanimity of votes (Art. 251[11](4) Company Law).

20. The shareholders who did not vote in favour of the cross-border merger are entitled to withdraw from the company and to request the purchase of their shares by the company. Such right of withdrawal shall be exercised in case of joint stock companies, partnerships limited by shares and limited liability companies within thirty days of the date of adopting the decision by the general meeting of shareholders (Arts. 251[12](2), 134(2) and 251[12](3) Company Law).

21. The right of withdrawal may be exercised by the shareholders only if (i) the law of all the Member States of the participating companies provides for a shareholders' protection system similar to the one discussed in no. 20 of this chapter and if (ii) the companies participating in the merger, governed by the law of another Member State not granting the shareholders a right of withdrawal from the company, have expressly accepted that the shareholders of the company – Romanian legal entity – may exercise such right, mention thereof being made in the decision of the general meeting approving the merger (Art. 251[12](4) Company Law).

Under the Romanian law, there are no formal requirements to be met as regards the decision of the general meeting of the shareholders or the minutes drafted (e.g. notarised form). Under Romanian law the notarised form of the act amending the constitutive act is required for the case when a land plot is transferred.

5 Pre-merger certificate

22. According to the Cross-border Merger Directive, each Member State shall designate an authority competent to scrutinise the legality of the cross-border merger as regards the part of the procedure which concerns each merging company subject to its national law. Such authority shall particularly ensure that the merging companies have approved the common draft terms in the same terms and, where appropriate, that the arrangements for employee participation have been determined accordingly, and it shall issue a certificate attesting the proper completion of the pre-merger acts and formalities (Arts. 10(1)(2) and 11(1) Directive).

23. Under the Romanian law, the legality of the cross-border merger is verified by the Trade Registry director/person designated by the general director of the National Trade Registry or by the tribunal commercial department. As such, in case of a merger by absorption or in case a new company is set up, the tribunal decides the registration with the Trade Registry of the additional act to the articles of association of the absorbing/newly established company – Romanian entity or European company headquartered in Romania – following the verification of the fulfilment of the legal requirements, i.e. the existence of the certificates or similar documents issued by the competent authorities from

the other Member States where the other companies participating in the merger are headquartered or, as the case may be, where the central management or main headquarters is, and the term within which such have been submitted to the Trade Registry Office, which is up to 6 months as of issuance (Art. 251^{13}(1) Company Law).

24. If the company resulting from the merger process is governed by the law of another Member State, including a European company headquartered in another Member State, the legality of the decision regarding the merger – as submitted by the management to the Trade Registry Office where the company, Romanian entity, is registered – shall be verified by the tribunal commercial department and a decision shall be pronounced attesting the fulfilment of the legal criteria, which decision shall be communicated to the company at its headquarters (Art. 251^{13}(5) Company Law). The decision may be made regardless of whether the shareholders' withdrawal procedure is pending, note being made that redemption of the shares is yet to be finalised. The withdrawals performed according to no. 20 of this chapter are opposable towards the resulting company and its shareholders (Art. 251^{13}(6) Company Law).

The companies participating in the process shall submit to the Trade Registry director/person designated by the general director of the National Trade Registry the common draft terms, as approved by the general meeting of shareholders, and the pre-merger certificate mentioned above.

25. If the absorbing company holds 90 per cent or more of the share capital of the absorbed company/companies, the decision of the tribunal, the issuance and communication of the certificate or similar document are no longer necessary, unless the law of the Member State of the absorbing company so provides (Art. 251^{18}(2) Company Law).

6 Effects of the decision

26. Under the Romanian law, the cross-border merger will produce its effects from the date of the registration with the Trade Registry of the act amending the articles of association, except for the case when, by the agreement of the parties, it is stipulated that the operation will produce its effects at a later date, which cannot be subsequent to the end of the current financial year of the absorbing company or prior to the end of the last financial year of the absorbing company or prior to the control of the legality of the merger performed by the tribunal mentioned above (Art. 251^{15}(2) Company Law). In case a new company or a European company is set up through the cross-border merger, the operation shall not be effective until the registration thereof with the Trade Registry or registration with the competent authority is performed.

The act amending the articles of association, attested by the tribunal, shall be published in the Official Gazette of Romania at the company's expense (Art. 251^{14}(1) Company Law).

The Trade Registry Office where the resulting company is registered shall notify the performance of the merger immediately, at the company's expense, to the corresponding authorities from the Member States of the other participating companies (Art. 251^{14}(3) Company Law). The absorbed companies shall be struck off from the relevant Trade Registry Office, based on the notification transmitted by the corresponding authority from the Member State of the absorbing/newly established company (Art. 251^{14}(4) Company Law).

27. In case the company resulting from the merger process is a European company headquartered in Romania, the National Trade Registry Office shall communicate to the Official Journal of the European Union, at the parties' expense, in order to be published, an announcement comprising the following elements: name of the company, registration number with the Trade Registry, registration date, number of the Official Gazette of Romania in which the decision of the tribunal for registering the company has been published (Art. 251^{14}(5) Company Law).

The merger may not be declared void by a court of law after the date it became effective, as mentioned above (Art. 251^{19}(2) Company Law), irrespective of whether the decision approving it has been published or not.

VI Minority shareholders

28. The decision of the general meeting of shareholders approving the cross-border merger (see no. 18 of this chapter) is also mandatory for the minority shareholders of the respective company. The minority shareholders shall receive shares in the resulting company, without having the possibility to raise objections against the merger process. However, please note that under the Company Law, there are several rights expressly granted to the minority shareholders (i.e. the right to be informed of the merger process, right to withdraw from the company in case they do not agree with the merger operation).

VII Protection of creditors

29. The creditors of the companies involved in the cross-border merger may oppose the merger process within thirty days of the date of publication of the common draft terms in the Official Gazette of Romania, provided that their receivables are certain, liquid, prior to the date of publication of the draft common terms and not due as of publication date, in the absence of any adequate guarantees or pledges for securing their receivables (Articles 251^{9} and 243 Company Law).

The opposition shall be submitted to the Trade Registry, which shall further deliver it within three days of submission to the tribunal in which jurisdiction the company has its headquarters.

Under recent amendments to the Company Law, in case of mergers performed after the entry into force of the enactment (i.e. October 2010), the opposition does not trigger the suspension of the merger, nor does it impede performance thereof (Arts. 251^9 and 243(3) Company Law).

VIII Employee participation[3]

30. With respect to employee participation, the Cross-border Merger Directive has been transposed into the Romanian legislation through the Company Law as amended and supplemented in view of transposing the Directive, by the Government Emergency Ordinance No. 52/2008 (amending and supplementing the Company Law and Law No. 26/1990 on the Trade Registry).

1 Employee participation in companies established in Romania resulting from a cross-border merger

31. Romanian law sets forth that for companies resulting from a cross-border merger that are established in Romania, a participation mechanism shall be set up, if such mechanism existed within one or more of the participating companies.

Moreover, Romanian legislation currently provides that if the absorbing/ newly established company is a European company having its headquarters in Romania, the directors of the companies participating in the merger shall ensure the observance of the employees' involvement in the affairs of the European company, in accordance with the provisions of Government Decision No. 187/2007 on the information, consultation and other modalities for the involvement of the employees in the affairs of a European company ('GD 187/2007').

2 Special negotiating body ('SNB')

32. According to the provisions of GD 187/2007, the Special Negotiating Body ('SNB') shall represent the employees of the legal entities participating in the European company and their subsidiaries, branches and other secondary offices. The members of the SNB are appointed by the trade unions, or in their absence, by the employees' representatives. In the absence of such employees' representatives, the members of the SNB shall be appointed with the majority of votes of the employees from Romania of the European company. However, practical problems could arise as GD 187/2007 does not provide for an election procedure.

GD 187/2007 does not necessarily require the members of the SNB to be employed by one of the participating companies or by an involved subsidiary or establishment.

33. In case a mechanism of employees' involvement in the affairs of a European company exists within one or more of the participating companies governed

3 Luminita Dima, Nestor Nestor Diculescu Kingston Petersen.

by the legislation of another Member State, according to Article 2(k) of the Directive (i.e. meaning the right to elect or appoint some of the members of the company's supervisory or administrative body, or the right to recommend and/or oppose the appointment of some or all of the members of the company's supervisory or administrative body), the absorbing/newly established company (a Romanian legal person) is obliged to also set up such a mechanism of involvement. Therefore, the relevant provisions of GD 187/2007 shall become applicable. Consequently, an SNB shall be created for the representation of the employees within the participating companies or within the subsidiaries, branches or other related secondary offices as follows: the members of the SNB are elected or appointed proportionally with the total number of employees of the participating companies, of the subsidiaries or of other secondary offices.

Moreover, in case the absorbing/newly established company is a Romanian legal entity, the management bodies of the companies participating in the merger in which modalities of employees' involvement exist may decide to apply the special provisions of GD 187/2007 or to observe such provisions as from the date of registration with the Trade Registry of the amendment to the articles of association of the absorbing company or as from the date of registration with the Trade Registry of the newly established company. In such case, the SNB may decide not to initiate negotiations or to cease the negotiations already started and to accept the application of the special provisions of GD 187/2007. Such decision may be taken with a two-thirds majority of its members representing two-thirds of the employees, including the votes of the members representing the employees of at least two different Member States.

3 Protection of employee representatives

34. Under GD 187/2007, SNB members or the members of the representative body, the employees' representatives having attributions within an information and consultation procedure and the employees' representatives within the control or management body of a European company who are employees of the subsidiaries or of its companies, or of a participating legal entity, of a European company, shall benefit from protection and guarantees while performing their attributions, allowing them to properly fulfil the obligations entrusted to them, in accordance with the provisions of the Romanian Labour Code and of the Trade Unions Law.

These legal provisions shall also be applicable with respect to the participation in the meetings of the SNB or of the representative body, as well as with respect to the payment of the employees' salaries during their absence necessary in view of fulfilling their attributions.

35. On the other side, according to the Company Law, when a mechanism of employees' involvement within the Romanian legal entity which was created

as a result of the cross-border merger exists, the directors or, if the case, the members of the directorate have the obligation to ensure the protection of the employees' rights resulting out of such mechanism in case that a merger will subsequently take place under the national legislation, for a three-year term as of the date the cross-border merger produced its effects.

IX Tax treatment[4]

36. Starting on 1 January 2007 (i.e. the date of Romania's accession to the European Union), Romania implemented into its legislation the Merger Tax Directive (2009/133/EC) of 19 October 2009. Thus, the Merger Tax Directive has become part of the Romanian Fiscal Code (i.e. Law 571/2003 as subsequently amended), as a specific part of the corporate income tax section.

In October 2009, the Romanian Fiscal Code was further amended in connection with the implementation of the Merger Tax Directive. These amendments are enforceable starting on 1 January 2010 and refer mainly to the implementation of the rules applicable to the transfer of the registered office of European Companies and European Cooperative Societies from Romania to another Member State.

However, even considering the said latest amendments of the Romanian Fiscal Code (applicable starting on 1 January 2010), some paragraphs and provisions of the Merger Tax Directive remain unimplemented in the Romanian fiscal legislation.

Furthermore, there are no details or guidance issued by the Romanian tax authorities on the application of the Merger Tax Directive to date.

37. The Romanian Fiscal Code allows reorganisations involving two or more companies, tax residents in different Member States, to be carried out in a tax-neutral way. Tax neutrality is achieved by exempting from tax the capital gains on the transferred assets and liabilities and is contingent on those assets and liabilities being effectively connected with a Romanian permanent establishment of the receiving company, beneficiary of the transfer of assets and liabilities. However, there are no techniques provided by the Romanian legislation on how to allocate the assets and liabilities to a permanent establishment.

Tax neutrality is allowed only if the capital gains/losses and depreciation are calculated by the receiving company as if the transaction had not taken place, according to the rules that would have applied to the transferring company (therefore, there is no step-up for tax purposes).

The provisions and reserves wholly or partly tax deductible at the level of the transferring company may be carried over, under the same deduction conditions, to the Romanian permanent establishment of the receiving company.

The transfer of the tax losses is not allowed in cross-border situations.

4 Marius Ionescu, Nestor Nestor Diculescu Kingston Petersen Tax Advisory.

38. Reorganisations include cross-border mergers and divisions, transfer of assets (branches of activity) and exchange of shares. Starting 1 January 2010, the transfer of the registered office of European Companies and European Cooperative Societies from Romania to another Member State is also included in the scope of the Romanian Fiscal Code.

39. The following conditions should generally be met in order for the reorganisations to be eligible for tax neutrality:

(i) Reorganisations should be performed between companies from two or more Member States, defined as any company of a Member State, which takes one of the forms presented in a specific list.[5] It is considered to be tax resident in a Member State, according to the tax laws of that Member State, without being considered under a double tax treaty concluded with a third state to be resident outside the European Union, and it is subject to a tax similar to the Romanian corporate income tax without the possibility of an option or of being exempt.

(ii) The reorganisation may not have as its principal objective or as one of its principal objectives tax evasion or tax avoidance.

(iii) The reorganisation may not result in a company, whether participating in the operation or not, no longer fulfilling the conditions required for the representation of employees in company bodies, according to the arrangements which were in force prior to that operation.

5 This list is similar to the relevant Annex to the Merger Tax Directive.

31

Spain

JAIME PEREDA ESPESO, JOSÉ GABRIEL MARTÍNEZ PAÑOS
Uría Menéndez

I Introduction

1. The Cross-border Merger Directive has been implemented in Spain pursuant to Law 3/2009 of April 3, on Structural Amendments relating to Commercial Companies (*Ley de Modificaciones Estructurales de las Sociedades Mercantiles*) ('Structural Amendments Law' or 'SAL'). Cross-border mergers within the EU are regulated by the specific rules applicable to these kinds of

mergers provided in the Structural Amendments Law (Arts. 54–67 SAL) and, on a subsidiary basis, by the general rules governing domestic mergers.

II Scope of the new rules

2. The Structural Amendments Law (Art. 54.1), following the Cross-border Merger Directive (Art. 1), defines as cross-border mergers within the EU mergers involving companies incorporated in accordance with the legislation of a Member State of the European Economic Area, whose registered office, central headquarters or principal place of business is located within the European Economic Area, where at least (i) two of the companies involved in the merger are subject to the legislation of different Member States and (ii) one of the companies involved in the merger is subject to Spanish legislation. The Structural Amendments Law also regulates mergers between companies of different nationalities which are not deemed cross-border mergers within the EU (i.e. international mergers not regulated by the Cross-border Merger Directive, such as, for example, a merger between a Spanish company and a company subject to the legislation of a non-Member State of the European Economic Area). These other kinds of international mergers, which are not subject to analysis in the present chapter, are not regulated under Articles 54 to 67 of the Structural Amendments Law, which only govern mergers provided for in the Cross-border Merger Directive.

3. The following companies subject to Spanish law may take part in a cross-border merger within the EU: joint stock companies (*sociedades anónimas*), partnerships limited by shares (*sociedades comanditarias por acciones*) and limited liability companies (*sociedades de responsabilidad limitada*).

4. The provisions relating to cross-border mergers within the EU included in the Structural Amendments Law (Arts. 54–67 SAL) do not apply to cross-border mergers involving a cooperative company or a company deemed a collective investment undertaking.

III Cash payment

5. In domestic mergers, the cash compensation to which the shareholders may be entitled as a result of the merger may not exceed 10 per cent of the nominal value of the shares or participations received in exchange (Art. 25.2 SAL). However, in cross-border mergers, if the legislation of one of the Member States should allow it, the cash payment included as part of the exchange may exceed 10 per cent of the nominal value or, in the absence thereof, of the accounting par value of the shares or participations subject to exchange (Art. 57 SAL).

Consequently, the rules governing cross-border mergers shall only apply to mergers involving a Spanish company where the cash payment exceeds 10 per cent of the nominal value or, in the absence thereof, the accounting par value of the shares or participations subject to exchange, if the legislation applicable to one of the foreign companies involved in the merger should allow this.

IV Legal consequences and enforceability of a cross-border merger

6. Pursuant to a cross-border merger, two or more companies become a single company by the block transfer of their assets and liabilities and the allocation to the shareholders of the companies subject to dissolution of shares or participations in the resulting entity or company, which may be newly formed or consist of one of the merging companies. Cross-border mergers have the same effects as domestic mergers:

(i) the companies involved in the merger (except for the surviving entity, if the merger does not involve the creation of a new entity) are dissolved without going into liquidation;
(ii) shareholders of the companies subject to dissolution become shareholders of the company resulting from the merger (whether a newly formed company or the surviving company); and
(iii) all assets and liabilities of the companies subject to dissolution are transferred to the company resulting from the merger, which acquires the rights and obligations thereof pursuant to universal succession.

7. Where the company resulting from the merger should be a Spanish company, the merger shall be enforceable against third parties in good faith from the date on which, after registration thereof with the Commercial Registry (see no. 29 below), it is published in the Official Gazette of the Commercial Registry(*Boletín Oficial del Registro Mercantil*). Notwithstanding the foregoing, during fifteen days following publication thereof in the Official Gazette of the Commercial Registry, the merger shall not be enforceable against persons who evidence that they were unable to become aware of the merger.

V Procedure

1 Draft terms of cross-border merger

8. The directors of each of the companies involved in the merger shall prepare the draft terms of cross-border merger (Art. 59.1 SAL). The draft terms of cross-border merger shall be without force or effect unless approved by the general shareholders' meetings of all companies involved in the merger within six months following the date thereof (Art. 30.3 SAL).

The draft terms of cross-border merger shall contain at least the particulars described in no. 19 of Chapter 1 of the first volume of this book (Arts. 59 and 31 SAL).

In the event of a takeover merger where the surviving company directly or indirectly holds all shares or participations in the share capital of the company or companies taken over, the draft terms of cross-border merger shall not require a reference to the exchange ratio of the merger or the date as of which the new shares or participations shall be entitled to a share in company profits (Art. 49.1.1 SAL), as these mergers do not, as a general rule, involve a capital increase in the surviving company. The same rules shall govern takeover mergers where the company taken over directly or indirectly holds all shares or participations in the surviving company (Art. 52 SAL).

9. The draft terms of cross-border merger shall be deposited with each Commercial Registry corresponding to each Spanish company involved in the merger. The fact of the deposit and the date thereof shall be published in the 'Official Gazette of the Commercial Registry'. The general shareholders' meetings to approve the merger may not be called prior to the deposit of the draft terms of cross-border merger, save in the event of a so-called universal general meeting, where, all shareholders being present, they unanimously decide to hold a general meeting (Art. 32.1 SAL).

10. The draft terms of cross-border merger shall be among the documents to be made available to the shareholders, debenture holders, holders of special rights and employee representatives upon calling the general shareholders' meeting to which the cross-border merger is to be submitted for approval (Art. 39.1 SAL).

2 Management report

11. The management body of each company involved in the merger shall draft a report explaining and justifying in detail the legal and financial issues of the draft terms of cross-border merger, with special reference to the exchange ratio and any special valuation difficulties which may exist, and the implications of the merger for shareholders, creditors and employees (Arts. 33 and 60 SAL).

12. The management report shall be made available to the shareholders and the employee representatives or, in the absence thereof, to the employees themselves, at least one month prior to the date of the general meeting which is to approve the draft terms of cross-border merger (Art. 60.1 SAL).

Where the management body of the Spanish company should receive in due time an opinion issued by the employee representatives, this opinion shall be attached to the report (Art. 60.2 SAL). However, it is unlikely that this will occur, as the management report will be made available usually to the shareholders and employee representatives at the same time as the calling of the general meeting, which shall similarly take place one month prior to the general meeting.

3 Experts' report on the draft terms of cross-border merger

13. The management body of each company involved in the merger must request the appointment of one or several independent experts so that they may

separately issue reports on the draft terms of cross-border merger (Art. 34.1 SAL). The Commercial Registrar corresponding to the registered offices of the Spanish companies involved in the merger shall be in charge of appointing their respective independent experts.

Notwithstanding the foregoing, the management bodies of all companies involved in the merger may request the designation of one or several experts to draft a single report on the draft terms of cross-border merger. Where the company resulting from the merger should be a Spanish company, the Commercial Registrar corresponding to the registered office of the surviving company or the registered office provided in the draft terms of cross-border merger as the registered office of the new company shall be competent to designate the expert or experts who are to draft the single report.

14. The expert report must give an opinion, at least, on the following issues: (i) whether or not the exchange ratio is justified; (ii) what are the methods used to set the exchange ratio and what values do such methods result in; (iii) any special valuation difficulties; and (iv) whether the assets and liabilities contributed by the companies subject to dissolution are at least the same as the share capital of the new company or the capital increase performed by the surviving company, where applicable (Art. 34.3 SAL).

The experts may, without any limitation whatsoever, obtain any information and documents believed to be useful from the companies involved in the merger, and perform any verifications deemed necessary (Art. 34.2 SAL).

15. The expert report on the draft terms of cross-border merger shall not be necessary in the following cases: (i) where it should be so resolved by all voting shareholders of the companies involved in the cross-border merger (Art. 34.5 SAL); (ii) in the event of a takeover merger where the surviving company directly holds all shares or participations in the share capital of the company or companies taken over (Arts. 34.5 and 49.1.2 SAL); (iii) in the event of a takeover merger where the company taken over directly holds all shares or participations in the share capital of the surviving company (Arts. 49.1.2 and 52.1 SAL); and (iv) in the event of a takeover merger where the surviving company is the direct holder of a share equal to or greater than 90 per cent, but not of the whole, of the share capital of the company or companies which are to be taken over, if the surviving company should offer to the shareholders of the companies taken over to acquire their shares or participations estimated at their fair value within one month counting from the date of registration of the merger with the Commercial Registry (Art. 50.1 SAL) (for such purposes, the draft terms of cross-border merger must indicate the acquisition price for such shares or participations).

16. The reports issued by the independent experts relating to the draft terms of cross-border merger are among the documents to be made available to shareholders, debenture holders, holders of special rights and employee representatives at

the time of calling the general shareholders' meeting to approve the cross-border merger (Art. 39.1 SAL).

4 Merger balance sheet

17. Each company involved in the merger may deem its last approved balance sheet to be its merger balance sheet, provided that such balance sheet should have been closed at the earliest six months prior to the date of the draft terms of cross-border merger. If the annual balance sheet should not meet this requirement, it will be necessary to draft a balance sheet closed subsequently to the first day of the third month prior to the date of the draft terms of cross-border merger, following the same methods and presentation criteria as the last balance sheet (Art. 36.1 SAL).

In both cases, the valuations provided in the last annual balance sheet may be amended on the basis of major changes in fair value which are not recorded in the relevant book entries (Art. 36.2 SAL).

18. If the company is under the obligation to audit its accounts, the merger balance sheet and, as the case may be, the valuation amendments included therein, must be verified by the company's auditor. Likewise, the merger balance sheet must be submitted to the approval of the general shareholders meeting which is to approve the merger, which, for such purposes, must be mentioned expressly in the agenda for the meeting (Art. 37 SAL).

19. The merger balance sheet is among the documents to be made available to shareholders, debenture holders, holders of special rights and employee representatives at the time of calling the general shareholders' meeting to approve the cross-border merger (Art. 39.1 SAL).

5 General meeting of shareholders

A. Information for shareholders

20. Upon the publication or individual notice of the calling of the shareholders' meetings of the Spanish companies to whose approval the cross-border merger is submitted, the following documents must be made available to their shareholders, debenture holders and holders of special rights, and likewise to the employee representatives, for examination thereof at the registered office of the relevant company (Art. 39.1 SAL):

(i) the draft terms of cross-border merger;
(ii) the management reports of each company on the draft terms of cross-border merger;
(iii) the independent expert reports on the draft terms of cross-border merger;
(iv) the annual accounts and management reports of the three preceding financial years for the companies involved in the merger, and the

corresponding auditors' reports for any companies subject to the obligation to audit their accounts;

(v) the merger balance sheet for each company involved in the merger, where different from the last approved annual balance sheet, including, as the case may be, the report by the company's auditor;

(vi) the current by-laws of the companies involved in the merger;

(vii) the draft public deed of incorporation of the newly formed company or, in the event of a takeover merger, the full text of the by-laws of the surviving company and any amendments to be made thereto;

(viii) the identity of the directors of the companies involved in the merger, the date on which they first began to perform their duties and, as the case may be, the same details concerning the persons to be proposed as directors as a result of the merger.

Shareholders and employee representatives may request the delivery or dispatch, free of charge, of a copy of these documents.

21. Publication of the calling of the shareholders' meeting or, as the case may be, individual notice thereof to the shareholders, must take place at least one month prior to the date set for the general meeting of the Spanish companies which are to decide on the cross-border merger. The calling of the meeting must include, inter alia, the minimum items required for the draft terms of cross-border merger (see no. 8 of this chapter). Likewise, the calling shall mention the right of shareholders, debenture holders and holders of special rights to examine the documents mentioned above (see no. 20 of this chapter) at the registered office and to receive or be sent free of charge the full text thereof (Art. 40.2 SAL).

22. The general meeting of each company involved in the merger must be informed of any major modifications in the assets and liabilities of any of the companies involved in the merger that occurred within the period between the date of the draft terms of cross-border merger and the date of the general shareholders' meeting to approve the merger. For such purposes, the management body of the company which has suffered such changes must make the management bodies of the remaining companies aware of them, so that they may inform their respective general shareholders' meetings (Art. 39.3 SAL).

B. Shareholders' approval

23. The merger must be approved by the general shareholders' meeting of each company involved, strictly complying with the draft terms of cross-border merger. Notwithstanding the foregoing, takeover mergers where the surviving company holds, directly or indirectly, all shares or participations in the share capital of the company or companies taken over shall not require the approval of the merger by the general shareholders' meetings of the companies taken over (Art. 49.1.4 SAL).

Where the merger takes place by creating a new company, the merger resolution must include the provisions legally required to incorporate it.

24. Unless the by-laws should provide for a specific quorum or majority, approval of the cross-border merger by a Spanish company shall require:

(i) For joint stock companies (*sociedades anónimas*) and limited partnerships by shares (*sociedades comanditarias por acciones*): (a) in the first call, presence of shareholders, in person or by proxy, representing at least 50 per cent of the voting capital (the approval of the merger resolution shall require the favourable vote of the majority of the share capital present at the meeting, in person or by proxy); and (b) in the second call, the presence of 25 per cent of such share capital shall be sufficient; however, if less than 50 per cent of the share capital should be present, the approval of the merger resolution shall require the favourable vote of two-thirds of the voting capital present at the general meeting, in person or by proxy (Arts. 194 and 201 of the Consolidated Text of the Capital Companies Law (*Texto Refundido de la Ley de Sociedades de Capital*), approved by Royal Legislative Decree 1/2010, of 2 July 2010).

(ii) For limited liability companies (*sociedades de responsabilidad limitada*): the favourable vote of at least two-thirds of the votes corresponding to participations in the share capital (Art. 199 of the Consolidated Text of the Capital Companies Law (*Texto Refundido de la Ley de Sociedades de Capital*), approved by Royal Legislative Decree 1/2010, of 2 July 2010).

The merger resolution shall likewise require the consent of all shareholders who, as a result of the cross-border merger, should assume unlimited liability for the corporate debts, and of all shareholders of the companies to be dissolved who are to assume personal obligations in the company resulting from the merger (Art. 41.1 SAL).

25. The general meeting of each company involved in the merger may subject their approval of the merger to the express ratification of its resolutions regarding employee participation in the company resulting from the merger (Art. 61 SAL).

26. Upon approval thereof, the merger resolution shall be published in the Official Gazette of the Commercial Registry and in a daily newspaper of wide circulation in the provinces where the relevant Spanish companies have their registered offices. Such announcement shall include the right assisting shareholders and creditors to obtain the full text of the merger resolution and the merger balance sheet, and the creditors' right to object to the merger (see no. 33 below). Notwithstanding the foregoing, publication of such announcements shall not be required where individual written notice of the resolution is given to all shareholders and creditors of the Spanish companies involved in the

merger, by a method which ensures receipt thereof, at the address provided in the documentation held by the companies (Art. 43 SAL).

6 Pre-merger certificate

27. The Commercial Registrar of the registered office of each Spanish company involved in the merger shall be in charge of verifying and certifying the proper performance of the acts and formalities by the relevant Spanish company prior to the merger (Art. 64 SAL). For these purposes, it shall issue a certificate to be delivered without delay to the relevant Spanish company involved in the merger.

28. Where the company resulting from the merger is subject to Spanish legislation, the Spanish Commercial Registrar, prior to proceeding to the registration of the merger, shall likewise ascertain whether the merger procedure is in compliance with the law as concerns the following: (i) performance of the merger, (ii) incorporation of the new company or amendments to the by-laws of the surviving company, (iii) approval of the draft terms of cross-border merger in the same terms by the companies involved in the merger and (iv), where applicable, appropriateness of any employee participation provisions. For such purposes, each of the companies involved in the merger shall forward to the relevant Spanish Commercial Registrar the draft terms of cross-border merger approved by its general shareholders' meeting and the certificate mentioned in Article 10 of the Cross-border Merger Directive (see no. 27 of this chapter) within six months of the date of issuance thereof (Art. 65.1 SAL).

7 Effects of the cross-border merger

29. Where the company resulting from the merger is subject to Spanish legislation, the merger shall be effective upon registration of the new company or, as the case may be, upon registration of the takeover with the competent Commercial Registry (Art. 46.1 SAL). Upon registration thereof, the Commercial Registry shall immediately give notice thereof to the Registries where the remaining companies involved are registered, in order that the latter may proceed to the cancellation thereof (Art. 66.3 SAL).

30. In cases where employee participation is required (see no. 35 below), the merger may not be registered unless an employee participation agreement has been entered into (see no. 37 below), or the negotiation period has expired without entering into an agreement (see no. 40 below) or the competent bodies of the companies involved in the merger have chosen to submit directly to the subsidiary provisions set forth in Law 31/2006 of 18 October 2006 on Employee Implication in European Joint Stock Companies and Cooperatives (*Ley de Implicación de los Trabajadores en las Sociedades Anónimas y Cooperativas Europeas*) ('Law 31/2006 of 18 October 2009' or 'EIL') (see no. 37 of this chapter).

VI Minority shareholders

31. Once approved, the cross-border merger shall be binding on all shareholders of the Spanish companies involved, even if they have voted against the merger resolution. Notwithstanding the foregoing, when the registered office of the resulting company is located in a Member State other than Spain, the shareholders of Spanish companies involved in a cross-border merger who have voted against the merger may exercise a right of separation and therefore request the redemption or acquisition of their shares or participations at their fair value (Art. 62 SAL).

VII Protection of creditors

32. The merger may not take place until one month has elapsed from the publication of the last announcement of the merger approval resolution or, in the event of written notice thereof to all shareholders and creditors, from the date of dispatch of the notice to the last of them.

33. During the month following the date of publication of the last announcement relating to the approval of the merger resolution or the last notice sent to the shareholders and creditors (see no. 26 of this chapter), creditors of each company involved in the merger whose credits arose prior to the date of publication of the draft terms of cross-border merger and remain outstanding at such time may object to the merger.

Creditors whose credits are sufficiently secured shall not be entitled to object to the merger (Art. 44 SAL).

Debenture holders may exercise their right to object to the merger in the same terms as the remaining creditors, unless the merger is approved by the general assembly of debenture holders.

34. In such cases where the creditors are entitled to object to the merger, the merger shall not be effective until the company provides security to the creditors' satisfaction or, otherwise, until notice should be given to such creditors of the execution of a joint and several guarantee in favour of the company by a credit institution duly entitled to provide it, for the amount of the credit held by the creditor, until expiration of the action to enforce such credit right.

VIII Employee participation

35. Employee participation rights, as provided in the Cross-border Merger Directive, have been implemented into Spanish law pursuant to the Law on Structural Amendments, which has introduced a new Title IV to Law 31/2006 of 18 October 2006 (Arts. 39 to 45).

36. As a general rule, Spanish law does not recognise employee participation rights (i.e. the right assisting employee representatives (i) to elect or designate

certain members of the management or supervisory body of the company or (ii) to recommend or object to the designation of a part or all members of the management or supervisory body). This right is only acknowledged to companies with a registered office in Spain where, meeting certain requirements, the company in question should be a European company or a company resulting from a cross-border merger within the EU.

In the event that the company resulting from the cross-border merger should have its registered office in Spain, the scope of employee participation rights shall be determined in accordance with Law 31/2006 of 18 October 2006; the application of the legislation of any other Member State where the company resulting from the merger or the companies involved in the merger should have any workplaces shall be excluded (Art. 39.2 EIL).

The regulation governing employee participation provided in Law 31/2006 of 18 October 2006 shall apply to companies resulting from the cross-border merger with a registered office in Spain in the following case: where at least one of the companies involved in the merger, during the six months prior to the publication of the draft terms of cross-border merger, employs an average number of employees greater than 500 and is managed with employee participation (Art. 39.1 EIL provides two residual instances).

37. Employee participation rights are the result of a negotiation between, on the one hand, a negotiating commission representing the employees and, on the other, the competent management bodies of the companies involved in the merger.

Notwithstanding the foregoing, the competent management bodies of the companies involved in the merger may choose the direct submission by the company resulting from the merger to the subsidiary rules concerning employee participation (see no. 39 of this chapter). In this case there will be no negotiation process and employee participation rights shall be as provided in the aforementioned subsidiary rules (Art. 40.1 EIL).

38. As a general rule, the members of the negotiating commission shall be elected in accordance with the respective domestic legislation and practice, in proportion to the number of employees employed in each Member State by the companies involved in the merger and their affected subsidiaries and workplaces, at a rate of one position for each 10 per cent or fraction thereof of the total number of employees in all Member States (Art. 7.1 EIL). Law 31/2006 of 18 October 2006 also includes measures to correct this rule, for the purpose of ensuring the representation of the employees of all companies subject to dissolution as a result of the merger in the negotiating commission (Arts. 7.2, 7.3 and 7.4 EIL).

39. If no agreement should be reached during the negotiation process (see no. 37 of this chapter), Law 31/2006 of 18 October 2006 sets forth certain subsidiary provisions concerning employee participation which, to summarise, entail the right of the employees of the company resulting from the merger to elect,

designate, recommend or object to the designation of a number of members of the company's management or supervision body equal to the highest proportion then in force in the companies involved in the merger prior to registration thereof (Art. 20.1b) EIL).

40. The subsidiary provisions regarding employee participation (see no. 39 above) shall apply when the negotiating commission and the competent bodies of the companies involved in the merger are unable to reach an agreement during the negotiation period (six months from the creation of the negotiating commission, which may be extended by another six months) provided that the following three circumstances apply:

(i) that the negotiating commission has not resolved not to begin negotiations or to end any negotiations already begun and to follow the employee participation rules currently applicable under Spanish law;
(ii) that the competent bodies of each of the companies involved in the merger decide to accept the application of the subsidiary provisions. If they should resolve not to accept the application thereof, the merger may not take place;
(iii) that, prior to the merger, an employee participation system should have been applied in one of the companies involved, affecting at least 33.3 per cent of the total number of employees of all companies involved, or a lower proportion, if so resolved by the negotiating commission.

IX Tax treatment

1 Implementation of the Merger Tax Directive in Spain

41. The current tax provisions related to cross-border mergers are set forth in the Merger Tax Directive (2009/133/EC) of 19 October 2009.

42. The Merger Tax Directive was first implemented in Spain through Law 29/1991, of 16 December 1991 (*Ley de adecuación de determinados conceptos impositivos a las Directivas y Reglamentos de las Comunidades Europeas*), which came into force on January 1992. After certain amendments to the relevant legislation, the tax provisions of the Merger Tax Directive are currently regulated in Chapter VIII of Title VII of the Royal Law Decree 4/2004 of 5 March 2004, approving the Spanish Corporate Income Tax Law (*Real Decreto Legislativo 4/2004, de 5 de marzo, por el que se aprueba el Texto Refundido de la Ley del Impuesto sobre Sociedades*) (the 'CIT Law').

43. On the implementation of the Merger Tax Directive, Spain went beyond EU requirements and extended the Merger Tax Directive rules not just to reorganisations carried out by EU resident companies but also to those taking place exclusively among Spanish companies and to those involving companies in non-EU Member States.

44. The objective of the Merger Tax Directive (and that of the special tax regime contained in the CIT Law) is to neutralise those tax costs that may represent an obstacle to corporate restructuring transactions (such as mergers, divisions, partial divisions, transfers of assets and exchanges of shares), which are regarded as necessary and beneficial for the domestic and EU economy. Such objective is achieved by allowing for the deferral of the tax due on capital gains which arise in connection with the restructuring transaction at the level of the companies involved and at the level of the shareholders of said companies as well, together with a general exemption on any indirect tax due.

45. The corporate documentation supporting the restructuring transaction must expressly include the option by the taxpayers involved for the application of the tax neutrality regime to the restructuring transaction. Additionally, such option must be notified to the Spanish tax authorities within three months following the registration of the relevant transaction in the Spanish Commercial Registry (i.e. no prior authorisation by the Spanish tax authorities is required in order to enjoy the benefits of the tax neutrality regime).

46. Finally, the CIT Law contains an anti-avoidance provision in accordance to which the tax neutrality system will not be applicable if the main purpose of the corporate restructuring transaction is tax avoidance. In particular, the tax neutrality regime will not be applicable when the restructuring transaction is not based upon sound commercial reasons (such as the reorganisation or rationalisation of the activities of the companies involved) but is carried out merely to obtain a tax advantage.

2 Definition of merger under the CIT Law

47. In accordance with the CIT Law (which, as said above, implements the Merger Tax Directive), a merger is an operation whereby:

(i) one or more entities, on being dissolved without going into liquidation, transfer all their assets and liabilities to another existing entity in exchange for the issue to their shareholders of securities representing the capital of that other company and, if applicable, a cash payment not exceeding 10 per cent of the nominal value, or in the absence of a nominal value, of the accounting par value of those securities;

(ii) two or more entities, on being dissolved without going into liquidation, transfer all their assets and liabilities to a new entity that they form, in exchange for the issue to their shareholders of securities representing the capital of that new entity and, if applicable, a cash payment not exceeding 10 per cent of the nominal value, or in the absence of a nominal value, of the accounting par value of those securities; or

(iii) an entity, on being dissolved without going into liquidation, transfers all its assets and liabilities to the company holding all the securities representing 100 per cent of its capital.

3 Taxation of the income generated on the merger

48. The income generated by the transferring entity as a result of the merger will not be subject to taxation in Spain provided that it refers to the following:

(i) Income arising from transfers by entities resident in Spain of assets and rights located therein. When the acquiring entity is resident outside of Spain, only the income deriving from a transfer of assets and rights that are allocated to a permanent establishment located in Spain shall be excluded from taxation.
(ii) Income arising from transfers by entities resident in Spain to entities resident in Spain of permanent establishments located outside of the EU.
(iii) Income arising from transfers by entities which are not resident in Spain of permanent establishments located in Spain. When the acquiring entity is resident outside of Spain, only the income deriving from a transfer of assets and rights that are allocated to a permanent establishment located in Spain shall be excluded from taxation.
(iv) Income arising from the transfer by entities resident in Spain of permanent establishments located in the EU to entities resident in the EU which take one of the forms set out in the Annex to the Merger Tax Directive and which are subject to and not exempt from one of the taxes mentioned in Article 3 of the Merger Tax Directive.

49. On the other hand, income generated by the shareholders of the merged entities will not be subject to Spanish taxation provided said shareholders are resident in Spain or in an EU Member State, or in any other state provided that, in the latter case, the acquiring entity is resident in Spain.

4 Tax value and acquisition date of the acquired assets and rights as well as of the securities issued to the shareholders of the transferring entity

50. Generally speaking, the assets and rights acquired by the acquiring company as a consequence of the merger will maintain for tax purposes the same value and acquisition date that they had in the transferring entity.

Similarly, the securities representing the capital of the acquiring entities allotted to the shareholders of the transferring entity will maintain for tax purposes the value and acquisition date of the securities transferred by said shareholders.

5 Indirect taxation consequences of the merger

51. In accordance with the provisions of Royal Law Decree 1/1993 of 24 September 1993, approving the Spanish Transfer and Stamp Taxes Law (*Real Decreto Legislativo 1/1993, de 24 de septiembre, por el que se aprueba el Texto Refundido de la Ley del Impuesto sobre Transmisiones Patrimoniales y Actos Jurídicos Documentados*), mergers (as defined in the CIT Law) will not

be subject to Spanish capital tax (*Impuesto sobre Operaciones Societarias*) and will be exempt from Spanish transfer tax (*Impuesto sobre Transmisiones Patrimoniales*) and Spanish stamp tax (*Impuesto sobre Actos Jurídicos Documentados*).

Finally, in accordance with Law 37/1992 of 28 December 1992, approving the Spanish Value Added Tax Law (*Ley del Impuesto sobre el Valor Añadido*), the merger will not be subject to Spanish value added tax since it entails the transfer of all the assets and liabilities of the transferring entity.

32

Sweden

JAN BERTIL ANDERSSON
Jönköping International Business School
Linköping University

I Introduction

1. The Cross-border Merger Directive has been implemented in Sweden by changes to the Swedish Companies Act of 2005 which came into force on 15 February 2008 (CA 2005). This Act amended the Companies Act by introducing a new section on cross-border mergers in the chapter 23 of the CA 2005 concerning merger of companies. It also to a large extent provides that the provisions applicable to domestic mergers also apply to cross-border mergers (see 23:36 CA 2005).

II Scope of the new rules

2. The rules on cross-border mergers apply to both public limited companies and private limited companies governed by the CA 2005. Furthermore, they apply

to any corresponding legal person which has its real seat within the European Economic Area (EEA). In the preliminary work preceding the implementation of the Tenth Company Law Directive the Swedish government discussed extensively which types of legal persons the rules on cross-border mergers apply to. The conclusion was that the Directive and thus the implemented rules must apply to the aforementioned companies (*privata och publika aktiebolag*), but also to Swedish mutual associations (*ekonomiska föreningar*).[1] Furthermore, the Swedish rules obviously apply to the European Company (SE) as well as the European Cooperative Society (SCE).

The rules for cross-border mergers involving mutual associations are found in the 1987 Act on mutual associations (*lag* [1987:667] *om ekonomiska föreningar*).

The Swedish legislation only allows mergers between business associations of the same kind with one exception (Art. 23:36 CA 2005). Thus, a cross-border merger which involves a Swedish company (public and private is considered the same for this purpose) is only allowed with an EEA company of the same kind. Furthermore, a Swedish mutual association may only participate in a cross-border merger with an EEA mutual association of the same kind. However, the Swedish legislation allows a merger between a mutual association which has a wholly owned subsidiary in the form of a company. Therefore, the same right to do a cross-border merger applies to a holding mutual association or subsidiary company which has its real seat within the EEA.

The cross-border rules do not apply to certain financial companies.

3. In the well known case of *SEVIC*[2] the court of the European Community found that national rules that only allow mergers between national companies and thereby hinder cross-border mergers under certain conditions might be contrary to the freedom of establishment. To the extent the Cross-border Merger Directive and national rules based thereon do not allow a cross-border merger between certain types of associations, such a merger may still be possible according to the *SEVIC* case, although the principles of this case are still to this day uncertain.

4. Swedish companies in liquidation can take part in a cross-border merger if the remaining assets have not been distributed among the shareholders at the time of the merger (Art. 23:4 and Art. 23:36 CA 2005).

III Consideration for shares

5. A cross-border merger is possible as long as the consideration to the shareholders in the company which will be dissolved includes at least more than 50 per cent shares in the acquiring company (Art. 23:2 and Art. 23:36 CA 2005).

1 However, two particular type of mutual association may not participate in cross-border mergers: mutual associations with the purpose of owning houses for living (*bostadsrättsföreningar*) and cooperative tenant associations (*kooperativa hyresgästföreningar*).

2 European Court of Justice, 13 December 2005, Case C411/03 ('*SEVIC*').

IV Legal consequences and enforceability of a cross-border merger

6. A cross-border merger results in all assets and liabilities being transferred to the surviving entity by operation of law, without liquidation of the participating companies, where the shareholders of the dissolving company receive shares in the acquiring company. It has the same legal effects as an internal (domestic) merger under the Merger Directive, i.e.:

(i) the participating companies (with the exception of the surviving company if no new company is established) cease to exist;
(ii) the shareholders of the companies which cease to exist become shareholders in the surviving company; and
(iii) all assets and liabilities, including rights and obligations, are transferred to the surviving company (Art. 23:1 and Art. 23:36 CA 2005).

7. A cross-border merger has legal effect from the date which has been fixed by the state where the acquiring company will have its real seat. If the acquiring company will have its real seat in Sweden the merger will have legal effect on the date when the merger is registered in the Swedish company register (Art. 23:49 CA 2005). The registration of the merger is enforceable against third parties as from the publication date of the merger in the Swedish State Gazette, unless the company can prove that the third parties in question knew of the merger earlier. For fifteen days following publication, third parties can claim that the merger is not enforceable against them if they can prove that it was impossible for them to have known of it (Art. 27:4 CA 2005).

V Procedure

1 Draft terms of cross-border merger

8. The management organs of the merging companies – in the Swedish company the board of directors – shall prepare draft terms of the cross-border merger. The board of directors of the Swedish company shall sign the draft plan (Art. 23:37 CA 2005).

This document need not to be in notarised form. The draft terms should include the information described in no. 18 of Chapter 1 of the first volume of this book. In the event a parent company merges with its wholly owned subsidiary, the information mentioned in Chapter 1, no. 39 can be omitted.

Failure to include the above-mentioned information can lead to liability for damages for members of the management organ, i.e., the directors or managers, depending on the type of company (Art. 29:1 CA 2005).

9. The draft terms of cross-border merger must be filed by the participating Swedish companies with the Swedish Companies Registration Office (*Bolagsverket*) to be registered in the Swedish company register. This must be done within one month from the date the plan was drafted. If several Swedish

companies participate in the cross-border merger, the acquiring Swedish company must register the draft. If the acquiring company is not a Swedish company, the oldest of the Swedish companies must register the draft (Art. 23:14 and Art. 23:42 CA 2005).

2 Board of directors' report

10. The board of directors of each merging company must prepare a written and justified report to the company's shareholders. This report should provide a legal and economic explanation and justification for the reasons for the merger as well as an explanation of how the ratio for the exchange of securities and shares representing capital and the amount of any cash payment have been decided. Furthermore, the report must contain a statement on the merger's consequences for shareholders, creditors and employees. In the event the trade unions prepare an opinion on the merger and this opinion is submitted to management in a timely manner, it must be attached to the management report.

3 Auditor's report

11. The auditor of each participating company should prepare a report on the draft terms of the cross-border merger as well as the report by the board of directors.

12. In its report the auditor should certify whether, in its opinion, the share exchange ratio is relevant and reasonable. The auditor's report should at least (i) indicate the methods used to determine the share exchange ratio; (ii) indicate whether these methods are appropriate in the case at hand and mention the resulting value yielded by each method; and (iii) give an opinion on the relative importance of each method in determining the value eventually retained. The report should, furthermore, indicate the particular difficulties, if any, encountered in the valuation process (Art. 23:11 and Art. 23:36 CA 2005).

In order to prepare its report, the auditor may request from the merging companies any information deemed necessary (Art. 23:13 and Art. 23:36 CA 2005).

13. The auditor's report must be made available to the shareholders of the merging companies at the latest one month before the general meeting called to approve the draft terms of the cross-border merger (see no. 14 of this chapter for more details). It must not be made public otherwise.

4 General meeting of shareholders

A Information for shareholders

14. The draft terms of cross-border merger, the board of directors' report and the auditor's report shall be available to the shareholders, trade union representatives who represents employees, and employees who are not represented by any

union. These documents must be made available at the latest one month before the general meeting where the shareholders are called to vote on the draft terms of the cross-border merger. The shareholders have the right to obtain the documents without cost and the documents should also be sent to them without cost as long as they provide a postal address (Art. 23:43 CA 2005).

B Shareholder approval

15. As regards Swedish participating companies, the draft terms of the cross-border merger must be approved by the general meeting of shareholders. However, for the absorption of a wholly owned subsidiary by its parent company, shareholder approval is not required at the level of the subsidiary (Art. 23:51 CA 2005).

16. In order to approve the cross-border merger, the merger must be approved by a qualified majority of two-thirds of the votes represented and cast; the articles may provide for a larger majority. If there are different classes of shares, i.e. shares with different rights, the qualified majority requirements must be met for each class of shares.

17. The general meeting of a merging company may decide to make its decision subject to express ratification of the arrangements with respect to the participation of employees in the company resulting from the merger by a later shareholder meeting (Art. 23:44 CA 2005).

18. If any of the shareholder meetings which have to approve the cross-border merger do not approve the draft plan of the merger in full, the merger cannot proceed (Art. 23:18 and Art. 23:36 CA 2005).

19. The general meeting of each Swedish participating company must not be held before a notary, but there must be a protocol of the shareholders' meeting.

5 Application for merger to take effect and merger certificate

20. The application for the cross-border merger to enter into effect must be filed by the participating Swedish company with the Swedish Companies Registration Office (*Bolagsverket*). This must be done within one month from the date the plan was approved by the shareholders' meeting. If several Swedish companies participate in the cross-border merger, the acquiring Swedish company must register the application. If the acquiring company is not a Swedish company, the oldest of the Swedish companies must register the application (Art. 23:20 and Art. 23:45 CA 2005).

21. When there is a legally binding decision to give effect to the cross-border merger according to Swedish law and the participating companies have done what is required of them by the CA 2005, the Swedish Companies Registration Office shall for each participating company issue a cross-border merger certificate which expresses that the merger procedure has been followed in accordance

with Swedish law. Such a certificate shall not, however, be issued if the cross-border merger has been challenged in a Swedish court and the case has not been finally resolved (Art. 23:46 CA 2005).

6 Effects of the decision

22. A cross-border merger only enters into effect on the date which has been ascertained by the state where the acquiring company will have its real seat. If the acquiring company will have its real seat in Sweden the merger is legally effective on the date it is registered in the company register by the Swedish Companies Registration Office. The application must be made by the board of directors of the acquiring company no later than six months after the date of the issue of the cross-border merger certificate (Art. 23:48–49 CA 2005).

VI Minority shareholders

23. A decision to carry out a cross-border merger approved by the majority discussed under no. 16 of this chapter is binding on the company's minority shareholders. They have no choice but to go along with the merger and will receive shares in the surviving or new company. Swedish law does not provide for any special remedies for minority shareholders unless any of the dissolving companies is a public company and the acquiring company is a private company in which case the merger must be approved by all shareholders present at the shareholders' meeting representing at least nine-tenths of all the shares in the company. The same rule applies if any of the dissolving companies is a public company and its shares are traded on a regulated market inside the EEA or equivalent market outside the EEA and the consideration for the shares is shares which are not traded on such a market (Art. 23:17 and Art. 23:36 CA 2005). However, the aforementioned minority protection applies to all mergers, i.e. also domestic mergers.

VII Protection of creditors

24. Creditors of the merging companies whose claims existed prior to the approval of the merger have the right to be informed of the merger. Such notice must be sent by each of the participating companies to all known creditors and shall state that the company will seek approval of the cross-border merger to take effect and that the creditors are entitled to oppose the merger (Art. 23:19 and Art. 23:36 CA 2005).

25. The Swedish Companies Registration Office shall, after the participating companies have made the application to give effect to the cross-border merger, summon the participating companies' creditors. The creditors may oppose the merger and require the claim to be settled in advance or ask for security for their claim. In the event of a dispute, the matter shall be referred to the court.

The court shall approve the application if the company has satisfied those creditors who opposed the merger (Art. 23:22–24 and Art. 23:36 CA 2005).

VIII Employee participation

26. With respect to employee participation, the Cross-border Merger Directive has been implemented in Swedish law by the 2008 Act concerning employee participation in cross-border mergers (*lag* ([2008:9] *om arbetstagares medverkan vid gränsöverskridande fusioner*).

IX Tax treatment

27. Sweden has implemented the Merger Tax Directive (2009/133/EC) of 19 October 2009.

PART VI

Application in the EEA Member States

33

Iceland

ÓLAFUR ARINBJÖRN SIGURÐSSON
LOGOS

I Introduction

1. The Cross-border Merger Directive has been implemented in Iceland by Act No. 54/2007. The Act amends the Act on Public Limited Companies No. 2/1995, the Act on Private Limited Companies No. 138/1994, the Act on Cooperatives No. 22/1991 and the Act on Non-Profit Organisations Engaged in Business Operations No. 33/1999. Since public limited companies and private limited companies are more common than other Icelandic companies that may be subject to cross-border merger, this section only refers to provisions of law governing the said type of companies.

II Scope of the new rules

2. The rules on cross-border mergers apply to all limited liability companies, i.e. public limited-liability companies (*hlutafélög*) (hf), partnerships limited by shares (*samlagshlutafélög*) and private limited liability companies (*einkahlutafélög*) (ehf). The rules also apply to all other companies that are subject to private law, including cooperatives (*samvinnufélög*) (svf) and entities that are subject to public law, including non-profit organisations engaged in business operations (*sjálfseignarstofnanir sem stunda atvinnurekstur*). Under Icelandic law all companies that can participate in a domestic merger are to be able to participate in a cross-border merger.

III Legal consequences and enforceability of a cross-border merger

3. Under Icelandic company law, cross-border merger means a merger where merger companies are subject to the legislation of at least two states in the European Economic Area, a Member State of the Convention Establishing the European Free Trade Association or the Faroe Islands as well as other countries in accordance with authority contained in Regulations laid down by the Minister of Economic Affairs in consultation with the Minister of Finance. The legal effects of a cross-border merger are the same as of a domestic merger, i.e.:

(i) one company is entirely merged with another company by means of takeover of assets and liabilities (merger by takeover); and
(ii) two or more companies merge into a new company (merger with the establishment of a new company) (Art. 119 Act on Public Limited Companies/Art. 94 Act on Private Limited Companies).

4. Upon completion of all necessary pre-merger acts and formalities the Icelandic Register of Enterprises will forthwith issue a certificate thereon to the merger company or companies being subject to Icelandic law (Art. 133(1) Act on Public Limited Companies/Art. 107(1) of the Act on Private Limited Companies). A cross-border merger where the company continuing operations is subject to Icelandic law has effect as from the date when the Icelandic Register of Enterprises registers the merger (Art. 133(4) Act on Public Limited Companies/Art. 107(4) Act on Private Limited Companies). If a company continuing operations following a cross-border merger shall not be subject to Icelandic law the Icelandic Register of Enterprises registers the implementation of the cross-border merger for the companies ceasing operations but being subject to Icelandic law at the time the Register has received a notification from the register in the country where the company continues operations.

IV Procedure

1 Merger schedule

5. The board of directors of the merging companies shall jointly prepare and sign a merger schedule which shall contain information and provisions concerning the following:

(i) the names and forms of the companies, i.e. whether a name or a conceivable foreign byname shall be maintained as an extra name of the takeover company;
(ii) the companies' address;
(iii) remuneration for the shares in the company which will be taken over;
(iv) as of which time the shares which are conceivably handed over as payment grant the right to dividend and special conditions pertaining to that right;
(v) which rights in the takeover company are obtained by conceivable owners of shares and bonds with special rights in the company which is taken over;
(vi) other conceivable arrangements for the benefit of the owners of the shares and bonds referred to in item (v);
(vii) delivery of share certificates in respect of shares delivered in lieu of payment;
(viii) as of which time limit the rights and duties of the company which has been taken over shall in terms of accounting be considered to have ceased;
(ix) some special arrangements which directors, managers and members of a representative committee, assessors and supervisory parties of the companies enjoy;
(x) draft articles of association if a new company is to be formed upon the merger (Art. 120 Act on Public Limited Companies/Art. 95 Act on Private Limited Companies).

Furthermore, a merger schedule, in respect to a cross-border merger, shall contain information concerning the likely effects of the merger on the company's activities (Art. 133(b) Act on Public Limited Companies/Art. 107(b) Act on Private Limited Companies).

2 Statement of the board of directors

6. The board of directors of each of the companies shall prepare a statement wherein the merger schedule is explained and substantiated. The statement shall deal with the economic and legal reasons forming the basis of the merger schedule as well as the determination of remuneration for the shares, including specific difficulties in connection with the decision.

An audited joint balance sheet and profit and loss account shall be attached to the statement showing the entire assets and liabilities of each individual company, the changes which the merger is considered to entail and a draft commencement balance sheet of the takeover company. The layout of the joint balance sheet and profit and loss account for the companies shall be based on the date of settlement which may not be more than six months prior to signatures being affixed to the merger schedule (Art. 121 Act on Public Limited Companies/Art. 96 Act on Private Limited Companies).

Furthermore, in respect to a cross-border merger, the statement of the board of directors shall also contain information on the merger's effect on the company's shareholders, creditors and employees (Art. 133(c) Act on Public Limited Companies/Art. 107(c) Act on Private Limited Companies).

3 Specialist assessor's report

7. Each participating company that is a limited liability company shall have one or more impartial specialist assessors render a report on the merger schedule (Art. 122(1) Act on Public Limited Companies/Art. 97(1) Act on Private Limited Companies). The assessors are to be either state-authorised public accountants, attorneys at law or other specially qualified persons who are appointed by a court of law in the relevant company's venue. In case a participating company is a private limited liability company, a state-authorised public accountant or an inspector shall render a report on the merger schedule (Art. 97 Act on Private Limited Companies). Both in the case of public and private limited companies, the companies may have one or more joint assessors, auditors or inspectors.

The specialist report shall contain a declaration stating to what extent the remuneration for the shares in the company which is taken over is reasonable and substantiated. The declaration shall describe the method or methods which were used upon determining the remuneration and include an assessment as to whether the method or methods were adequate in this instance. Furthermore, the declaration shall specify the price to which each method individually leads as well as which internal interpretation shall be applied to methods upon the determination of prices. In case the determination of price has been subject to special difficulties these shall be specified in the declaration (Art. 122(3) Act on Public Limited Companies/Art. 97(3) Act on Private Limited Companies).

If all shareholders in the companies participating in the merger so approve, the preparation of a specialist assessor report can be avoided. However, a declaration shall always be made stating to what extent the merger may diminish the possibilities of creditors for recourse in the individual companies participating in the merger (Art. 122(4) and (5) Act on Public Limited Companies/Art. 97(4) Act on Private Limited Companies).

4 Notification to Register of Enterprises

8. Not later than one month following signing of a merger schedule each participating merger company shall send to the Icelandic Register of Enterprises a copy of the schedule certified by the company's board of directors. Simultaneously there shall also be sent to the Register the specialist assessor's declaration referred to in Section 3 above (Art. 123(1) Act on Public Limited Companies/ Art. 98(1) Act on Private Limited Companies).

9. Information on the receipt of documents referred to in no. 8 shall be published in the Icelandic Legal Gazette *(Lögbirtingablaðið)*. In case assessors do in their declaration consider that the merger may diminish the possibilities of creditors for recourse notification shall contain information pertaining thereto and the attention of creditors shall be directed to their rights (Art. 123(2) Act on Public Limited Companies/Art. 98(2) Act on Private Limited Companies).

10. The Register of Enterprises shall, at the expense of the notifying party, have published in the Legal Gazette the main subject of that which has been recorded, e.g. specialised assessor's declaration, about creditors' inferior possibilities of achieving recourse due to a merger schedule. With respect to public limited companies, in case of reference to the aforementioned special assessor's declaration, the attention of creditors shall be alerted to their right to security in accordance with Article 126 of the Act on Public Limited Companies and Article 101 of the Act on Private Limited Companies. In other instances, the Register of Enterprises can arrange for the publication of more than a reference in the main subject of an extraordinary announcement if it deems this necessary (Art. 151(1) Act on Public Limited Companies/Art. 124(1) Act on Private Limited Companies).

11. That which has been recorded and published in the Legal Gazette shall be considered to be known to a person, unless circumstances be such that he may be deemed to have been unaware thereof and unable to know about it. The provisions of the first sentence do not, however, apply to arrangements which are made within sixteen days following upon publication if the person concerned proves that he has been unable to acquire knowledge about that which was published (Art. 151(2) Act on Public Limited Companies/Art. 124(2) Act on Private Limited Companies).

12. In case publication in the Legal Gazette has not been undertaken, notice will not be valid except for those who may be proved to have been aware thereof (Art. 151(3) Act on Public Limited Companies/Art. 124(3) Act on Private Limited Companies).

13. In case of lack of conformity between that which is recorded and that which is published in the Legal Gazette the relevant company cannot plead the published text vis-à-vis a third person. The third person may, on the other hand,

plead the published text vis-à-vis the company, unless it be proved that such person has been aware of that which was recorded (Art. 151(4) Act on Public Limited Companies/Art. 124(4) Act on Private Limited Companies).

5 Decision on the merger

A The decision in respect to a company which is taken over

14. A decision concerning merger of a company which has been taken over will be made by a shareholders' meeting. A decision on a merger will become valid only provided it obtains the approval of a minimum of two-thirds of the votes cast and also the approval of shareholders controlling at least two-thirds of the share capital in respect of which votes are wielded at the shareholders' meeting. In case an Icelandic participating company is subject to winding-up proceedings, a merger may be decided upon only provided allocation to shareholders has not been commenced and that the shareholders' meeting simultaneously decides that the work of the winding-up committee shall cease (Art. 124(1) Act on Public Limited Companies/Art. 99(1) Act on Private Limited Companies).

B The decision in respect to the takeover company

15. A decision on a merger in an Icelandic takeover company will be made by the board of directors of such company, unless a shareholders' meeting need effect amendments to the articles of association in other respects than that which pertains to the name of the takeover company. A shareholders' meeting will furthermore make a decision if shareholders holding 5 per cent or more of the share capital so require in writing within two weeks as of the time the receipt of a merger schedule has been announced in the Legal Gazette. In such an instance a decision on a merger will become valid only provided it obtains the approval of a minimum of two-thirds of the votes cast and also the approval of shareholders controlling at least two-thirds of the share capital in respect of which votes are wielded at the shareholders' meeting. The company's board of directors will call a shareholders' meeting within two weeks of the receipt of the requirement (Art. 124(2) Act on Public Limited Companies/Art. 99(2) Act on Private Limited Companies).

16. In the Icelandic participating takeover company a shareholders' meeting will decide upon the merger if the shareholders, in accordance with the company's articles of association, and in conformity with the provisions of the company legislation which allows shareholders to require a shareholders' meeting, request this (Art. 124(3) Act on Public Limited Companies/Art. 99(3) Act on Private Limited Companies).

C The timing of the shareholders' meeting

17. A shareholders' meeting in an Icelandic participating company may at the earliest be held a month following upon the publication of a notice of the receipt of

the merger plan and the special assessor's declaration in the Legal Gazette and no later than four months following upon the publication. In case the merger is not approved on the basis of such a merger plan or the meeting is not held within the time limit as per the first sentence the merger plan is deemed to be dismissed (Art. 124(4) Act on Public Limited Companies/Art. 99 (4) Act on Private Limited Companies).

D Information for shareholders and creditors

18. At the latest a month prior to the shareholders' meeting in an Icelandic participating company the following documents shall be submitted for inspection by shareholders at the offices of each individual merger company and furthermore handed to each registered shareholder free of charge upon request:

(i) a merger schedule;
(ii) annual accounts of all the merger companies covering the immediate past three years or a shorter period if the company has been operated more briefly;
(iii) balance sheet and profit and loss account in respect of the past portion of the current fiscal year prior to a commencement balance sheet being prepared for the takeover company;
(iv) statement by the board of directors, i.e. a balance sheet and profit and loss account and a commencement balance sheet;
(v) special assessor's report and declaration (Art. 124(5) Act on Public Limited Companies/Art. 99 (5) Act on Private Limited Companies).

19. Creditors that so request shall obtain information on the date when decision on the merger will be taken (Art. 124(5) Act on Public Limited Companies/Art. 99 (5) Act on Private Limited Companies).

6 Minority shareholders

20. Upon a cross-border merger shareholders in the Icelandic participating company or companies being merged with others, having at a shareholders' meeting voted against the merger with takeover or merger with the establishment of a new company, are entitled to claim that the company redeems its shares, provided that this be required within a month after a shareholders' meeting (Art. 133(e)(1) Act on Public Limited Companies/Art. 107(f)(1) Act on Private Limited Companies). In case it has been requested of shareholders prior to the voting that those wishing to avail themselves of the right of redemption indicate their will in that respect this is then subject to the condition that the parties concerned have given a declaration accordingly at the shareholders' meeting. The company shall purchase the shares from them at a price corresponding to the value thereof and, in case there is not a question of an accord, this shall be fixed by special assessors appointed by a court of law in the company's venue. Either party may consult courts of law about the special assessor's decision.

Legal action must be taken within three months of the time an assessment has been undertaken (Art. 131 Act on Public Limited Companies/Art. 106 Act on Private Limited Companies).

21. Only when a satisfactory security has been pledged in respect of the value of shares in accordance with Article 133(e)(1) of the Act on Public Limited Companies and Article 107(f)(1) of the Act on Private Limited Companies, the Register of Enterprises may issue a certificate to the effect that all necessary pre-merger acts and formalities have been completed (Art. 133(f) Act on Public Limited Companies/Art. 107(g) Act on Private Limited Companies). Special assessors appointed by a court of law at the company's venue will determine whether the security be sufficient. In case the special assessor's decision is referred to a court of law the institution of legal proceedings will not prevent the Register of Enterprises from issuing a certificate as per Article 133(f) of the Act on Public Limited Companies and Article 107(g) of the Act on Private Limited Companies unless the court of law rules otherwise (Art. 133(e)(2) Act on Public Limited Companies and Art. 107(f)(2) Act on Private Limited Companies).

7 Effects of the decision

22. Upon completion of all necessary pre-merger acts and formalities the Register of Enterprises will forthwith issue a certificate thereon to the merger company or companies being subject to Icelandic law (Art. 133(f)(1) Act on Public Limited Companies/Art. 107(g)(1) Act on Private Limited Companies).

23. If a company continuing operations following a cross-border merger shall be subject to Icelandic law, a certificate concerning each merger company from the registers of the foreign companies shall be sent to the Register of Enterprises. The certificate shall constitute final evidence to the effect that all necessary pre-merger acts and formalities in the country concerned have been completed and that the foreign register will register the merger as it pertains to the company ceasing operations, after the receipt of notification from the Icelandic Register of Enterprises. Upon receipt of the certificates concerning all the merger companies, the Register of Enterprises will register the implementation of the cross-border merger for the company continuing operations (Art. 133(f)(2) Act on Public Limited Companies/Art. 107(g)(2) Act on Private Limited Companies).

24. If a company continuing operations following upon a cross-border merger shall be subject to Icelandic law the Register of Enterprises will notify the registers where other merger companies are registered as soon as possible when the implementation of a cross-border merger concerning the company continuing operations has been registered (Art. 133(f)(2) Act on Public Limited Companies/Art. 107(g)(2) Act on Private Limited Companies).

25. A cross-border merger where the company continuing operations shall be subject to Icelandic law has effect as from the date when the Register of Enterprises registers the merger (Art. 133(f)(3) Act on Public Limited Companies/Art. 107(g)(3) Act on Private Limited Companies).

26. If a company continuing operations following a cross-border merger shall not be subject to Icelandic law, the Register of Enterprises registers the implementation of the cross-border merger for the companies ceasing operations but being subject to Icelandic law at the time the Register has received an identical notification from the foreign register concerned about the company continuing operations.

V Employee participation

27. With respect to employee participation, Article 16 of the Cross-border Merger Directive has been implemented in Icelandic law by the Act on Employee Participation in respect to Cross-Border Mergers of Limited Liability Companies No. 86/2009 (the 'Employee Participation Act'), which entered into force on 18 August 2009.

1 Employee participation in companies established in Iceland resulting from a cross-border merger

28. Iceland has implemented Directive 94/45/EC on the establishment of a European Works Council in legislation by Act No. 61/1999. In addition, Directive 2001/86/EC supplementing the Statute for a European Company with regard to the involvement of employees, has been implemented into Icelandic law by Act No. 27/2004. Furthermore, Directive 2003/72/EC on the European Cooperative Society was implemented into Icelandic law by Act No. 44/2007. Otherwise, Icelandic law does not provide for employee participation rights or the right for employees to sit on the board of directors of limited liability companies.

2 Special negotiating body ('SNB')

29. Where the rules in force concerning employee participation, if any, in the Member State where the company resulting from the cross-border merger has its registered office are set aside, a special negotiating body ('SNB') must be set up with a view to negotiating arrangements on employee participation in the company resulting from the cross-border merger with the management organs of the participating companies (Art. 16(3) Directive).

30. The Employee Participation Act provides specific rules for the appointment of the Icelandic member(s) of the SNB (Art. 6 Employee Participation Act).

In general, such member(s) are appointed by trade union representatives. Employees that are not represented by trade unions shall choose a representative that will participate in the election of the SNB. The voting power of the persons that have the right to elect a representative on the SNB depends on the number of employees behind them.

3 Protection of employee representatives

31. Article 18 of the Employee Participation Act stipulates that the representatives in the SNB shall not be subject to dismissal or reduction of their employment remuneration. In addition, such representatives shall have the right to leave from their employment so they can pursue their duties in respect to the SNB.

VI Tax treatment[1]

32. The Merger Tax Directive does not apply in Iceland and, furthermore, Iceland has not implemented into the Icelandic Income Tax Act no. 90/2003 any specific rules to deal with the cross-border mergers provided for in company law.

33. Practice indicates there can be hurdles as regards tax neutrality in cross-border reorganisations. There are strong legal arguments in favour of existing Icelandic tax rules being applied in the same manner as domestically to achieve tax neutral cross-border mergers. Such arguments are mainly based on the fundamental freedoms as extended to apply to Iceland by means of the EEA Agreement. Court practice indicates that Icelandic courts could opt for such a position while administrative practice on cross-border mergers indicates there are problem areas.

34. Provided that the domestic tax merger rules will be applied to cross-border mergers the following conditions must be met in order to be eligible for tax neutrality:

(i) the absorbing or receiving company must be a resident or an intra-EEA company;
(ii) the transaction must be carried out in accordance with Icelandic and foreign company law;
(iii) the shareholders in the absorbed company only receive shares in the new company but no cash payment;
(iv) the transaction may not have as its principal objective, or as one of its principal objectives, tax evasion or tax avoidance.

1 This part has been written by Jon Elvar Gudmundsson, a tax partner at LOGOS legal services.

34

Liechtenstein

ALEXANDER APPEL, MORITZ BLASY
Walch & Schurti

I Introduction

1. The Cross-border Merger Directive has been implemented in Liechtenstein by (i) the Act on the Amendment of the Persons and Companies Act[1] and (ii) the

1 Gesetz vom 16. September 2009 über die Abänderung des Personen- und Gesellschaftsrechts, LGBl. 2009/268.

Act on Employee Participation in Case of a Cross-border Merger of Limited Liability Companies ('FMG').[2]

The Act on the Amendment of the Persons and Companies Act introduced a new subsection on cross-border mergers into the section on (national) mergers of corporations as provided for in the Persons and Companies Act ('PGR'). This new sub-section on cross-border mergers consists of ten articles (Art. 352a to Art. 352k PGR) and is based on the general principle that the provisions on national mergers also apply with regard to cross-border mergers, if not stipulated otherwise in the new subsection on cross-border mergers (Art. 352b PGR).

The Directive's provisions on employee participation have been transposed by the Liechtenstein legislator by passing the FMG, a new (separate) law.

II Scope of the new rules

2. Pursuant to the new Article 352a PGR, the new sub-section on cross-border mergers applies only with regard to mergers between Liechtenstein corporations (*Aktiengesellschaften*) and limited liability companies which have been formed in accordance with the law of a Member State of the European Economic Area ('EEA') and which have their registered office, central administration or principal place of business within the EEA. Notably, the new sub-section on cross-border mergers does neither apply with regard to the Liechtenstein private limited company (*Gesellschaft mit beschränkter Haftung*) nor with regard to the Liechtenstein establishment (*Anstalt*).[3] Further, the new rules on cross-border mergers do not apply in relation to investment undertakings (funds) in terms of the Investment Undertakings Act.[4]

III Cash payment

3. In accordance with the new Article 352b PGR, the new subsection on cross-border mergers even applies to cross-border mergers if the law of at least one of the other involved EEA Member States allows an additional cash payment to exceed 10 per cent of the nominal value, or, in the absence of such nominal value, of the accounting par value of the shares or stakes in the capital of the company resulting from the cross-border merger (Art. 352b PGR).

Under the existing Liechtenstein national merger rules, mergers involving a cash payment exceeding 10 per cent of the nominal value cannot benefit from the rules applicable to mergers (Art. 351(1) PGR). As a consequence,

2 Gesetz vom 16. September 2009 über die Mitbestimmung der Arbeitnehmer bei einer grenzüberschreitenden Fusion von Kapitalgesellschaften, LGBl. 2009/269.

3 The Liechtenstein establishment (*Anstalt*) is a very flexible legal form unique to Liechtenstein which can be structured like a limited liability company.

4 Gesetz vom 19. Mai 2005 über Investmentunternehmen, LGBl. 2005/156.

a cross-border merger involving a Liechtenstein corporation can contain a cash payment exceeding 10 per cent of the nominal value only if the foreign law applicable to one of the other participating companies allows such cash payment.

IV Legal consequences

4. Like a national merger, a cross-border merger results in all assets and liabilities of the disappearing company(ies) being transferred to the surviving company (in case of a merger by takeover) or to the new company (in case of a merger by incorporation of a new company) *ex lege* and without liquidation of the participating companies (*Prinzip der Universalsukzession*). The shareholders of the company(ies) which cease(s) to exist become shareholders either of the surviving company (in case of a merger by takeover) or of the new incorporated company (in case of a merger by incorporation of a new company).

V Procedure

1 General

5. As already mentioned above, the general rules[5] regarding national mergers (Arts. 351 ff. PGR) are also applicable on cross-border mergers. This fundamental principle, as set forth in Article 4(1) of the Cross-border Merger Directive and as implemented by Article 352b PGR, applies in particular in relation to the procedure of a cross-border merger.

2 Draft terms of cross-border merger

6. Under Liechtenstein law, the draft terms of cross-border merger (*Fusionsplan*) must not only contain the information required by the general rules on national mergers (Art. 351a PGR) but in addition the specific information requested by Article 352c PGR. Therefore, the terms of cross-border merger must disclose the following:

(i) the legal type, the name and the registered seats of both the merging companies and the company resulting from the merger;
(ii) the agreement regarding the transfer of the assets of each transferring company to the absorbing company against the granting of shares in the absorbing company;
(iii) the ratio of shares to be exchanged and, if applicable, the amount of the cash payment;

5 For the purpose of this publication the general rules for mergers by takeover are described. However, for mergers in the course of which a new company is created the general rules are partly modified (cf. Art. 352 PGR).

(iv) the details for the transfer of shares of the absorbing company; the target date from which these shares entitle to a portion of the profits including all particular details in this regard as well as the target date from which any actions of the transferring company qualify as to be made for the account of the absorbing company;
(v) the rights which the absorbing company grants to single shareholders with special rights and to owners of other securities;
(vi) each particular advantage granted to a member of the administration or management of the companies involved in the merger or to an expert (auditor);
(vii) the prospective implications of the cross-border merger on employment;
(viii) the articles of the company resulting from the cross-border merger;
(ix) if applicable, detailed information on the procedure relating to participation of the employees;
(x) information regarding the value of the assets and liabilities which are conferred to the corporation resulting from the cross-border merger;
(xi) the target date of the annual accounts of the companies involved in the cross-border merger which are used to determine the conditions of such merger.

7. According to Article 351a sec. 3 PGR the terms of cross-border merger require the form of a public deed (*öffentliche Beurkundung*). In practice, an authorised official of the Liechtenstein Public Registry (*Grundbuch- und Öffentlichkeitsregisteramt*) usually draws up such public deed.

8. The publication notice of the draft terms of cross-border merger must in addition (i.e. besides the information requested by Art. 351 sec. 1 PGR) contain the following information:

(i) the legal form, name and registered seat of each of the merging companies;
(ii) the name/title of the register with which the documents to be disclosed for each of the merging companies need to be lodged in accordance with Article 3 sec. 2 of EU Directive 68/151/EWG as well as the pertinent registration numbers; and
(iii) for each of the merging companies information regarding the modalities for the creditors (and if applicable, for the minority shareholders) to exercise their rights, as well as the address under which complete information for these modalities can be obtained free of charge.

In Liechtenstein such publication notice has to be made in the public legal gazettes.

9. Article 352i PGR prohibits the exchange of shares in certain cases. According to this provision shares in the absorbing company cannot be exchanged against shares in the transferring company if such shares are held by:

(i) the absorbing company itself or by a person acting in its own name but for the account of the person acting for the absorbing company; or
(ii) the transferring company itself or by a person acting in its own name but for the account of the transferring company.

3 Management report

10. In accordance with Article 352d PGR the board of directors has to render a report (*Fusionsbericht*) to the general meeting of shareholders in which the board explains and gives reasons for the legal and economic aspects of the merger, in particular the implications to the shareholders, the creditors and the employees. Furthermore, this report must also comment on the terms of the merger and the ratio by which the shares are exchanged. Should particular difficulties in the evaluation of the shares arise, the report must include a specific reference in this regard (Art. 351b PGR).

This report must be made available to the shareholders and the employees' representatives or, in the absence of such, to the employees directly at the latest one month prior to the date of the general shareholders' meeting. The board of each merging company is obligated to add to this report any comments which have been submitted timely by the employees' representatives.

4 Report of the independent experts

11. For each of the involved companies an independent expert must examine the terms of the merger (*Fusionsplan*). The board is in charge to appoint such expert. It is sufficient if one expert carries out the examination for all involved companies if the boards of all these companies submit a joint application to the Public Register in which they request for this very expert to be appointed.

The expert report, which can also be submitted jointly, must contain a conclusion as to whether or not the ratio to exchange the shares proposed by the board is appropriate. In this context, the methods according to which such ratio has been identified and the grounds on which the application of such methods is appropriate must be disclosed. If several methods have been applied the report inter alia must disclose which ratio of exchange would be ascertained under the application of these various efforts (Art. 351c sec. 4 PGR).

5 Shareholder approval

12. Each participating company must file with the Public Registry the terms of merger at least one month prior to its general shareholders' meeting which shall approve the merger. Furthermore, such filing must be published by the Public Registry in accordance with Article 958 sec. 2 PGR.

In addition, each participating company must keep at least one month prior to the aforementioned shareholder meeting at its seat the following documents for inspection:

(i) the terms of merger;
(ii) for the last three business years the annual accounts and annual reports of all companies involved in the merger;
(iii) if the last annual accounts refer to a business year that has expired more than six months prior to the execution of the terms of merger, a balance sheet to a target date which does not lie prior to the first day of the third month which precedes the *Zwischenbilanz*;
(iv) the management report(s); and
(v) the report of the independent expert.

For the interim balance sheet specific regulations apply (Art. 351d sec. 3 PGR).

Shareholders are entitled to request that the corporation provides them without delay and free of charge with a copy of the aforementioned documents.

13. For the necessary shareholder approval the following general rules apply:

In accordance with Article 351e PGR the terms of merger and the possibly required amendments to the articles only become effective if the general meeting of shareholders of each merging company consents thereto separately. Such shareholder resolution requires a majority of at least two-thirds of the represented share capital. If at least 50 per cent of the share capital is validly represented a simple majority of votes is sufficient provided that the articles do not provide for a higher quorum (Art. 351e sec. 2 PGR).

14. However, the approval by the general meeting of shareholders of the absorbing company is not required if

(i) the terms of cross-border merger are made by the absorbing company at least one month prior to the shareholder meeting of the transferring company which shall resolve on the terms of merger;
(ii) each shareholder of the absorbing company can inspect at this moment in time and at the seat of the company the terms of merger, the annual accounts for the last three business years, the management report and the report(s) of the independent experts (Art. 351e sec. 3 PGR).

The shareholder meeting can make its consent to a cross-border merger conditional on the company resulting from the cross-border merger expressly confirming the modalities for the employees' participation.

6 Protection of minority shareholders

15. One or several shareholders which represent jointly at least 5 per cent of the share capital of the absorbing company are entitled to request the convocation of a general meeting of shareholders which shall resolve on the approval of the terms of merger (Art. 351e sec. 4 PGR). These minority shareholder rights only exist if the law does not require the consent of the shareholders' meeting of the absorbing company (Art. 351e sec. 3 PGR).

7 Pre-merger certificate

16. After completed scrutiny of the legality of a cross-border merger, the Public Registry issues a pre-certificate (*Vorabbescheinigung*) to the Liechtenstein corporation which participates in the cross-border merger. If the prerequisites are fulfilled, such issuance must be completed without delay. In such pre-certificate the Public Registry confirms that the legal requirements and formalities for the merger have been duly completed (Art. 352e PGR).

Furthermore, Article 352f PGR obligates the Public Registry to issue to the new company resulting from the cross-border merger, provided that such company is subject to Liechtenstein law, a certificate regarding the legality of the cross-border merger (*Rechtmässigkeitsbescheinigung*) after the respective scrutiny has been carried out. In this certificate the Public Registry confirms in particular that:

(i) the companies involved in the merger have consented to common and identical terms of cross-border merger; and
(ii) if applicable, that an agreement regarding the participation of the employees in the sense of the respective law has been concluded.

17. For the purpose of the issuance of this certificate all companies involved in the cross-border merger have to submit within six months upon issuance of their pre-certificates according to Article 352e PGR the terms of cross-border merger approved by each shareholder meeting and, to the extent applicable, proof that an agreement regarding the participation of employees has been concluded.

8 No prospectus obligation

18. Article 6 sec. 1 lit. a of the Prospectus Act exempts a public offer of securities which are offered within the framework of an exchange offer or of a merger from the obligation to draw up and file an offering memorandum (*Prospekt*) under the Prospectus Act. However, such exemption exists only if another document is made available the content of which is equivalent to that of an offering memorandum. Therefore, the inapplicability of the Prospectus Act on the aforementioned merger as such does not lead to a material disadvantage of the shareholders.

Nonetheless, in the event of a cross-border merger, any foreign legislation regarding the duty to submit an offering memorandum must also be taken into account. As a consequence, it is possible that an offering memorandum is required under such foreign legislation.

9 Entry into force, registration and publication

19. The general rules regarding the registration of the merger (Arts. 351g and 351h PGR) are partly inapplicable on a cross-border merger since not only the

Liechtenstein Public Registry but also the foreign authority which is in charge in the other involved jurisdictions must participate in the registration process.

In accordance with Article 12 of the Cross-border Merger Directive a cross-border merger can only become effective after the process of scrutiny regarding the legality of the cross-border merger has been completed. Therefore, Article 352h PGR specifies that the registration of a cross-border merger in the Public Register may only be carried out after the certificate regarding the legality of the cross-border merger (*Rechtmässigkeitsbescheinigung*) has been submitted.

10 No avoidance of the merger

20. Article 352h sec. 2 PGR deviates from the Liechtenstein national merger rules and implements Article 17 of the Directive. In a purely national merger the Liechtenstein courts can declare a defective merger null and void if (i) an involved party requests such judgment, (ii) the merger suffers from a material defect and (iii) such court action is filed at the latest six months after the publication of the merger (Art. 351m PGR).

In accordance with Article 352h sec. 2 PGR a cross-border merger can no longer be declared null and void (*nichtig*) after it has been registered in the Public Register. The Public Registry must without delay inform the foreign authorities with which the involved companies had to deposit their documents on the registration of the cross-border merger in the Liechtenstein Public Register.

VI Protection of creditors

21. The creditors of a Liechtenstein corporation which participates in a cross-border merger are, within the first six months after publication of the cross-border merger, entitled to obtain adequate safeguard. In order to be entitled to do so their claims may not have fallen due and they have to prove that the merger puts their claims at risk. The publication of the registration of the merger has to point out that the creditors have such right (Art. 351i PGR).

VII Employee participation

1 General

22. Unlike the other provisions of the Cross-border Merger Directive its provisions on employee participation were not implemented by amending the PGR but by enacting a separate and new law, the FMG. This was necessary since the PGR does not provide for an employee participation system and the Directive's rules on employee participation would therefore have been alien to the PGR's system.

2 Applicability of the FMG

23. Pursuant to Article 3 FMG, the general principle is that the company resulting from a cross-border merger (being either the surviving company or the newly incorporated company) shall not be subject to the rules of the FMG but to the rules concerning employee participation in force in the EEA Member State in which the resulting company has its registered seat (Art. 3 FMG). However, according to Article 4 FMG, the employee participation rules as set forth in the FMG shall apply if:

(i) at least one of the merging companies has, in the last six months before the publication of the draft terms of the cross-border merger, an average staff of more than 500 employees and is operating under an employee participation system;
(ii) the law governing the company resulting from the cross-border merger does not provide for at least the same level of employee participation as operated in the relevant merging companies; or
(iii) the law governing the company resulting from the cross-border merger does not provide for employees in establishments of the company resulting from the cross-border merger that are situated in other EEA Member States the same entitlement to exercise participation rights as enjoyed by those employees employed in the EEA Member State in which the company resulting from the cross-border merger has its registered office.

24. Since Liechtenstein law does not provide for an employee participation system,[6] a company resulting from a cross-border merger with its seat in Liechtenstein will always be subject to the employee participation rules as set forth in the FMG, if at least one of the companies participating in the respective cross-border merger has an employee participation system in place.

Moreover, according to Article 2 sec. 2 FMG the FMG can also be applicable if the employees of a (foreign) participating company have their place of work in Liechtenstein and if such participating company has its registered seat in a foreign country.

3 Agreed employee participation

25. If the FMG is applicable with regard to a certain cross-border merger, a special negotiating body ('SNB') must be set up. This SNB is competent to negotiate with the corporate management bodies of the participating companies arrangements on employee participation in the company resulting from the cross-border merger. Rules on the composition and the appointment of the SNB are set forth in detail in Section II of the FMG.

6 Apart from the Act on Employee Participation in the European Company (*Gesetz vom 25. November 2005 über die Beteiligung der Arbeitnehmer in der Europäischen Gesellschaft*, LGBl. 2006/27).

The parties to the negotiation process (the SNB and the management bodies of the participating companies) can freely determine a participation system for the resulting company (Art 21 FMG). Negotiation shall commence as soon as the SNB is established and may continue for six months thereafter (Art. 19(1) FMG). The parties can decide, by joint agreement, to extend the negotiations for a further six months (Art. 19(2) FMG).

4 Obligatory employee participation

26. In general, if the SNB and the management bodies of the participating companies fail to reach an agreement within the negotiation period, the employee participation system as set forth in Section IV of the FMG applies (Art. 23(1)(b) FMG). The parties can of course agree on the application of Section IV of the FMG (Art. 23(1)(a) FMG). However, the management bodies of the participating companies can also decide to skip the negotiation process and to apply Section IV of the FMG right away (Art. 23(1)(c) FMG).

The general rule of Section IV of the FMG is that the employees have the right to appoint a certain number of members of the administration or supervisory board of the resulting company. The number of members of the administration or supervisory board appointed by the employees has to be equal to the highest proportion in force in one of the involved companies (Art. 24(1) FMG). Pursuant to Article 27 FMG, the employee-appointed members of the administration or supervisory board are full members of the respective board with the same rights and obligations as the members representing the shareholders, including the right to vote.

VIII Tax treatment

27. The three countries which are EEA but not EU Member States only implement those EU Directives that have 'EEA relevance'. The EU Directives relating to tax harmonisation do not fall within the scope of the EEA. Hence, the Merger Tax Directive is neither directly applicable in Liechtenstein nor had to be implemented into Liechtenstein law. As a consequence, it is possible to include a Liechtenstein corporation in an EEA cross-border merger, governed by the respective harmonised national rules implementing the Directive, but a tax-neutral implementation of such merger is neither guaranteed on the EEA level nor provided for on the national (Liechtenstein) level.

The former Liechtenstein Tax Law[7] provided for a 4 per cent coupon tax on distributions or liquidation proceeds made by a Liechtenstein company whose capital was divided into stakes or shares. Such coupon tax qualified as a withholding tax as the duty to remit fell on the Liechtenstein company.

7 Art. 88e (3) des Gesetzes vom 30. Januar 1961 über die Landes- und Gemeindesteuern LGBl. 1961/7.

As a result of the entry into force of the new Tax Act[8] the coupon tax was abolished. However there are interim provisions which provide for a coupon tax duty if reserves which had been accumulated prior to 1 January 2011 are distributed after that date. The new Tax Act provides for a suspension of taxation in certain restructuring events and grants such privilege to mergers.[9] One of the requirements for such privilege is that the new company resulting from the merger remains subject to taxation in Liechtenstein. If, as in an outbound cross-border merger, this is not the case, specific provisions can grant a similar suspension also for such mergers.[10]

However, in any event one will have to await which practice the tax administration will develop in this regard. In a specific cross-border merger transaction it is certainly advisable to discuss any tax implications in advance with the tax administration.

IX Conclusion

28. In a jurisdiction with a very small national territory such as Liechtenstein, the chances of dealing with parties in other jurisdictions are somewhat higher than in countries with large domestic markets. Companies and professionals of all areas are accustomed to cross-border business dealings. As a consequence, Liechtenstein has a vital interest in facilitating not only for its market players but also for their foreign business partners the possibility of a clear and efficient cross-border merger system. It is in this light that the new rules will have to be tested.

8 Gesetz vom 23. September 2010 über die Landes- und Gemeindesteuern (Steuergesetz), LGBl. 2011 Nr. 340.

9 Art. 52 Abs. 1 lit.c Steuergesetz.

10 Art. 52 Abs. 3 and Art. 51 Abs. 2 Steuergesetz.

PART VII

Annexes

Annex I

DIRECTIVE 2005/56/EC OF THE EUROPEAN PARLIAMENT AND OF THE COUNCIL

of 26 October 2005

on cross-border mergers of limited liability companies

(Text with EEA relevance)

THE EUROPEAN PARLIAMENT AND THE COUNCIL OF THE EUROPEAN UNION,

Having regard to the Treaty establishing the European Community, and in particular Article 44 thereof,

Having regard to the proposal from the Commission,

Having regard to the opinion of the European Economic and Social Committee ([1]),

Acting in accordance with the procedure laid down in Article 251 of the Treaty ([2]),

Whereas:

(1) There is a need for cooperation and consolidation between limited liability companies from different Member States. However, as regards cross-border mergers of limited liability companies, they encounter many legislative and administrative difficulties in the Community. It is therefore necessary, with a view to the completion and functioning of the single market, to lay down Community provisions to facilitate the carrying-out of cross-border mergers between various types of limited liability company governed by the laws of different Member States.

(2) This Directive facilitates the cross-border merger of limited liability companies as defined herein. The laws of the Member States are to allow the cross-border merger of a national limited liability company with a limited liability company from another Member State if the national law of the relevant Member States permits mergers between such types of company.

(3) In order to facilitate cross-border merger operations, it should be laid down that, unless this Directive provides otherwise, each company taking part in a cross-border merger, and each third party concerned, remains subject to the provisions and formalities of the national law which would be applicable in the case of a national merger. None of the provisions and formalities of national law, to which reference is made in this Directive, should introduce restrictions on freedom of establishment or on the free movement of capital save where

([1]) OJ C 117, 30.4.2004, p. 43.

([2]) Opinion of the European Parliament of 10 May 2005 (not yet published in the Official Journal) and Council Decision of 19 September 2005.

these can be justified in accordance with the case-law of the Court of Justice and in particular by requirements of the general interest and are both necessary for, and proportionate to, the attainment of such overriding requirements.

(4) The common draft terms of the cross-border merger are to be drawn up in the same terms for each of the companies concerned in the various Member States. The minimum content of such common draft terms should therefore be specified, while leaving the companies free to agree on other items.

(5) In order to protect the interests of members and others, both the common draft terms of cross-border mergers and the completion of the cross-border merger are to be publicised for each merging company via an entry in the appropriate public register.

(6) The laws of all the Member States should provide for the drawing-up at national level of a report on the common draft terms of the cross-border merger by one or more experts on behalf of each of the companies that are merging. In order to limit experts' costs connected with cross-border mergers, provision should be made for the possibility of drawing up a single report intended for all members of companies taking part in a cross-border merger operation. The common draft terms of the cross-border merger are to be approved by the general meeting of each of those companies.

(7) In order to facilitate cross-border merger operations, it should be provided that monitoring of the completion and legality of the decision-making process in each merging company should be carried out by the national authority having jurisdiction over each of those companies, whereas monitoring of the completion and legality of the cross-border merger should be carried out by the national authority having jurisdiction over the company resulting from the cross-border merger. The national authority in question may be a court, a notary or any other competent authority appointed by the Member State concerned. The national law determining the date on which the cross-border merger takes effect, this being the law to which the company resulting from the cross-border merger is subject, should also be specified.

(8) In order to protect the interests of members and others, the legal effects of the cross-border merger, distinguishing as to whether the company resulting from the cross-border merger is an acquiring company or a new company, should be specified. In the interests of legal certainty, it should no longer be possible, after the date on which a cross-border merger takes effect, to declare the merger null and void.

(9) This Directive is without prejudice to the application of the legislation on the control of concentrations between undertakings, both at Community level, by Regulation (EC) No 139/2004 ([3]), and at the level of Member States.

(10) This Directive does not affect Community legislation regulating credit intermediaries and other financial undertakings and national rules made or introduced pursuant to such Community legislation.

(11) This Directive is without prejudice to a Member State's legislation demanding information on the place of central

([3]) Council Regulation (EC) No 139/2004 of 20 January 2004 on the control of concentrations between undertakings (the EC Merger Regulation) (OJ L 24, 29.1.2004, p. 1).

administration or the principal place of business proposed for the company resulting from the cross-border merger.

(12) Employees' rights other than rights of participation should remain subject to the national provisions referred to in Council Directive 98/59/EC of 20 July 1998 on collective redundancies ([4]), Council Directive 2001/23/EC of 12 March 2001 on the safeguarding of employees' rights in the event of transfers of undertakings, businesses or parts of undertakings or businesses ([5]), Directive 2002/14/EC of the European Parliament and of the Council of 11 March 2002 establishing a general framework for informing and consulting employees in the European Community ([6]) and Council Directive 94/45/EC of 22 September 1994 on the establishment of a European Works Council or a procedure in Community-scale undertakings and Community-scale groups of undertakings for the purposes of informing and consulting employees ([7]).

(13) If employees have participation rights in one of the merging companies under the circumstances set out in this Directive and, if the national law of the Member State in which the company resulting from the cross-border merger has its registered office does not provide for the same level of participation as operated in the relevant merging companies, including in committees of the supervisory board that have decision-making powers, or does not provide for the same entitlement to exercise rights for employees of establishments resulting from the cross-border merger, the participation of employees in the company resulting from the cross-border merger and their involvement in the definition of such rights are to be regulated. To that end, the principles and procedures provided for in Council Regulation (EC) No 2157/2001 of 8 October 2001 on the Statute for a European company (SE) ([8]) and in Council Directive 2001/86/EC of 8 October 2001 supplementing the Statute for a European company with regard to the involvement of employees ([9]), are to be taken as a basis, subject, however, to modifications that are deemed necessary because the resulting company will be subject to the national laws of the Member State where it has its registered office. A prompt start to negotiations under Article 16 of this Directive, with a view to not unnecessarily delaying mergers, may be ensured by Member States in accordance with Article 3(2)(b) of Directive 2001/86/EC.

(14) For the purpose of determining the level of employee participation operated in the relevant merging companies, account should also be taken of the proportion of employee representatives amongst the members of the management group, which covers the profit units of the companies, subject to employee participation.

(15) Since the objective of the proposed action, namely laying down rules with common features applicable at transnational level, cannot be sufficiently achieved by the Member States and can therefore, by reason of the scale and impact of the proposed action, be better achieved at Community level, the Community may

([4]) OJ L 225, 12.8.1998, p. 16.

([5]) OJ L 82, 22.3.2001, p. 16.

([6]) OJ L 80, 23.3.2002, p. 29.

([7]) OJ L 254, 30.9.1994, p. 64. Directive as amended by Directive 97/74/EC (OJ L 10, 16.1.1998, p. 22).

([8]) OJ L 294, 10.11.2001, p. 1. Regulation as amended by Regulation (EC) No 885/2004 (OJ L 168, 1.5.2004, p. 1).

([9]) OJ L 294, 10.11.2001, p. 22.

adopt measures in accordance with the principle of subsidiarity as set out in Article 5 of the Treaty. In accordance with the principle of proportionality as set out in that Article, this Directive does not go beyond what is necessary to achieve that objective.

(16) In accordance with paragraph 34 of the Interinstitutional Agreement on better law-making ([10]), Member States should be encouraged to draw up, for themselves and in the interest of the Community, their own tables which will, as far as possible, illustrate the correlation between this Directive and the transposition measures and to make them public,

HAVE ADOPTED THIS DIRECTIVE:

Article 1

Scope

This Directive shall apply to mergers of limited liability companies formed in accordance with the law of a Member State and having their registered office, central administration or principal place of business within the Community, provided at least two of them are governed by the laws of different Member States (hereinafter referred to as cross-border mergers).

Article 2

Definitions

For the purposes of this Directive:

1. 'limited liability company', hereinafter referred to as 'company', means:

([10]) OJ C 321, 31.12.2003, p. 1.

(a) a company as referred to in Article 1 of Directive 68/151/EEC ([11]), or

(b) a company with share capital and having legal personality, possessing separate assets which alone serve to cover its debts and subject under the national law governing it to conditions concerning guarantees such as are provided for by Directive 68/151/EEC for the protection of the interests of members and others;

2. 'merger' means an operation whereby:

(a) one or more companies, on being dissolved without going into liquidation, transfer all their assets and liabilities to another existing company, the acquiring company, in exchange for the issue to their members of securities or shares representing the capital of that other company and, if applicable, a cash payment not exceeding 10 % of the nominal value, or, in the absence of a nominal value, of the accounting par value of those securities or shares; or

(b) two or more companies, on being dissolved without going into liquidation, transfer all their assets and liabilities to a company that they form, the new company, in exchange for the issue to their members of

([11]) First Council Directive 68/151/EEC of 9 March 1968 on coordination of safeguards which, for the protection of the interests of members and others, are required by Member States of companies within the meaning of the second paragraph of Article 58 of the Treaty, with a view to making such safeguards equivalent throughout the Community (OJ L 65, 14.3.1968, p. 8). Directive as last amended by the 2003 Act of Accession.

securities or shares representing the capital of that new company and, if applicable, a cash payment not exceeding 10 % of the nominal value, or in the absence of a nominal value, of the accounting par value of those securities or shares; or

(c) a company, on being dissolved without going into liquidation, transfers all its assets and liabilities to the company holding all the securities or shares representing its capital.

Article 3

Further provisions concerning the scope

1. Notwithstanding Article 2(2), this Directive shall also apply to cross-border mergers where the law of at least one of the Member States concerned allows the cash payment referred to in points (a) and (b) of Article 2(2) to exceed 10 % of the nominal value, or, in the absence of a nominal value, of the accounting par value of the securities or shares representing the capital of the company resulting from the cross-border merger.

2. Member States may decide not to apply this Directive to cross-border mergers involving a cooperative society even in the cases where the latter would fall within the definition of 'limited liability company' as laid down in Article 2(1).

3. This Directive shall not apply to cross-border mergers involving a company the object of which is the collective investment of capital provided by the public, which operates on the principle of risk-spreading and the units of which are, at the holders' request, repurchased or redeemed, directly or indirectly, out of the assets of that company. Action taken by such a company to ensure that the stock exchange value of its units does not vary significantly from its net asset value shall be regarded as equivalent to such repurchase or redemption.

Article 4

Conditions relating to cross-border mergers

1. Save as otherwise provided in this Directive,

(a) cross-border mergers shall only be possible between types of companies which may merge under the national law of the relevant Member States, and

(b) a company taking part in a cross-border merger shall comply with the provisions and formalities of the national law to which it is subject. The laws of a Member State enabling its national authorities to oppose a given internal merger on grounds of public interest shall also be applicable to a cross-border merger where at least one of the merging companies is subject to the law of that Member State. This provision shall not apply to the extent that Article 21 of Regulation (EC) No 139/2004 is applicable.

2. The provisions and formalities referred to in paragraph 1 (b) shall, in particular, include those concerning the decision-making process relating to the merger and, taking into account the cross-border nature of the merger, the protection of creditors of the merging companies, debenture holders and the holders of securities or shares, as well as of employees as regards rights other than those governed by Article 16. A Member State may, in the case of companies

participating in a cross-border merger and governed by its law, adopt provisions designed to ensure appropriate protection for minority members who have opposed the cross-border merger.

Article 5

Common draft terms of cross-border mergers

The management or administrative organ of each of the merging companies shall draw up the common draft terms of cross-border merger. The common draft terms of cross-border merger shall include at least the following particulars:

(a) the form, name and registered office of the merging companies and those proposed for the company resulting from the cross-border merger;

(b) the ratio applicable to the exchange of securities or shares representing the company capital and the amount of any cash payment;

(c) the terms for the allotment of securities or shares representing the capital of the company resulting from the cross-border merger;

(d) the likely repercussions of the cross-border merger on employment;

(e) the date from which the holding of such securities or shares representing the company capital will entitle the holders to share in profits and any special conditions affecting that entitlement;

(f) the date from which the transactions of the merging companies will be treated for accounting purposes as being those of the company resulting from the cross-border merger;

(g) the rights conferred by the company resulting from the cross-border merger on members enjoying special rights or on holders of securities other than shares representing the company capital, or the measures proposed concerning them;

(h) any special advantages granted to the experts who examine the draft terms of the cross-border merger or to members of the administrative, management, supervisory or controlling organs of the merging companies;

(i) the statutes of the company resulting from the cross-border merger;

(j) where appropriate, information on the procedures by which arrangements for the involvement of employees in the definition of their rights to participation in the company resulting from the cross-border merger are determined pursuant to Article 16;

(k) information on the evaluation of the assets and liabilities which are transferred to the company resulting from the cross-border merger;

(l) dates of the merging companies' accounts used to establish the conditions of the cross-border merger.

Article 6

Publication

1. The common draft terms of the cross-border merger shall be published in the manner prescribed by the laws of each Member State in accordance with Article 3 of Directive 68/151/EEC for each of the merging companies at least one month before the date of the general meeting which is to decide thereon.

2. For each of the merging companies and subject to the additional requirements imposed by the Member State to which the company concerned is subject, the following particulars shall be published in the national gazette of that Member State:

   (a) the type, name and registered office of every merging company;

   (b) the register in which the documents referred to in Article 3(2) of Directive 68/151/EEC are filed in respect of each merging company, and the number of the entry in that register;

   (c) an indication, for each of the merging companies, of the arrangements made for the exercise of the rights of creditors and of any minority members of the merging companies and the address at which complete information on those arrangements may be obtained free of charge.

Article 7

Report of the management or administrative organ

The management or administrative organ of each of the merging companies shall draw up a report intended for the members explaining and justifying the legal and economic aspects of the cross-border merger and explaining the implications of the cross-border merger for members, creditors and employees.

The report shall be made available to the members and to the representatives of the employees or, where there are no such representatives, to the employees themselves, not less than one month before the date of the general meeting referred to in Article 9.

Where the management or administrative organ of any of the merging companies receives, in good time, an opinion from the representatives of their employees, as provided for under national law, that opinion shall be appended to the report.

Article 8

Independent expert report

1. An independent expert report intended for members and made available not less than one month before the date of the general meeting referred to in Article 9 shall be drawn up for each merging company. Depending on the law of each Member State, such experts may be natural persons or legal persons.

2. As an alternative to experts operating on behalf of each of the merging companies, one or more independent experts, appointed for that purpose at the joint request of the companies by a judicial or administrative authority in the Member State of one of the merging companies or of the company resulting from the cross-border merger or approved by such an authority, may examine the common draft terms of cross-border merger and draw up a single written report to all the members.

3. The expert report shall include at least the particulars provided for by Article 10(2) of Council Directive 78/855/EEC of 9 October 1978 concerning mergers of public limited liability companies ([12]). The experts shall be entitled to secure from each of the merging companies all information they consider necessary for the discharge of their duties.

([12]) OJ L 295, 20.10.1978, p. 36. Directive as last amended by the 2003 Act of Accession.

4. Neither an examination of the common draft terms of cross-border merger by independent experts nor an expert report shall be required if all the members of each of the companies involved in the cross-border merger have so agreed.

Article 9

Approval by the general meeting

1. After taking note of the reports referred to in Articles 7 and 8, the general meeting of each of the merging companies shall decide on the approval of the common draft terms of cross-border merger.

2. The general meeting of each of the merging companies may reserve the right to make implementation of the cross-border merger conditional on express ratification by it of the arrangements decided on with respect to the participation of employees in the company resulting from the cross-border merger.

3. The laws of a Member State need not require approval of the merger by the general meeting of the acquiring company if the conditions laid down in Article 8 of Directive 78/855/EEC are fulfilled.

Article 10

Pre-merger certificate

1. Each Member State shall designate the court, notary or other authority competent to scrutinise the legality of the cross-border merger as regards that part of the procedure which concerns each merging company subject to its national law.

2. In each Member State concerned the authority referred to in paragraph 1 shall issue, without delay to each merging company subject to that State's national law, a certificate conclusively attesting to the proper completion of the pre-merger acts and formalities.

3. If the law of a Member State to which a merging company is subject provides for a procedure to scrutinise and amend the ratio applicable to the exchange of securities or shares, or a procedure to compensate minority members, without preventing the registration of the cross-border merger, such procedure shall only apply if the other merging companies situated in Member States which do not provide for such procedure explicitly accept, when approving the draft terms of the cross-border merger in accordance with Article 9(1), the possibility for the members of that merging company to have recourse to such procedure, to be initiated before the court having jurisdiction over that merging company. In such cases, the authority referred to in paragraph 1 may issue the certificate referred to in paragraph 2 even if such procedure has commenced. The certificate must, however, indicate that the procedure is pending. The decision in the procedure shall be binding on the company resulting from the cross-border merger and all its members.

Article 11

Scrutiny of the legality of the cross-border merger

1. Each Member State shall designate the court, notary or other authority competent to scrutinise the legality of the cross-border merger as regards that part of the procedure which concerns the completion of the cross-border merger and, where appropriate, the formation of a new company resulting from the cross-border merger where the company created by the cross-border merger is subject to

its national law. The said authority shall in particular ensure that the merging companies have approved the common draft terms of cross-border merger in the same terms and, where appropriate, that arrangements for employee participation have been determined in accordance with Article 16.

2. To that end each merging company shall submit to the authority referred to in paragraph 1 the certificate referred to in Article 10(2) within six months of its issue together with the common draft terms of cross-border merger approved by the general meeting referred to in Article 9.

Article 12

Entry into effect of the cross-border merger

The law of the Member State to whose jurisdiction the company resulting from the cross-border merger is subject shall determine the date on which the cross-border merger takes effect. That date must be after the scrutiny referred to in Article 11 has been carried out.

Article 13

Registration

The law of each of the Member States to whose jurisdiction the merging companies were subject shall determine, with respect to the territory of that State, the arrangements, in accordance with Article 3 of Directive 68/151/EEC, for publicising completion of the cross-border merger in the public register in which each of the companies is required to file documents.

The registry for the registration of the company resulting from the cross-border merger shall notify, without delay, the registry in which each of the companies was required to file documents that the cross-border merger has taken effect. Deletion of the old registration, if applicable, shall be effected on receipt of that notification, but not before.

Article 14

Consequences of the cross-border merger

1. A cross-border merger carried out as laid down in points (a) and (c) of Article 2(2) shall, from the date referred to in Article 12, have the following consequences:

   (a) all the assets and liabilities of the company being acquired shall be transferred to the acquiring company;

   (b) the members of the company being acquired shall become members of the acquiring company;

   (c) the company being acquired shall cease to exist.

2. A cross-border merger carried out as laid down in point (b) of Article 2(2) shall, from the date referred to in Article 12, have the following consequences:

   (a) all the assets and liabilities of the merging companies shall be transferred to the new company;

   (b) the members of the merging companies shall become members of the new company;

   (c) the merging companies shall cease to exist.

3. Where, in the case of a cross-border merger of companies covered by this Directive, the laws of the Member States require the completion of special formalities before the transfer of certain assets, rights and obligations by the merging companies becomes effective against third parties,

those formalities shall be carried out by the company resulting from the cross-border merger.

4. The rights and obligations of the merging companies arising from contracts of employment or from employment relationships and existing at the date on which the cross-border merger takes effect shall, by reason of that cross-border merger taking effect, be transferred to the company resulting from the cross-border merger on the date on which the cross-border merger takes effect.

5. No shares in the acquiring company shall be exchanged for shares in the company being acquired held either:

   (a) by the acquiring company itself or through a person acting in his or her own name but on its behalf;

   (b) by the company being acquired itself or through a person acting in his or her own name but on its behalf.

Article 15

Simplified formalities

1. Where a cross-border merger by acquisition is carried out by a company which holds all the shares and other securities conferring the right to vote at general meetings of the company or companies being acquired:

   - Articles 5, points (b), (c) and (e), 8 and 14(1), point (b) shall not apply,

   - Article 9(1) shall not apply to the company or companies being acquired.

2. Where a cross-border merger by acquisition is carried out by a company which holds 90 % or more but not all of the shares and other securities conferring the right to vote at general meetings of the company or companies being acquired, reports by an independent expert or experts and the documents necessary for scrutiny shall be required only to the extent that the national law governing either the acquiring company or the company being acquired so requires.

Article 16

Employee participation

1. Without prejudice to paragraph 2, the company resulting from the cross-border merger shall be subject to the rules in force concerning employee participation, if any, in the Member State where it has its registered office.

2. However, the rules in force concerning employee participation, if any, in the Member State where the company resulting from the cross-border merger has its registered office shall not apply, where at least one of the merging companies has, in the six months before the publication of the draft terms of the cross-border merger as referred to in Article 6, an average number of employees that exceeds 500 and is operating under an employee participation system within the meaning of Article 2(k) of Directive 2001/86/EC, or where the national law applicable to the company resulting from the cross-border merger does not

   (a) provide for at least the same level of employee participation as operated in the relevant merging companies, measured by reference to the proportion of employee representatives amongst the members of the administrative or supervisory organ or their committees or of the management group which covers the profit units of the company, subject to employee representation, or

(b) provide for employees of establishments of the company resulting from the cross-border merger that are situated in other Member States the same entitlement to exercise participation rights as is enjoyed by those employees employed in the Member State where the company resulting from the cross-border merger has its registered office.

3. In the cases referred to in paragraph 2, the participation of employees in the company resulting from the cross-border merger and their involvement in the definition of such rights shall be regulated by the Member States, *mutatis mutandis* and subject to paragraphs 4 to 7 below, in accordance with the principles and procedures laid down in Article 12(2), (3) and (4) of Regulation (EC) No 2157/2001 and the following provisions of Directive 2001/86/EC:

   (a) Article 3(1), (2) and (3), (4) first subparagraph, first indent, and second subparagraph, (5) and (7);

   (b) Article 4(1), (2), points (a), (g) and (h), and (3);

   (c) Article 5;

   (d) Article 6;

   (e) Article 7(1), (2) first subparagraph, point (b), and second subparagraph, and (3). However, for the purposes of this Directive, the percentages required by Article 7(2), first subparagraph, point (b) of Directive 2001/86/EC for the application of the standard rules contained in part 3 of the Annex to that Directive shall be raised from 25 to 33 1/3%;

   (f) Articles 8, 10 and 12;

   (g) Article 13(4);

   (h) part 3 of the Annex, point (b).

4. When regulating the principles and procedures referred to in paragraph 3, Member States:

   (a) shall confer on the relevant organs of the merging companies the right to choose without any prior negotiation to be directly subject to the standard rules for participation referred to in paragraph 3(h), as laid down by the legislation of the Member State in which the company resulting from the cross-border merger is to have its registered office, and to abide by those rules from the date of registration;

   (b) shall confer on the special negotiating body the right to decide, by a majority of two thirds of its members representing at least two thirds of the employees, including the votes of members representing employees in at least two different Member States, not to open negotiations or to terminate negotiations already opened and to rely on the rules on participation in force in the Member State where the registered office of the company resulting from the cross-border merger will be situated;

   (c) may, in the case where, following prior negotiations, standard rules for participation apply and notwithstanding these rules, determine to limit the proportion of employee representatives in the administrative organ of the company resulting from the cross-border merger. However, if in one of the merging companies employee representatives constituted at least one third of the administrative or supervisory board, the limitation may never result in a lower proportion of employee representatives in the administrative organ than one third.

5. The extension of participation rights to employees of the company resulting from the cross-border merger employed in other Member States, referred to in paragraph 2(b), shall not entail any obligation for Member States which choose to do so to take those employees into account when calculating the size of workforce thresholds giving rise to participation rights under national law.

6. When at least one of the merging companies is operating under an employee participation system and the company resulting from the cross-border merger is to be governed by such a system in accordance with the rules referred to in paragraph 2, that company shall be obliged to take a legal form allowing for the exercise of participation rights.

7. When the company resulting from the cross-border merger is operating under an employee participation system, that company shall be obliged to take measures to ensure that employees' participation rights are protected in the event of subsequent domestic mergers for a period of three years after the cross-border merger has taken effect, by applying *mutatis mutandis* the rules laid down in this Article.

Article 17

Validity

A cross-border merger which has taken effect as provided for in Article 12 may not be declared null and void.

Article 18

Review

Five years after the date laid down in the first paragraph of Article 19, the Commission shall review this Directive in the light of the experience acquired in applying it and, if necessary, propose its amendment.

Article 19

Transposition

Member States shall bring into force the laws, regulations and administrative provisions necessary to comply with this Directive by 15 December 2007.

When Member States adopt these measures, they shall contain a reference to this Directive or shall be accompanied by such reference on the occasion of their official publication. The methods of making such reference shall be laid down by Member States.

Article 20

Entry into force

This Directive shall enter into force on the 20th day following its publication in the *Official Journal of* the *European Union.*

Article 21

Addressees

This Directive is addressed to the Member States.

Done at Strasbourg, 26 October 2005.

For the *European Parliament*	*For* the *Council*
The President	*The President*
J. BORRELL FONTELLES	D. ALEXANDER

Annex II

COUNCIL DIRECTIVE 2009/133/EC

of 19 October 2009

on the common system of taxation applicable to mergers, divisions, partial divisions, transfers of assets and exchanges of shares concerning companies of different Member States and to the transfer of the registered office of an SE or SCE between Member States

(codified version)

THE COUNCIL OF THE EUROPEAN UNION,

Having regard to the Treaty establishing the European Community, and in particular Article 94 thereof,

Having regard to the proposal from the Commission,

Having regard to the opinion of the European Parliament [1],

Having regard to the opinion of the European Economic and Social Committee [2],

Whereas:

(1) Council Directive 90/434/EEC of 23 July 1990 on the common system of taxation applicable to mergers, divisions, partial divisions, transfers of assets and exchanges of shares concerning companies of different Member States and to the transfer of the registered office, of an SE or SCE, between Member States [3] has been substantially amended several times [4]. In the interests of clarity and rationality the said Directive should be codified.

(2) Mergers, divisions, partial divisions, transfers of assets and exchanges of shares concerning companies of different Member States may be necessary in order to create within the Community conditions analogous to those of an internal market and in order thus to ensure the effective functioning of such an internal market. Such operations ought not to be hampered by restrictions, disadvantages or distortions arising in particular from the tax provisions of the Member States. To that end it is necessary, with respect to such operations, to provide for tax rules which are neutral from the point of view of competition, in order to allow enterprises to adapt to the requirements of the internal market, to increase their productivity and to improve their competitive strength at the international level.

(3) Tax provisions disadvantage such operations, in comparison with those

(1) Opinion of 13 January 2009 (not yet published in the Official Journal).

(2) OJ C 100, 30.4.2009, p. 153.

(3) OJ L 225, 20.8.1990, p. 1.

(4) See Annex II, Part A.

concerning companies of the same Member State. It is necessary to remove such disadvantages.

(4) It is not possible to attain this objective by an extension at Community level of the systems in force in the Member States, since differences between these systems tend to produce distortions. Only a common tax system is able to provide a satisfactory solution in this respect.

(5) The common tax system ought to avoid the imposition of tax in connection with mergers, divisions, partial divisions, transfers of assets or exchanges of shares, while at the same time safeguarding the financial interests of the Member State of the transferring or acquired company.

(6) In respect of mergers, divisions or transfers of assets, such operations normally result either in the transformation of the transferring company into a permanent establishment of the company receiving the assets or in the assets becoming connected with a permanent establishment of the latter company.

(7) The system of deferral of the taxation of the capital gains relating to the assets transferred until their actual disposal, applied to such of those assets as are transferred to that permanent establishment, permits exemption from taxation of the corresponding capital gains, while at the same time ensuring their ultimate taxation by the Member State of the transferring company at the date of their disposal.

(8) While the companies listed in Annex I, Part A are corporate taxpayers in their Member State of residence, some of them may be considered to be fiscally transparent by other Member States. In order to preserve the effectiveness of this Directive, Member States treating non-resident corporate taxpayers as fiscally transparent should grant the benefits of this Directive to them. However, Member States should have the option not to apply the relevant provisions of this Directive when taxing a direct or indirect shareholder of those taxpayers.

(9) It is also necessary to define the tax regime applicable to certain provisions, reserves or losses of the transferring company and to solve the tax problems occurring where one of the two companies has a holding in the capital of the other.

(10) The allotment to the shareholders of the transferring company of securities of the receiving or acquiring company should not in itself give rise to any taxation in the hands of such shareholders.

(11) The decision of an SE or SCE to reorganise its business by transferring its registered office should not be unduly hampered by discriminatory tax rules or by restrictions, disadvantages or distortions arising from national tax legislation which is contrary to Community Law. The transfer, or an event connected with the transfer, may give rise to some form of taxation in the Member State from which the office is transferred. Where the assets of the SE or of the SCE remain effectively connected with a permanent establishment in the Member State from which the registered office was transferred, that permanent establishment should enjoy benefits similar to those provided for by Articles 4, 5 and 6. Moreover, the taxation of shareholders on the occasion of the transfer of the registered office should be excluded.

(12) This Directive does not deal with losses of a permanent establishment in another Member State recognised in the Member State of residence of an SE or SCE. In

particular, where the registered office of an SE or SCE is transferred to another Member State, such transfer does not prevent the former Member State of residence from reinstating losses of the permanent establishment in due time.

(13) It is necessary to allow Member States the possibility of refusing to apply this Directive where the merger, division, partial division, transfer of assets, exchange of shares or transfer of the registered office of an SE or SCE has as its objective tax evasion or avoidance or results in a company, whether or not it participates in the operation, no longer fulfilling the conditions required for the representation of employees in company organs.

(14) One of the aims of this Directive is to eliminate obstacles to the functioning of the internal market, such as double taxation. In so far as this is not fully achieved by the provisions of this Directive, Member States should take the necessary measures to achieve this aim.

(15) This Directive should be without prejudice to the obligations of the Member States relating to the time-limits for transposition into national law and application of the Directives set out in Annex II, Part B,

HAS ADOPTED THIS DIRECTIVE:

CHAPTER I

GENERAL PROVISIONS

Article 1

Each Member State shall apply this Directive to the following:

(a) mergers, divisions, partial divisions, transfers of assets and exchanges of shares involving companies from two or more Member States;

(b) transfers of the registered office from one Member State to another Member State of a European company (Societas Europaea or SE), as established in Council Regulation (EC) No 2157/2001 on the Statute for a European company (SE) ([5]), and a European Cooperative Society (SCE), as established in Council Regulation (EC) No 1435/2003 on the Statute for a European Cooperative Society (SCE) ([6]).

Article 2

For the purposes of this Directive, the following definitions shall apply:

(a) 'merger' means an operation whereby:

(i) one or more companies, on being dissolved without going into liquidation, transfer all their assets and liabilities to another existing company in exchange for the issue to their shareholders of securities representing the capital of that other company, and, if applicable, a cash payment not exceeding 10 % of the nominal value, or, in the absence of a nominal value, of the accounting par value of those securities;

(ii) two or more companies, on being dissolved without going into liquidation, transfer all their assets and liabilities to a company that they form, in exchange for the issue to their shareholders of securities representing the capital of that new company, and, if applicable, a cash payment not exceeding 10 % of the nominal value, or in the absence of a

([5]) OJ L 294, 10.11.2001, p. 1.
([6]) OJ L 207, 18.8.2003, p. 1.

nominal value, of the accounting par value of those securities;

(iii) a company, on being dissolved without going into liquidation, transfers all its assets and liabilities to the company holding all the securities representing its capital;

(b) 'division' means an operation whereby a company, on being dissolved without going into liquidation, transfers all its assets and liabilities to two or more existing or new companies, in exchange for the pro rata issue to its shareholders of securities representing the capital of the companies receiving the assets and liabilities, and, if applicable, a cash payment not exceeding 10 % of the nominal value or, in the absence of a nominal value, of the accounting par value of those securities;

(c) 'partial division' means an operation whereby a company transfers, without being dissolved, one or more branches of activity, to one or more existing or new companies, leaving at least one branch of activity in the transferring company, in exchange for the pro-rata issue to its shareholders of securities representing the capital of the companies receiving the assets and liabilities, and, if applicable, a cash payment not exceeding 10 % of the nominal value or, in the absence of a nominal value, of the accounting par value of those securities;

(d) 'transfer of assets' means an operation whereby a company transfers without being dissolved all or one or more branches of its activity to another company in exchange for the transfer of securities representing the capital of the company receiving the transfer;

(e) 'exchange of shares' means an operation whereby a company acquires a holding in the capital of another company such that it obtains a majority of the voting rights in that company, or, holding such a majority, acquires a further holding, in exchange for the issue to the shareholders of the latter company, in exchange for their securities, of securities representing the capital of the former company, and, if applicable, a cash payment not exceeding 10 % of the nominal value, or in the absence of a nominal value, of the accounting par value of the securities issued in exchange;

(f) 'transferring company' means the company transferring its assets and liabilities or transferring all or one or more branches of its activity;

(g) 'receiving company' means the company receiving the assets and liabilities or all or one or more branches of the activity of the transferring company;

(h) 'acquired company' means the company in which a holding is acquired by another company by means of an exchange of securities;

(i) 'acquiring company' means the company which acquires a holding by means of an exchange of securities;

(j) 'branch of activity' means all the assets and liabilities of a division of a company which from an organisational point of view constitute an independent business, that is to say an entity capable of functioning by its own means;

(k) 'transfer of the registered office' means an operation whereby an SE or an SCE, without winding up or creating a new legal person, transfers its registered office from one Member State to another Member State.

Article 3

For the purposes of this Directive, 'company from a Member State' shall mean any company which:

(a) takes one of the forms listed in Annex I, Part A;

(b) according to the tax laws of a Member State is considered to be resident in that Member State for tax purposes and, under the terms of a double taxation agreement concluded with a third country, is not considered to be resident for tax purposes outside the Community; and

(c) is subject to one of the taxes listed in Annex I, Part B, without the possibility of an option or of being exempt, or to any other tax which may be substituted for any of those taxes.

CHAPTER II

RULES APPLICABLE TO MERGERS, DIVISIONS, PARTIAL DIVISIONS, TO TRANSFERS OF ASSETS AND EXCHANGES OF SHARES

Article 4

1. A merger, division or partial division shall not give rise to any taxation of capital gains calculated by reference to the difference between the real values of the assets and liabilities transferred and their values for tax purposes.

2. For the purpose of this Article, the following definitions shall apply:

   (a) 'value for tax purposes': the value on the basis of which any gain or loss would have been computed for the purposes of tax upon the income, profits or capital gains of the transferring company if such assets or liabilities had been sold at the time of the merger, division or partial division but independently of it;

   (b) 'transferred assets and liabilities': those assets and liabilities of the transferring company which, in consequence of the merger, division or partial division, are effectively connected with a permanent establishment of the receiving company in the Member State of the transferring company and play a part in generating the profits or losses taken into account for tax purposes.

3. Where paragraph 1 applies and where a Member State considers a non-resident transferring company as fiscally transparent on the basis of that Member State's assessment of the legal characteristics of that company arising from the law under which it is constituted and therefore taxes the shareholders on their share of the profits of the transferring company as and when those profits arise, that Member State shall not tax any income, profits or capital gains calculated by reference to the difference between the real values of the assets and liabilities transferred and their values for tax purposes.

4. Paragraphs 1 and 3 shall apply only if the receiving company computes any new depreciation and any gains or losses in respect of the assets and liabilities transferred according to the rules that would have applied to the transferring company or companies if the merger, division or partial division had not taken place.

5. Where, under the laws of the Member State of the transferring company, the receiving company is entitled to have any new depreciation or any gains or losses

in respect of the assets and liabilities transferred computed on a basis different from that set out in paragraph 4, paragraph 1 shall not apply to the assets and liabilities in respect of which that option is exercised.

Article 5

The Member States shall take the necessary measures to ensure that, where provisions or reserves properly constituted by the transferring company are partly or wholly exempt from tax and are not derived from permanent establishments abroad, such provisions or reserves may be carried over, with the same tax exemption, by the permanent establishments of the receiving company which are situated in the Member State of the transferring company, the receiving company thereby assuming the rights and obligations of the transferring company.

Article 6

To the extent that, if the operations referred to in Article 1(a) were effected between companies from the Member State of the transferring company, the Member State would apply provisions allowing the receiving company to takeover the losses of the transferring company which had not yet been exhausted for tax purposes, it shall extend those provisions to cover the takeover of such losses by the receiving company's permanent establishments situated within its territory.

Article 7

1. Where the receiving company has a holding in the capital of the transferring company, any gains accruing to the receiving company on the cancellation of its holding shall not be liable to any taxation.

2. The Member States may derogate from paragraph 1 where the receiving company has a holding of less than 15 % in the capital of the transferring company.

From 1 January 2009 the minimum holding percentage shall be 10%.

Article 8

1. On a merger, division or exchange of shares, the allotment of securities representing the capital of the receiving or acquiring company to a shareholder of the transferring or acquired company in exchange for securities representing the capital of the latter company shall not, of itself, give rise to any taxation of the income, profits or capital gains of that shareholder.

2. On a partial division, the allotment to a shareholder of the transferring company of securities representing the capital of the receiving company shall not, of itself, give rise to any taxation of the income, profits or capital gains of that shareholder.

3. Where a Member State considers a shareholder as fiscally transparent on the basis of that Member State's assessment of the legal characteristics of that shareholder arising from the law under which it is constituted and therefore taxes those persons having an interest in the shareholder on their share of the profits of the shareholder as and when those profits arise, that Member State shall not tax those persons on income, profits or capital gains from the allotment of securities representing the capital of the receiving or acquiring company to the shareholder.

4. Paragraphs 1 and 3 shall apply only if the shareholder does not attribute to the securities received a value for tax purposes higher than the value the

securities exchanged had immediately before the merger, division or exchange of shares.

5. Paragraphs 2 and 3 shall apply only if the shareholder does not attribute to the sum of the securities received and those held in the transferring company, a value for tax purposes higher than the value the securities held in the transferring company had immediately before the partial division.

6. The application of paragraphs 1, 2 and 3 shall not prevent the Member States from taxing the gain arising out of the subsequent transfer of securities received in the same way as the gain arising out of the transfer of securities existing before the acquisition.

7. For the purpose of this Article, 'value for tax purposes' shall mean the value on the basis of which any gain or loss would be computed for the purposes of tax upon the income, profits or capital gains of a shareholder of the company.

8. Where, under the law of the Member State in which he is resident, a shareholder may opt for tax treatment different from that set out in paragraphs 4 and 5, paragraphs 1, 2 and 3 shall not apply to the securities in respect of which such an option is exercised.

9. Paragraphs 1, 2 and 3 shall not prevent a Member State from taking into account when taxing shareholders any cash payment that may be made on the merger, division, partial division or exchange of shares.

Article 9

Articles 4, 5 and 6 shall apply to transfers of assets.

CHAPTER III

SPECIAL CASE OF THE TRANSFER OF A PERMANENT ESTABLISHMENT

Article 10

1. Where the assets transferred in a merger, a division, a partial division or a transfer of assets include a permanent establishment of the transferring company which is situated in a Member State other than that of the transferring company, the Member State of the transferring company shall renounce any right to tax that permanent establishment.

The Member State of the transferring company may reinstate in the taxable profits of that company such losses of the permanent establishment as may previously have been set off against the taxable profits of the company in that Member State and which have not been recovered.

The Member State in which the permanent establishment is situated and the Member State of the receiving company shall apply the provisions of this Directive to such a transfer as if the Member State where the permanent establishment is situated were the Member State of the transferring company.

This paragraph shall also apply in the case where the permanent establishment is situated in the same Member State as that in which the receiving company is resident.

2. By way of derogation from paragraph 1, where the Member State of the transferring company applies a system of taxing worldwide profits, that Member State shall have the right to tax any profits or capital gains of the permanent establishment resulting from the merger, division, partial division or transfer of assets, on condition that it gives relief for the tax that, but for

the provisions of this Directive, would have been charged on those profits or capital gains in the Member State in which that permanent establishment is situated, in the same way and in the same amount as it would have done if that tax had actually been charged and paid.

CHAPTER IV

SPECIAL CASE OF TRANSPARENT ENTITIES

Article 11

1. Where a Member State considers a non-resident transferring or acquired company to be fiscally transparent on the basis of that Member State's assessment of the legal characteristics of that company arising from the law under which it is constituted, it shall have the right not to apply the provisions of this Directive when taxing a direct or indirect shareholder of that company in respect of the income, profits or capital gains of that company.

2. A Member State exercising the right referred to in paragraph 1 shall give relief for the tax which, but for the provisions of this Directive, would have been charged on the fiscally transparent company on its income, profits or capital gains, in the same way and in the same amount as that Member State would have done if that tax had actually been charged and paid.

3. Where a Member State considers a non-resident receiving or acquiring company to be fiscally transparent on the basis of that Member State's assessment of the legal characteristics of that company arising from the law under which it is constituted, it shall have the right not to apply Article 8(1), (2) and (3).

4. Where a Member State considers a non-resident receiving company to be fiscally transparent on the basis of that Member State's assessment of the legal characteristics of that company arising from the law under which it is constituted, that Member State may apply to any direct or indirect shareholders the same treatment for tax purposes as it would if the receiving company were resident in that Member State.

CHAPTER V

RULES APPLICABLE TO THE TRANSFER OF THE REGISTERED OFFICE OF AN SE OR AN SCE

Article 12

1. Where:

   (a) an SE or an SCE transfers its registered office from one Member State to another Member State; or

   (b) in connection with the transfer of its registered office from one Member State to another Member State, an SE or an SCE, which is resident in the first Member State, ceases to be resident in that Member State and becomes resident in another Member State;

   that transfer of registered office or the cessation of residence shall not give rise to any taxation of capital gains, calculated in accordance with Article 4(1), in the Member State from which the registered office has been transferred, derived from those assets and liabilities of the SE or SCE which, in consequence, remain effectively connected with a permanent establishment of the SE or of the SCE in the Member State from which the registered office has been transferred and play a part in generating the profits or losses taken into account for tax purposes.

2. Paragraph 1 shall apply only if the SE or the SCE computes any new depreciation and any gains or losses in respect of the assets and liabilities that remain effectively connected with that permanent establishment, as though the transfer of the registered office had not taken place or the SE or the SCE had not so ceased to be tax resident.

3. Where, under the laws of the Member State from which the registered office was transferred, the SE or the SCE is entitled to have any new depreciation or any gains or losses in respect of the assets and liabilities remaining in that Member State computed on a basis different from that set out in paragraph 2, paragraph 1 shall not apply to the assets and liabilities in respect of which that option is exercised.

Article 13

1. Where:

   (a) an SE or an SCE transfers its registered office from one Member State to another Member State; or

   (b) in connection with the transfer of its registered office from one Member State to another Member State, an SE or an SCE, which is resident in the first Member State, ceases to be resident in that Member State and becomes resident in another Member State;

   the Member States shall take the necessary measures to ensure that, where provisions or reserves properly constituted by the SE or the SCE before the transfer of the registered office are partly or wholly exempt from tax and are not derived from permanent establishments abroad, such provisions or reserves may be carried over, with the same tax exemption, by a permanent establishment of the SE or the SCE which is situated within the territory of the Member State from which the registered office was transferred.

2. To the extent that a company transferring its registered office within the territory of a Member State would be allowed to carry forward or carry back losses which had not been exhausted for tax purposes, that Member State shall allow the permanent establishment, situated within its territory, of the SE or of the SCE transferring its registered office, to take over those losses of the SE or SCE which have not been exhausted for tax purposes, provided that the loss carry forward or carry back would have been available in comparable circumstances to a company which continued to have its registered office or which continued to be tax resident in that Member State.

Article 14

1. The transfer of the registered office of an SE or of an SCE shall not, of itself, give rise to any taxation of the income, profits or capital gains of the shareholders.

2. The application of paragraph 1 shall not prevent the Member States from taxing the gain arising out of the subsequent transfer of the securities representing the capital of the SE or of the SCE that transfers its registered office.

CHAPTER VI

FINAL PROVISIONS

Article 15

1. A Member State may refuse to apply or withdraw the benefit of all or any part of the provisions of Articles 4 to 14 where it appears that one of the operations referred to in Article 1:

(a) has as its principal objective or as one of its principal objectives tax evasion or tax avoidance; the fact that the operation is not carried out for valid commercial reasons such as the restructuring or rationalisation of the activities of the companies participating in the operation may constitute a presumption that the operation has tax evasion or tax avoidance as its principal objective or as one of its principal objectives;

(b) results in a company, whether participating in the operation or not, no longer fulfilling the necessary conditions for the representation of employees on company organs according to the arrangements which were in force prior to that operation.

2. Paragraph 1(b) shall apply as long as and to the extent that no Community law provisions containing equivalent rules on representation of employees on company organs are applicable to the companies covered by this Directive.

Article 16

Member States shall communicate to the Commission the texts of the main provisions of national law which they adopt in the field covered by this Directive.

Article 17

Directive 90/434/EEC, as amended by the acts listed in Annex II, Part A, is repealed, without prejudice to the obligations of the Member States relating to the time-limits for transposition into national law and application of the Directives set out in Annex II, Part B.

References to the repealed Directive shall be construed as references to this Directive and shall be read in accordance with the correlation table in Annex III.

Article 18

This Directive shall enter into force on the 20th day following its publication in the *Official Journal of the European Union*.

Article 19

This Directive is addressed to the Member States.

Done at Luxembourg, 19 October 2009.

For the Council
The President
E. ERLANDSSON

ANNEX I

PART A

LIST OF COMPANIES REFERRED TO IN ARTICLE 3(a)

(a) companies (SE) incorporated under Regulation (EC) No 2157/2001 and Council Directive 2001/86/EC of 8 October 2001 supplementing the Statute for a European company with regard to the involvement of employees (7) and cooperative societies (SCE) incorporated under Regulation (EC) No 1435/2003 and Council Directive 2003/72/EC of 22 July 2003 supplementing the Statute for a European Cooperative Society with regard to the involvement of employees (8);

(b) companies under Belgian law known as 'société anonyme'/'naamloze vennootschap', 'société en commandite par actions'/'commanditaire vennootschap op aandelen', 'société privée à responsabilité limitée'/'besloten vennootschap met beperkte aansprakelijkheid' 'société coopérative à responsabilité limitée'/'coöperatieve vennootschap met beperkte aansprakelijkheid', 'société coopérative à responsabilité illimitee'/'coöperatieve vennootschap met onbeperkte aansprakelijkheid', 'société en nom collectif'/'vennootschap onder firma', 'société en commandite simple'/'gewone commanditaire vennootschap', public undertakings which have adopted one of the abovementioned legal forms, and other companies constituted under Belgian law subject to the Belgian corporate tax;

(c) companies under Bulgarian law known as 'събирателното дружество', 'командитното дружество', 'дружеството с ограничена отговорност', 'акционерното дружество', 'командитното дружество с акции', 'кооперации', 'кооперативни съюзи', and 'държавни предприятия' constituted under Bulgarian law and carrying on commercial activities;

(d) companies under Czech law known as 'akciová společnost' and 'společnost s ručením omezeným';

(e) companies under Danish law known as 'aktieselskab' and 'anpartsselskab' and other companies subject to tax under the Corporation Tax Act, in so far as their taxable income is calculated and taxed in accordance with the general tax legislation rules applicable to 'aktieselskaber';

(f) companies under German law known as 'Aktiengesellschaft', 'Kommanditgesellschaft auf Aktien', 'Gesellschaft mit beschrankter Haftung', 'Versicherungsverein auf Gegenseitigkeif, ˛rwerbs- und Wirtschaftsgenossenschaft', 'Betriebe gewerblicher Art von juristischen Personen des Öffentlichen Rechts', and other companies constituted under German law subject to German corporate tax;

(g) companies under Estonian law known as 'täisühing', 'usaldusühing', 'osaühing', 'aktsiaselts' and 'tulundusühistu';

---

(7) OJ L 294, 10.11.2001, p. 22.

(8) OJ L 207, 18.8.2003, p. 25.

(h) companies incorporated or existing under Irish law, bodies registered under the Industrial and Provident Societies Act, building societies incorporated under the Building Societies Acts and trustee savings banks within the meaning of the Trustee Savings Banks Act, 1989;

(i) companies under Greek law known as 'ανώνυμη εταιρεία' and 'εταιρεία περιορισμένης ευθύνης (Ε.Π.Ε.)';

(j) companies under Spanish law known as 'sociedad anünima', 'sociedad comanditaria por acciones', 'sociedad de responsabilidad limitada', and those public law bodies which operate under private law;

(k) companies under French law known as 'société anonyme', 'société en commandite par actions', 'société à responsabilité limitée', 'sociétés par actions simplifiées', 'sociétés d'assurances mutuelles', 'caisses d'épargne et de prévoyance', 'sociétés civiles' which are automatically subject to corporation tax, 'coopératives', 'unions de coopératives', industrial and commercial public establishments and undertakings, and other companies constituted under French law subject to the French corporate tax;

(l) companies under Italian law known as 'società per azioni', 'società in accomandita per azioni', 'società a responsabilità limitata', 'società cooperative', 'società di mutua assicurazione', and private and public entities whose activity is wholly or principally commercial;

(m) companies (εταιρείες) under Cypriot law as defined in the income tax laws;

(n) companies under Latvian law known as 'akciju sabiedrība' and 'sabiedrība ar ierobežotu atbildību';

(o) companies incorporated under the law of Lithuania;

(p) companies under Luxembourg law known as 'société anonyme', 'société en commandite par actions', 'société à responsabilité limitée', 'société coopérative', 'société coopérative organisée comme une société anonyme', 'association d'assurances mutuelles', 'association d'épargne-pension', 'entreprise de nature commerciale, industrielle ou minière de l'État, des communes, des syndicats de communes, des établissements publics et des autres personnes morales de droit public', and other companies constituted under Luxembourg law subject to the Luxembourg corporate tax;

(q) companies under Hungarian law known as 'közkereseti társaság', 'betéti társaság', 'közös vállalat', 'korlátolt felelősségű társaság', 'részvénytársaság', 'egyesülés', 'közhasznú társaság' and 'szövetkezet';

(r) companies under Maltese law known as 'Kumpaniji ta' Responsabilita Limitata' and 'Socjetajiet en commandite li l-kapital taghhom maqsum f'azzjonijiet';

(s) companies under Dutch law known as 'naamloze vennootschap', 'besloten vennootschap met beperkte aansprakelijkheid', 'open commanditaire vennootschap', 'coöperatie', 'onderlinge waarborgmaatschappij', 'fonds voor gemene rekening', 'vereniging op coöperatieve grondslag' and 'vereniging welke op onderlinge grondslag als verzekeraar of kredietinstelling optreedt', and other companies constituted under Dutch law subject to the Dutch corporate tax;

(t) companies under Austrian law known as 'Aktiengesellschaft', 'Gesellschaft mit beschrankter Haftung', and 'Erwerbs- und Wirtschaftsgenossenschaften';

(u) companies under Polish law known as as 'spółka akcyjna' and 'spółka z ograniczoną odpowiedzialnością';

(v) commercial companies or civil law companies having a commercial form as well as other legal persons carrying on commercial or industrial activities, which are incorporated under Portuguese law;

(w) companies under Romanian law known as 'societăţi pe acţiuni', 'societăţi în comandită pe acţiuni' and 'societăţi cu răspundere limitată';

(x) companies under Slovenian law known as 'delniška družba', 'komanditna družba' and 'družba z omejeno odgovornostjo';

(y) companies under Slovak law known as 'akciová spoločnosť', 'spoločnosť s ručením obmedzeným' and 'komanditná spoločnosť';

(z) companies under Finnish law known as 'osakeyhtiö'/'aktiebolag', 'osuuskunta'/'andelslag', 'säästöpankki'/'sparbank' and 'vakuutusyhtiö'/'försäkringsbolag';

(aa) companies under Slovak law known as 'akciová spoločnosť', 'spoločnosť s ručením obmedzeným' and 'komanditná spoločnosť';

(ab) companies under Finnish law known as 'osakeyhtiö'/'aktiebolag', 'osuuskunta'/'andelslag', 'säästöpankki'/'sparbank' and 'vakuutusyhtiö'/'försäkringsbolag';

PART B

LIST OF TAXES REFERRED TO IN ARTICLE 3(C)

- impôt des sociétés/vennootschapsbelasting in Belgium,
- корпоративен данък in Bulgaria,
- daň z příjmů právnických osob in the Czech Republic,
- selskabsskat in Denmark,
- Körperschaftssteuer in Germany,
- tulumaks in Estonia,

- corporation tax in Ireland,
- φόρος εισοδήματος νομικών προσώπων κερδοσκοπικού χαρακτήρα in Greece,
- impuesto sobre sociedades in Spain,
- impôt sur les sociétés in France,
- imposta sul reddito delle società in Italy,
- φόρος εισοδήματος in Cyprus,
- uzņēmumu ienākuma nodoklis in Latvia,
- pelno mokestis in Lithuania,
- impôt sur le revenu des collectivités in Luxembourg,
- társasági adó in Hungary,
- taxxa fuq l-income in Malta,
- vennootschapsbelasting in the Netherlands,
- KÖrperschaftssteuer in Austria,
- podatek dochodowy od osób prawnych in Poland,
- imposto sobre o rendimento das pessoas colectivas in Portugal,
- impozit pe profit in Romania,
- davek od dobička pravnih oseb in Slovenia,
- daň z príjmov právnických osôb in Slovakia,
- yhteisöjen tulovero/inkomstskatten för samfund in Finland,
- statlig inkomstskatt in Sweden,
- corporation tax in the United Kingdom.

Annex III

List of national laws implementing the Cross-border Merger Directive

This Annex contains a list of the current national legislation implementing the Cross-border Merger Directive.

AUSTRIA

Bundesgesetz über die grenzüberschreitende Verschmelzung von Kapitalgesellschaften in der Europäischen Union

Bundesgesetz, mit dem ein Bundesgesetz über die grenzüberschreitende Verschmelzung von Kapitalgesellschaften in der Europäischen Union erlassen wird sowie das Firmenbuchgesetz, das Gerichtsgebührengesetz, das Rechtspflegergesetz, das GmbH-Gesetz, das Aktiengesetz 1965, das Umwandlungsgesetz, das Unternehmensgesetzbuch und das Übernahmegesetz geändert werden (Gesellschaftsrechts-Änderungsgesetz 2007 – GesRÄG 2007, *Bundesgesetzblatt* I Nr. 72/2007

BELGIUM

Code des sociétés/Wetboek van vennootschappen

BULGARIA

Търговски закон, обнародван в Държавен вестник бр. 48 от 1999 г., с последващи изменения и допълнения

Закон за публичното предлагане на ценни книжа, обнародван в Държавен вестник бр. 114 от 1999 г., с последващи изменения и допълнения

Кодекс на труда, обнародван в Държавен вестник бр. 26 от 1986 г., с последващи изменения и допълнения.

CYPRUS

Ο περί Εταιρειών (Τροποποιητικός) (Αρ. 4) Νόμος 186(I)/2007, Επίσημη Εφημερίδα της Κυπριακής Δημοκρατίας Αρ. 4154, παράρτημα πρώτο, μέρος I της 31ης Δεκεμβρίου 2007

CZECH REPUBLIC

Zákon č. 125/2008 Sb., o přeměnách obchodních společností a družstev. Částka: 40/2008 Sb., na s. 1570, *Rozesláno*, 16 April 2008.

DENMARK

Lovbekendtgørelse nr. 649 af 15 June 2006 (aktieselskabsloven) med senere ændringer

Lovbekendtgørelse nr. 650 af 15. juni 2006 (anpartsselskabsloven) med senere ændringer

Lovbekendtgørelse nr. 651 af 15. juni 2006 (erhvervsvirksomhedsloven) med senere ændringer

Lovbekendtgørelse nr. 652 af 15. juni 2006 (erhvervsfondsloven) med senere ændringer

ESTONIA

Äriseadustiku ja sellega seonduvate seaduste muutmise seadus, 21 November 2007, *Riigi Teataja* I, 13 December 2007, 65, 405

FINLAND

Laki henkilöstön edustuksesta yritysten hallinnossa annetun lain muuttamisesta / Lag om ändring av lagen om personalrepresentation i företagens förvaltning, 1128/2007 (*Suomen Saadoskokoelma (SK)*, 1128, of 11 December 2007)

Laki sijoitusrahastolain muuttamisesta / Lag om ändring av lagen om placeringsfonder, 1426/2007 (*Suomen Saadoskokoelma (SK)*, 1426, of 31 December 2007)

Laki arvopaperimarkkinalain muuttamisesta / Lag om ändring av värdepappersmarknadslagen, 1424/2007 (*Suomen Saadoskokoelma (SK)*, 1424, of 31 December 2007)

Laki säästöpankkilain muuttamisesta / Lag om ändring av sparbankslagen, 1423/2007 (*Suomen Saadoskokoelma (SK)*, 1423, of 31 December 2007)

Laki osuuspankeista ja muista osuuskuntamuotoisista luottolaitoksista annetun lain muuttamisesta / Lag om ändring av lagen om andelsbanker och andra kreditinstitut i andelslagsform,1422/2007 *(Suomen Saadoskokoelma (SK)*, 1422, of 31 December 2007)

Laki liikepankeista ja muista osakeyhtiömuotoisista luottolaitoksista annetun lain muuttamisesta / Lag om ändring av lagen om affärsbanker och andra kreditinstitut i aktiebolagsform, 1421/2007 (*Suomen Saadoskokoelma (SK)*, 1421, of 31 December 2007)

Laki kaupparekisterilain 3 ja 18 a §:n muuttamisesta / Lag om ändring av 3 och 18 a § i handelsregisterlagen, 1418/2007 (*Suomen Saadoskokoelma (SK)*, 1418, of 31 December 2007)

Laki osuuskuntalain muuttamisesta / Lag om ändring av lagen om andelslag, 1417/2007 (*Suomen Saadoskokoelma (SK)*, 1417, of 31 December 2007)

Laki osakeyhtiölain muuttamisesta / Lag om ändring av aktiebolagslagen, 1415/2007 (*Suomen Saadoskokoelma (SK)*, 1415, of 31 December 2007)

FRANCE

Loi no 2008–649 du 3 juillet 2008 portant diverses dispositions d'adaptation du droit des sociétés au droit communautaire, 2008–649 *(Journal Officiel de la République Française (JORF)*, of 4 July 2008)

Décret no 2008–1116 du 31 octobre 2008 relatif à la participation des salariés dans les sociétés issues de fusions transfrontalières, 2008–1116 (*Journal Officiel de la République Française (JORF)*, of 1 November 2008)

Décret no 2008–1117 du 31 octobre 2008 relatif à la participation des salariés dans les sociétés issues de fusions transfrontalières (dispositions relevant d'un décret), 2008–1117 (*Journal Officiel de la République Française (JORF)*, of 1 November 2008)

Décret no 2009–11 du 5 janvier 2009 relatif aux fusions transfrontalières de sociétés, 2009–11 (*Journal Officiel de la République Française (JORF)*, of 7 January 2009)

GERMANY

Zweites Gesetz zur Änderung des Umwandlungsgesetzes, 19 April 2007, *Bundesgesetzblatt Jahrgang* 2007 Teil I Nr. 15, 24 April 2007.

GREECE

Διασυνοριακές συγχωνεύσεις κεφαλαιουχικών εταιρειών και άλλες διατάξεις, 3777/2009 (Greek Government Gazette, volume A, no. 127, 28 July 2009)

HUNGARY

2007. évi CXL. törvény a tőkeegyesítő társaságok határokon átnyúló egyesüléséről

ICELAND

Lög um breytingu á lögum um hlutafélög og lögum um einkahlutafélög (*millilandasamruni og millilandaskipting*) of 17 March 2007

IRELAND

Statutory Instrument No. 157 of 2008, European Communities (Cross-border Mergers) Regulation 2008

ITALY

Attuazione della direttiva 2005/56/CE, relativa alle fusioni transfrontaliere delle società di capitali, (*Gazzetta Ufficiale della Repubblica Italiana* of 17 June 2008)

LATVIA

Eiropas komercsabiedrbu likums, 2005.gada 10.mart (*Latvijas Vstnesis* of 24 March 2005)

LIECHTENSTEIN

Gesetz vom 16. September 2009 über die Abänderung des Personen- und Gesellschaftsrechts (*LGBl.* 2009/268)

Gesetz vom 16. September 2009 über die Mitbestimmung der Arbeitnehmer bei einer grenzüberschreitenden Fusion von Kapitalgesellschaften (*LGBl.* 2009/269)

LITHUANIA

Lietuvos Respublikos administracinių teisės pažeidimų kodeksas Nr. ADM (*Valstybės žinios*, 1985, Nr. 1–1)

Lietuvos Respublikos vienos valstybės ribas peržengiančio ribotos atsakomybės bendrovių jungimosi įstatymas Nr. X-1367 (*Valstybės žinios*, 2007, Nr. 140–5747)

Lietuvos Respublikos įstatymas dėl darbuotojų dalyvavimo bendrovėje po vienos valstybės ribas peržengiančio ribotos atsakomybės bendrovių jungimosi Nr. X-1607 (*Valstybės žinios*, 2008, Nr. 76–3001)

Lietuvos Respublikos Vyriausybės 2003 m. lapkričio 12 d. nutarimas Nr. 1407 „Dėl Juridinių asmenų registro įsteigimo ir Juridinių asmenų registro nuostatų patvirtinimo' (*Valstybės žinios*, 2003, Nr. 107).

LUXEMBOURG

Loi du 10 juin 2009 relative aux fusions transfrontalières de sociétés de capitaux, à la simplification des modalités de constitution des sociétés anonymes et de maintien et de modification de leur capital, portant transposition: de la directive 2005/56/CE du Parlement européen et du Conseil du 26 octobre 2005 sur les fusions transfrontalières des sociétés de capitaux; de la directive 2006/68/CE du Parlement européen et du Conseil du 6 septembre 2006 modifiant la directive 77/91/CEE du Conseil en ce qui concerne la constitution de la société anonyme ainsi que le maintien et les modifications de son capital; de la directive 2007/63/CE du Parlement européen et du Conseil du 13 novembre 2007 modifiant les directives 78/855/CEE et 82/891/CEE du Conseil pour ce qui est de l'exigence d'un rapport d'expert indépendant à réaliser à l'occasion des fusions ou des scissions des sociétés anonymes, ainsi que modification de la loi modifiée du 10 août 1915 concernant les sociétés commerciales, et du Code du travail (*Mémorial Luxembourgeois* A, of 29 June 2009)

MALTA

L.N. 415 of 2007 CA (CAP. 386) Cross-Border Mergers of Limited Liability Companies Regulations, 2007 (The Malta government gazette of 14 December 2007)

L.N. 165 of 2008 ERA, 2002 (CAP. 452) Employee Involvement (Cross-Border Mergers of Limited Liability Companies) Regulations 2008 (The Malta government gazette of 1 July 2008)

THE NETHERLANDS

Wet van 27 juni 2008 tot wijziging van boek 2 van het Burgerlijk Wetboek in verband met de implementatie van richtlijn nr. 2005/56/EG van het Europese Parlement en de Raad van de Europese Unie betreffende grensoverschrijdende fusies van kapitaalvennootschappen (PbEU L 310), *Staatsblad* 27 June 2008

NORWAY

Lov 21. desember 2007 nr. 129 om endringer i aksjeloven, allmennaksjeloven og enkelte andre lover (fusjon og fisjon over landegrensene, *Norsk Lovtidend Avd. 1*, 2007 no. 13, p. 1868

Forskrift 9. januar 2008 nr. 50 om arbeidstakernes rett til representasjon ved fusjon over landegrensene av selskaper med begrenset ansvar, *Norsk Lovtidend Avd.* 1, 2008 no. 1, p. 267

POLAND

Ustawa z dnia 25 kwietnia 2008 r.o zmianie ustawy – Kodeks spółek handlowych (.Dz.U.08.86.524 z dnia 20 maja 2008 r.)

PORTUGAL

Lei n.° 19/2009, de 12 de Maio de 2009, a qual altera o Código das Sociedades Comerciais e o Código do Registo Comercial, transpondo para a ordem jurídica interna as Directivas n.os 2005/56/CE, do Parlamento Europeu e do Conselho, de 26 de Outubro, relativa às fusões transfronteiriças das sociedades de responsabilidade limitada, e 2007/63/CE, do Parlamento Europeu e do Conselho, de 13 de Novembro, que altera as Directivas n.os 78/855/CEE e 82/891/CEE, do Conselho, no que respeita à exigência de um relatório de peritos independentes aquando da fusão ou da cisão de sociedades anónimas, e estabelece o regime aplicável à participação dos trabalhadores na sociedade resultante da fusão (*Diário da Republica I*, of 12 May 2009)

REPUBLIC OF SLOVENIA

Zakon o gospodarskih družbah (ZGD-1) (*Uradni list RS*, of 19 April 2006)

Zakon o spremembah in dopolnitvah Zakona o gospodarskih družbah (ZGD-1A) (*Uradni list RS* of 30 January 2008)

Zakon o spremembah in dopolnitvah Zakona o gospodarskih družbah (ZGD-1B) (*Uradni list RS* of 8 July 2008)

Zakon o spremembah in dopolnitvah Zakona o gospodarskih družbah (ZGD-1C) (*Uradni list RS* of 5 June 2009)

Zakon o soodločanju delavcev pri čezmejnih združitvah kapitalskih družb (ZSDČZKD) (*Uradni list RS* of 6 June 2008)

ROMANIA

Ordonanţă de urgenţă nr. 52/2008 pentru modificarea şi completarea Legii nr. 31/1990 privind societăţile comerciale şi pentru completarea Legii nr. 26/1990 privind registrul comerţului (*Monitorul Oficial* nr. 333 of 30 April 2008)

Lege nr. 31/1990 privind societăţile comerciale, republicată, cu modificările şi completările ulterioare (*Monitorul Oficial* nr. 1066 of 17 November 2004)

SLOVAK REPUBLIC

Zakon z 27. novembra 2007 c. 657/2007 Z.z., ktorym sa meni a doplna zakon c. 513/1991 Zb. Obchodny zakonnik v zneni neskorsich predpisov a o zmene a doplneni zakona c. 530/2003 Z.z. o obchodnom registri v zneni neskorsich prepisov, uverejneny dna 31. decembra 2007 v c. 266/2007 Zbierky zakonov Slovenskej republiky

SPAIN

Ley 3/2009, de 3 de abril, sobre modificaciones estructurales de las sociedades mercantiles (*Boletín Oficial del Estado (B.O.E)* of 4 April 2009)

SWEDEN

Lag (2008:3) om ändring i lagen (1987:667) om ekonomiska föreningar (*Svensk författningssamling* (SFS), 2008:3)

Lag (2008:14) om ändring i aktiebolagslagen (2005:551) (*Svensk författningssamling* (SFS), 2008:14)

Förordning (2008:24) om ändring i aktiebolagsförordningen (2005:559) (*Svensk författningssamling* (SFS), 2008:24)

Lag (2008:13) om ändring i lagen (1987:1245) om styrelserepresentation för de privatanställda (*Svensk författningssamling* (SFS), 2008:13)

Lag (2008:12) om ändring i aktiebolagslagen (2005:551) (*Svensk författningssamling* (SFS), 2008:12)

Lag (2008:9) om arbetstagares medverkan vid gränsöverskridande fusioner (*Svensk författningssamling* (SFS), 2008:9)

Lag (2008:8) om ändring i lagen (2004:575) om europabolag (*Svensk författningssamling* (SFS), 2008:8)

Lag (2010:1516) om ändring i aktiebolagslagen (2005:551) (*Svensk författningssamling* (SFS), 2010:1516)

UNITED KINGDOM

Statutory Instrument 2007 No. 2974 The Companies (Cross-Border Mergers) Regulations 2007

Index

For EU product safety concerns, contact us at Calle de José Abascal, 56–1°,
28003 Madrid, Spain or eugpsr@cambridge.org.

www.ingramcontent.com/pod-product-compliance
Lightning Source LLC
LaVergne TN
LVHW011523200926
848484LV00001B/123

* 9 7 8 0 5 2 1 4 8 7 6 0 3 *